SYDNEY SMITH was born at ⬛⬛⬛
1771. He was educated at Winchester and New College, Oxford, being a fellow of the latter from 1791 until his marriage
in 1800. In 1794 he took Orders on his appointment to the
curacy of Netheravon on Salisbury Plain. After three years he
became tutor to the son of Mr. Michael Hicks Beach, M.P.,
the squire of Netheravon, and left for Edinburgh with the
boy in 1798. While there, he and several others founded the
Edinburgh Review which first appeared in 1802. From 1803 to
1809 he lived in London as a preacher and lecturer where his
wit and sincerity won many friendships including those of
Lord and Lady Holland. In 1809 he moved to Yorkshire,
having accepted the living of Foston where, in addition to his
duties as a clergyman, he became a farmer, a magistrate and
even the village doctor. In 1829 he exchanged the living of
Foston for Combe Florey in Somerset. He was Rector of
Combe Florey from 1839 to 1845 during which time he lived
mainly in London as Lord Grey had appointed him to a
canonry of St Paul's in 1831. He died in his London residence
at Grosvenor Square on 22 February 1845.

NOWELL C. SMITH was an Hon. Fellow of New College,
Oxford.

AUBERON WAUGH has been a regular contributor to the
Spectator, the *New Statesman*, the *Evening Standard* and
Private Eye. He is the author of several novels and non-fiction
works including the *Four Crowded Years : the Diaries of
Auberon Waugh*, 1976.

THE WORLD'S CLASSICS

Selected Letters of Sydney Smith

Edited by
NOWELL C. SMITH

With an Introduction by
AUBERON WAUGH

Oxford New York Toronto Melbourne
OXFORD UNIVERSITY PRESS
1981

Oxford University Press, Walton Street, Oxford OX2 6DP

London Glasgow New York Toronto
Delhi Bombay Calcutta Madras Karachi
Kuala Lumpur Singapore Hong Kong Tokyo
Nairobi Dar es Salaam Cape Town
Melbourne Wellington

and associate companies in
Beirut Berlin Ibadan Mexico City

British Library Cataloguing in Publication Data

Smith, Sydney, b. 1771
Selected letters of Sydney Smith.
1. Smith, Sydney, b. 1771 – Correspondence
2. Authors, English – Correspondence
3. Philosophers – England – Correspondence
I. Smith, Nowell C
824'.7   PR5458.A44   80-40829
ISBN 0-19-281031-2
ISBN 0-19-281535-0 Pbk

Printed in Great Britain by
Hazell Watson & Viney Limited
Aylesbury, Bucks

CONTENTS

INTRODUCTION

AUBERON WAUGH

'WHAT is real piety?' wrote Sydney Smith to Mrs Baring in July 1834. 'What is true attachment to the Church? How are these fine feelings best evinced? The answer is plain: by sending strawberries to a clergyman. Many thanks.'

As a clergyman, Sydney Smith was always more suspicious of excessive zeal than he was of a shortage in that quality. He despised alike the Puseyites and Methodists, evangelicals and Roman Catholic enthusiasts. But, as his biographer in the *Dictionary of National Biography* remarks, 'he was sensitive to the charge of indifference to the creed which he professed. He took pains to protest against any writing by his allies which might shock believers.'

On occasions, a certain robust sectarianism emerges. One of his last jokes, on being taken ill in the autumn of 1844 with what proved to be his final illness, was to complain of languor: 'I feel so weak, both in body and mind, that I verily believe, if the knife were put into my hand, I should not have strength or energy enough to stick it into a Dissenter.'

The truth is that he was an exceptionally tolerant man, believing in personal freedom before all else, and was prepared to tolerate almost anything but extremes of religious fanaticism. One should not be too censorious about his lack of any obvious enthusiasm for religion when one reflects that he had no wish to become a clergyman in the first place. He was forced into Holy Orders by his Father's refusal to support him while he read for the Bar.

Smith spent most of his adult life exiled in the 'healthy grave' of the countryside, where he always feared that 'creation would expire before teatime'. Twenty of the most active years of his life, from 1809–29, were spent in the hell-hole of Foston, Yorkshire. This was a result of the Residence Act of 1808 which obliged clergymen to live in their livings. No clergyman had resided in Foston for 150 years, and the parsonage was a hovel. Smith's good-humoured acceptance of his fate – at a time when, fresh from his triumphs in Edinburgh, he was just beginning to take London by storm – seems a model of Christian humility. He became a farmer, directing his labour with the help of a telescope and speaking trumpet, inventing a universal scratcher for cattle. Later he became a magistrate, and was noted for his leniency to poachers and ability to make up quarrels. Finally he became the village doctor, dispensing medicines to the local peasantry with as much success, one imagines, as the qualified general practitioner of the day.

Posterity may be grateful for these long periods of exile in the country, since they resulted in the letters reproduced here – letters written for the most part, with no greater purpose in mind than to amuse and to keep himself amused. Other wits, lacking a Boswell, survive only a short time in the memory of their friends or in a few anecdotes. Good conversation was always, I suspect, the enemy of literature. Smith's proudest boast was that 'I never wrote anything very dull in my life', but he never wrote a masterpiece, either. He survives in his daughter's *Memoir*, in various anecdotes which have been culled from other sources, but chiefly, at first hand, in his letters.

He came to Combe Florey, Somerset, in 1829, soon after the death of his son, Douglas, in his early twenties. Smith was heartbroken, and this incident seems to have been the one great sorrow of his life. As he wrote on Douglas's tomb: 'His life was blameless. His death was the first sorrow he ever occasioned his parents, but it was deep and lasting.' By coincidence, Combe Florey was only a mile and a half away from the place where his father finally settled. Robert Smith, the father, bought, spoiled and then sold nineteen different houses in England, ultimately dying in Bishops Lydeard, Somerset in 1827 at the age of eighty-eight.

These last fifteen years would appear to have been the happiest in Smith's life. He rejoiced in the milder climate of Combe Florey and in the financial independence which came to him with a canonry at St. Paul's. Ten years were spent in comparative affluence, after the death of his brother Courtenay, left him richer by £50,000. For a man who remarked: 'I can safely say I have been happier for every guinea I have gained', he should have been very happy indeed. Rebuilding the Rectory at Combe Florey, he created his first library – 'a pretty odd room, dignified by the name of library' – about twenty-eight feet long and eight feet high – ending in a bay-window supported by pillars, looking into the garden, and which he had obtained by throwing a pantry, a passage and a shoe-hole together.

This room, which still survives, was his pride and his delight. It was here that he remarked: 'No furniture is so charming as books, even if you never open them or read a single word.' It was in the garden outside that he paraded two donkeys with deers' antlers fastened on their heads, exclaiming: 'There, Lady —— ! You said the only thing this place wanted to make it perfect was deer; what do you say now?'

Beyond the garden is a steep valley with a beautiful hanging wood on one side. It was here, in order to impress on a visitor the mildness of the Combe Florey climate, that he tied oranges and lemons on the beech and oak trees. One cannot be sure, but it was probably in the library that Lord John Russell sat, while on a visit to his friend, while his 'butler' – a devoted Yorkshirewoman whom he called 'Bunch' – charged a penny a time for villagers to look at him through the keyhole.

Although Smith was always disappointed not to have been given the opportunity to refuse a bishopric – one wonders, in fact, whether he would have refused it – the strongest impression we receive is that of a profoundly happy man. There are many stories of his kindness; perhaps the most endearing is how, immediately after his marriage when he was completely penniless, he received a present of £750 from his friend and patron, Hicks Beach. This was to set him up in married life, but quixotically he gave £100 of it away on the spot to an old lady in distress.

Politically he was a Whig of the best possible sort. He abhorred the slave trade and campaigned energetically for Reform in 1832, but his greatest political commitment was to Catholic emancipation. This was especially praiseworthy in a man who had no High Church leanings and, indeed, very few religious interests at all, since it contributed to his unpopularity with the Church establishment and almost certainly explains why he was never offered a bishopric. One of the first things Lord Grey said on entering Downing Street was 'Now I shall be able to do something for Sydney Smith'; in the same way, according to Smith's daughter, 'Lord Melbourne said there was nothing he more deeply regretted, in looking back on his past career, than the not having made Sydney Smith a bishop.'

Although a good Whig in every respect and an exceptionally charitable man, Smith's aversion to radicals and levellers was absolute. Perhaps some of his best and angriest polemical writing can be seen in his letter to Bishop Blomfield of 5 September 1840. It may offer a partial explanation for Smith's earlier enthusiasm for reform. It is also one of the most savage rebukes to a trendy bishop ever composed, with just enough of the bitterness of the unpromoted parson to keep it human:

> It is very easy, my Lord, to swing about in the House of Lords, and to be brave five years after the time, and to point out to their Lordships the clear difference between moral and physical fear, and to be nodded to by the Duke of Wellington, but I am not to be paid by such coin. I believe that the old fashioned, orthodox, hand-shaking, bowel-disturbing passion of fear had a good deal to do with the whole reform. You choose to forget it, but I remember the period when Bishops never remained unpelted, they were pelted going, coming, riding, walking, consecrating and carousing. . . . If you were not frightened by all this, I was, and would have given half my preferment to save the rest. . . .
>
> You are fast hastening on, with the acclamations and gratitude of the Whigs, to Lambeth, and I am hastening, after a life of 70 years, with gout and asthma, to the grave. I am most sincere, therefore, when I say that in the management of this business you have (in my opinion) made a very serious and fatal mistake: you have shaken the laws of property, and prepared the ruin of the church by lowering the character of its members, and encouraging the aggression of its enemies.

Mr Everett, the American minister, remarked that 'if he had not been known as the wittiest man of his day, he would have been accounted one of the wisest'. Perhaps he had time to develop his wisdom because, as he put it, 'a joke goes a long way in the country'. Some of his aphorisms have a homely wisdom which can only be described as sublime, like this common man's guide to politics: 'Don't be led away by nonsense. All things are dearer under a bad government and cheaper under a good one.' That is all the common voter knows and all he needs to know. It would excite the same noises of approval in Taunton today as it did in Taunton in 1830 – the year of the riots in Bristol and July Revolution in France. However else he might be described, Smith was never a revolutionist.

Smith's biographer, Pearson, sums up his political attitude thus: 'He believed in freedom; it was probably the only thing he did entirely believe in; but he knew in his bones (what we are now only beginning to find out) that no politician could be trusted with a people's liberties.'

The most significant part of that observation, I should judge, is contained within the parentheses. Time and again, in reading Smith, one sees with delighted surprise a discovery one has just made oneself. Different people will respond differently, but I find it rather gratifying that Smith was sixty before he discovered what I have understood since my thirty-fifth birthday, that digestion is the great secret of life. The poor man was plagued by gout – not a funny illness and seldom caused by over-indulgence, as ignorant people suppose. Smith assumed that his gout was some sort of punishment. This is how he describes it, writing from Combe Florey to Lady Carlisle (at Castle Howard) on the same day as he wrote the magnificent letter to Bishop Blomfield, already quoted:

... I am pretty well, except for gout, asthma, and pains in all the bones, and all the flesh, of my body. What a very singular disease gout is! It seems as if the stomach fell down into the feet. The smallest lameness, and the innocent ankle and blameless instep are tortured for the vices of the nobler organs. The stomach ... punishes for the least offences. A plum, a glass of champagne, excess in joy, excess in grief – any crime, however small, is sufficient for redness, swelling, spasms and large shoes.

As we follow Smith's mind, wandering from subject to subject from childhood to old age – 'what is childhood but a series of happy delusions?'; 'We are both tolerably well bulging out like old houses but with no immediate intention of tumbling down' – one begins to see that Smith may be more than an amiable, eccentric old clergyman who lived his span, ate his peaches and died. What he is, surely, is the *ideal* English clergyman, the model from which every amiable English clergyman in English literature has been drawn. More than this, he is the embodiment of our national genius, or at any rate one fairly major expression of it. Long before the politicians variously and preposterously decided that we were a nation of gritty, classless workers anxious to improve ourselves by modern methods, or a nation of helpless incompetents in need of constant visiting and encouragement by the caring professions – long before any of this nonsense there was Smith. And Smith remains – as close, through his letters, to the poor educated man living in an Islington bedsitter as he is to me, who live two hundred yards away from the house where he lived, fifty yards away from the little village church where he preached, and look out over the acres which he once farmed.

But it would be the worst possible sin against his memory to read his letters in a mood of resentful nostalgia. In almost the same breath as he inveighed against secret ballots, averring that universal suffrage would cure every ill 'as a teaspoonful of prussic acid is a certain cure for the most formidable diseases', he welcomed the arrival of the railway in the West of England with unconcealed delight. There are undoubtedly many aspects of the contemporary scene about which he would rejoice, even if he would complain bitterly about many others. His advice on melancholy should be engraved in every conservative Englishman's memory, because although Smith was as sceptical of most human progress as he was appalled by cruelty or intolerance, although, in his own words, he always anticipated the worst, he remained a profoundly happy man. Here it is, taken from his daughter's *Memoir* with the proviso that she herself supplies, that 'without the look, the voice, the manner, the laugh, the thousand little delicate touches, the quick repartee, the connecting link from which these observations sprang – without the master's spirit to animate the whole – without all this, I feel it is but a body without a soul'. We can only imagine what the old boy was like, and benefit from his wisdom:

Never give way to melancholy: nothing encroaches more; I fight against it vigorously. One great remedy is, to take short views of life. Are you happy now? Are you likely to remain so till this evening? or next week? or next month? or next year? Then why destroy present happiness by a distant misery, which may never come at all, or you may never live to see it? For every substantial grief has twenty shadows, and most of them shadows of your own making.

PREFACE

THE following Selection is taken from the two volumes of *The Letters of Sydney Smith* published by the Clarendon Press in 1953. It was called for by the chorus of pleasure with which the letters were received. The difficulty has been to make a selection where, generally speaking, one letter is as good as another; but I have tried to represent the course of Sydney's life, his principal friendships, his various interests, and his remarkable combination of solid judgement and irresistible fun. Many readers will probably wish to enjoy the larger collection. Those who desire a biography cannot do better than read Mr Hesketh Pearson's *The Smith of Smiths* (Hamish Hamilton, 1934, and Penguin Books) which is at once comprehensive and appropriately vivacious.

I have retained Sydney's erratic spelling, haphazard use of capitals, and frequent omission of stops. His text is strewn with dashes of every length, impossible to represent, which take the place, but on no system, of conventional punctuation. To substitute uniform dashes would give a very wrong impression; merely to omit them would have made the text unreadable. I have therefore substituted such punctuation as seemed necessary. The numbering of the letters here follows that in the Clarendon Press edition, to which the reader is referred for any further textual information.

N. C. S.

November 1955

ABBREVIATIONS

M	vol. i of *Memoirs and Letters of the Rev. Sydney Smith* (1855).
P	the text of the letters as printed in vol. ii of *Memoirs and Letters* above.
R	*Life and Times of the Rev. Sydney Smith*, by Stuart J. Reid (1884).
H. of H.	*The Home of the Hollands*, by the Earl of Ilchester (1937).
C. of H.H.	*Chronicles of Holland House*, by the same (1937).
A.C.	*Archibald Constable and his literary correspondents*, by T. Constable (1873).
E.R.	*The Edinburgh Review*.
G.M.	*The Gentleman's Magazine*.
A.R.	*The Annual Register*.
D.N.B.	*The Dictionary of National Biography*.
O.E.D.	*The Oxford English Dictionary*.

SYDNEY SMITH IN
HIS LETTERS

SYDNEY SMITH was born at Woodford in Essex on 3 June 1771, the second son of a handsome, clever, restless, and selfish father (himself the son of a London merchant) and of a good, charming, and vivacious mother of Huguenot descent. He was educated at Winchester and New College, Oxford, being Prefect of Hall at the former college in 1788 and a Fellow of the latter from 1791 till his marriage in 1800. In 1794 he took Orders on his appointment to the curacy of Netheravon on Salisbury Plain. The vicar was non-resident. The squire usually resided at Netheravon for a part of the year, but his principal home was Williamstrip Park, near Fairford, Glos. He was Mr. Michael Hicks Beach, M.P. for Cirencester, who had taken the name Beach on marrying Miss Beach, the heiress to the Netheravon property. The Hicks Beaches were conscientious landlords and found in Sydney Smith an able and energetic agent in improving the conditions of the parishioners. A cordial friendship sprang up between the curate and the squire's family, which led to Sydney becoming tutor to the squire's elder boy Michael and going to live in Edinburgh with him in 1798.

The following is the first extant letter of Sydney Smith:

1. M. H. BEACH

Netheravon, July 26th, Saturday, 1794

Sr

I am extremely obliged to you for your kind invitation to Williamstrip. I mean to continue in my present situation for two years, and will certainly pay my compliments to you in Gloucestershire before the expiration of that time; but I am afraid it cannot be this Summer. I have engagements at Winchester, Weymouth, Bath, and Oxford and expect my Brother at Netheravon. My stock of theological doctrine which at present is most alarmingly small will necessarily occupy a great deal of my time; and I mean to try if I cannot persuade the poor people to come to church, for really at present (as was said of Burke at Hastings' Trial) my preaching is like the voice of one crying in the Wilderness.

You may assure yourself Sr that the Parsonage house, owing to the uncommon heat of the Summer is perfectly dry. I have suffered a little from the smell of paint, but that is entirely gone off at present.

I shall have great pleasure in transmitting the compliments of yourself and Mrs. Beach to my Aunts, and be assured Sr I cannot do it without mentioning in the warmest terms, the great politeness and attention I have experienced at Netheravon. I am Sr with the greatest respect, your obliged humble St.

Sydney Smith

2. M. H. Beach

Netheravon, Monday, 10 ⟨Nov. 1794⟩

Dr Sr

If I can get my churches* served for one Sunday I shall have great pleasure in coming to see you at Williamstrip. I rather think I shall be able to effect this, and if I do not write you to the contrary I will be with you next Monday night. Your offer of a horse to carry my portmanteau I cannot accept, and for two reasons which I think will justify me in not accepting it. The first is you have no horse here, the next, I have no Portmanteau. I shall send my things to Bath* in a small trunk, from thence by the mail to Fairford, from whence I hope the Mr. of the Inn will have ingenuity enough to forward it by a porter to Williamstrip. For this acute and well contrived scheme of sending my things I arrogate to myself very little merit, it was chiefly contrived by yr charioteer, a man of senatorial gravity and prudence. I beg my Compts to Mrs. Beach and am my dr Sr yours very sincerely

Sydney Smith

[Sydney Smith left Netheravon in the spring of 1796. The next certain date in his life is that of a letter of 23 August 1797, in which we find him engaged to become tutor to Mr. Hicks

Beach's elder son Michael on his leaving Eton. In the meantime we know that he had stayed at Bath, where his father was living, and in London and at Williamstrip, and that he had busied himself with finding a governess for the Hicks Beach daughters. It is a fair assumption that he also saw something of his sister Maria's friend and schoolfellow, Miss Catherine Pybus of Cheam House, Cheam. His daughter tells us in the *Memoir* that at the time of their marriage they had been 'long engaged'. It is not easy to imagine him for more than a year unemployed; but we do not know what steps he may have taken towards earning a living, nor at what date he was invited to become Michael's tutor.

The first plan for the tutorship was that they should go to Germany, but this was abandoned owing to the state of Europe. Napoleon had just overrun Italy, humiliated the Pope, enslaved Switzerland, and was now threatening the German States. Edinburgh was accordingly selected as the place of sojourn for tutor and pupil, with important results for the life at least of the tutor and for the course of English literary journalism. For at Edinburgh, then in the heyday of its fame as 'the Athens of the North', Sydney Smith became intimate with Francis Jeffrey, Henry Brougham, Francis Horner, and others, and with them conceived and put into successful execution the *Edinburgh Review*. He also preached occasionally, and with great effect, at the Episcopalian Charlotte Chapel, and in 1800 published his first book of *Six Sermons*.]

11. M. H. BEACH

Bowood, Friday ⟨Dec. 1st, 1797⟩

My dear Sr

They have sent for me here to marry my Brother* to Miss Vernon daughter of Lady Ossory and Dick Vernon. and as you know young Ladies are rather squeamish, I am afraid they will not buckle to in time enough for me to keep my appointment with Michael. I am very sorry to interrupt the scheme, but such a cause will I am sure be a very sufficient excuse to you. I shall return to Oxford from hence and then set off immediately for

Netheravon of which I will give you notice in time. I would write to you more at large, but it is dinner time and this Aristocrat or rather Democrat* gives such good dinners, that they are by no means to be neglected, and especially not by such an Epicure as me. I am my dear Sr yours very sincerely

Sydney Smith

19. M. H. BEACH

Edinburgh, June 30th, Saturday Evening, 1798

My dear Sr

Anxious as you and Mrs Beach are for the welfare and improvement of yr Son, I do not think it fair to keep you much longer than a fortnight at a time without a Letter, and at about that interval you may always expect to hear from me. – I can promise you one thing in my correspondence, I will always tell you the truth in every thing which concerns yr Son, whether that truth be likely to give you pleasure, or pain; I have endeavored to make this my System in life, and (if I understand you right) it is that, which you yourself have pursued. Our beginning has been very auspicious; as far as we have hitherto gone, I am extremely pleased and satisfied with Michael. My first serious conversation with him, was upon the subject of his toilette, and the very great portion of time he daily consumed in adorning himself. This Michael took in high anger, and was extreemly sulky, and upon my renewing the conversation sometime after, he was still more so. Without the smallest appearance of anger, or vexation on my part, I turned his Sulkiness into ridicule, and compleatly laughed him into good humor. He acknowledged it was very foolish, and unmanly to be sulky about any thing, promised that he would hear any future remarks of mine upon his conduct with chearfulness, and that he would endeavor to dress himself as quickly as he could, and to these promises he has certainly conformed himself. Mithoffer* was extreemly fond of standing at his elbow while he was dressing, and reaching him every thing he wanted. This I have put a stop to; habits of indolence are soon learnt, Michael is a very apt Scholar in these particulars; Where

activity and energy are not innate they are infused by slow
degrees, and by a vigilant attention to little particulars. Very soon
after our arrival here, I checked his propensity of getting to bed,
so very early. He has since then generally sat up till between 10
and 11, and got up most mornings at about 6. The great apprehension I entertained of Michael was, that he would hear every
thing I said to him with a kind of torpid Silence, and that I
should never be able to learn whether he acquiesced voluntarily,
or from compulsion in my proposals, or get him by any means to
state candidly his objections, and prefer openly and ingenuously
his observations. From an entire ignorance of his opinions and
disposition, I should then have always been working in the dark.
This difficulty however upon a better acquaintance with him has
vanished; he talks over a subject boldly with me, and makes his
objections like a man.

I have found him very docile in a great many little particulars,
and I think very highly of the goodness of his heart, and disposition. I think much better of his understanding than I did.
His *acquirements* at Eaton have certainly not been very brilliant;
he reads Greek with great difficulty and cannot construe the
most easy Latin Book. He spells carelessly, and writes English
awkwardly, and ungrammatically. In my attention to his improvement, I shall by no means neglect the 2 latter particulars. I
am always for laying a good solid foundation. The plan I have
begun with is Latin, (very easy) for two hours in the morning,
and the history of England for two hours in the afternoon. Twice
a week instead of reading Latin, he writes me some English, as an
exercise in Style, and when we get into our new Lodgings I mean
that a master shall attend him in some thing or other for an hour
every day; and then I think his time will be sufficiently employed.
He very honestly confesses his love of horses, and hounds and his
dislike of study but expresses his great willingness to fag as well
as he can, and allows I have not been too hard upon him. In
adjusting the time of study, my object was to occupy him fairly,
without exciting his disgust; I think I have succeeded. This my
dear Sr is the detail I have to give you respecting yr Son, and
these are the observations I have made upon him during our
short acquaintance. I have no doubt *at present* of his safety, and

improvement in this place; when I *have*, you shall instantly know it. The Eruptions on his face are certainly better than they were, which I attribute to Sea Bathing. He continues to take his Essence of the Woods. - Our present acquaintance are - Ld Webb Seymour,* whom we both like very much; Mr Stewart* professor of moral philosophy, in this university and I believe generally considered to be one of the first men in it, and a Mr Dalzel* Greek professor of whom we have seen very little. We have received, and thank you for the letter to Baron N.* The Town is extreemly empty and is to continue so till November. The greater part of the people to whom we have Letters are absent.

You have undertaken a very arduous task, in engaging to frank my outward and homeward bound Letters, I am really quite ashamed of the trouble I am giving you. No Smells were ever equal to Scotch Smells. It is the School of Physic; walk the Streets, and you would imagine that every Medical man had been administering Cathartics to every man woman and child in the Town. Yet the place is uncommonly beautiful, and I am in a constant balance between admiration and trepidation –

> Taste guides my Eye, where e'er new beauties spread
> While prudence whispers, 'look before you tread'.

⟨   ⟩* my dear Sr I am with best regards to Mrs B, and the various branches of yr family yrs very sincerely

Sydney Smith

The Courier shall quaff fragrant bohea at 6s per Lb. I beg leave to present you with the following most beautiful Extempore upon the subject by me

> His antient privilege restored by thee
> The joyous courier quaffs the gratis tea,
> Uplifts the mantling cup and curses me,
> Th' unfeeling Spoiler of his sweet Bohea.

21. Mrs. Beach

38, South Hanover-street, Edinburgh,
1798, Sunday, Aug. 26th

My dear Madam,

You are the first Lady I ever met with, who thought she wrote a bad Letter; I know nothing would please you so much, as my coincidence in this opinion, but you know I am never complaisant, when I cannot be so conscientiously. Michael finishes his Latin Studies at the end of this month, and I mean to exercise him for some time in English composition, a pursuit in which we shall have perhaps more success from his conviction of its importance. The evenings we have thitherto employed in English history and shall continue to do so for some time. Michael takes a Lesson in dancing every day. I get him now and then to shew me a step or two; I cannot bear the repetition of this spectacle every day, as it never fails to throw me into a fit of laughing little short of suffocation, in which Michael joins and so ends the exhibition. You ask me how Michael bore the difficulties of our highland expedition. It is no part of Michael's character to be easily intimidated by these kind of difficulties; he has an admirable constitution and a soldier-like indifference to luxurious accomodations, not that he does not enjoy them when present, but that he does not regret them when they cannot be obtained. I am sorry to say he was not the first to complain. You mention some Ben (in Gaelic a hill), but from the entangled appearance of the Letters I cannot discover the name, and shall therefore call it Ben Blot; we did not see it. To mount a very high hill, is an adventure of dubious success; you are very often repaid with fog and vapor for your trouble. You may depend upon it my dr Madam that my observations upon the Clergy are just. Religion (I am sorry to say) is much like Heraldry, an antiquated concern; a few people attend to the one and the other, but the world laugh at them for engaging in such a superannuated pursuit. In 50 years more the whole art of going to church – how the Squire's Lady put on her best hat and cloak, and how the Squire bowed to the parson after church and how the parson dined with the Squire, and all these ceremonies of worship will be in the hands of the antiquarian, will be elucidated by laborious investigation, and explained by appropriate drawings. I am glad you like your atlas. I shall attend to what you say about Mr. Talbot. Edinburgh is very empty, consequently our Studies are not much interrupted by visiting. We have dined with Baron Norton once. He seems to be a very hearty good sort of man; he has more the appearance of an English country gentleman than of a Baron of the Scotch Exchequer. Mithoffer continues to behave extreemly well. As he is not a very good judge of meat, I have been forced to go to Market myself 2 or 3 times, but now the courier is very much improved. We all tried to make a pye by our joint efforts, the Cook, Mithoffer and I; the Crust was as hard as a biscuit and we could not eat it. There is always some beef in the Salt tub, and I look into the family affairs like a fat old Lady of 40. The Cook has 6d a day and the other girl her board only.

Will you be so good as to let me know whether the Letter I mentioned has been written by Messrs Hoares. I hope the presentation of colors was a gallant spectacle; Buonaparte's absence in Ægypt will retard for some time the event of his meeting with Mr Hicks. I beg my best regards to Mr B. and family and remain my dr Mdm yrs very sincerely

S. Smith

26. Mrs. Beach

38, South Hanover-street, 1798
⟨endorsed in pencil Nov. 4⟩

My dear Madam

There is in the first place at Edinburgh a workhouse where those poor who want support are sent, and which is supported by a voluntary assessment of all the inhabitants.

At the Church doors there is a collection made every Sunday, which is distributed at the discretion of the minister and Elders, and this is all the public Support that the poor receive. The antipathy to the workhouse is very great, and the Collections not considerable and there must be as I fancy there certainly is a great deal of misery here.

In one respect the police of Scotland is very bad. I suppose there are at least 3 beggars in this Country for every one in England, and there is not here the same just reason for putting an end to the abuse. They beg in a very quiet, gentle way, and thus lose the most productive art of their profession, Importunity. Have you ever made any efforts to introduce a better System of cooking among the poor? It would be a great charity. The basis of the food of the English poor is fine Wheaten bread and it is utterly impossible that a man, his wife and 4 Children can have 3 Meals a day of dry bread for 5d or 6d, which they can of broth and even for less.

If their manner of appropriating their money was better than it is and more provident, their pay would certainly be sufficient. I am in hopes to carry these ideas into execution, at some future time, and become Master Cook, as well ⟨as⟩ Master parson of my village.*

The people here understand this much better than in England. Michael is extreemly well, he got William's Letter this morning. He has met here with an Eaton friend, whom he seems to like, and as he appears to be a very good lad I can have no objection to his cultivating such an acquaintance.

I now consider the war between France and England no longer as an occasional quarrel, or tempory dispute but as an antipathy and natural horror of the same kind as subsists between the kite and the Crow, or the Church warden and the pauper, the weazle and the rat, the parson and the deist, the bailiff and the half-pay Captain &c. &c., who have persecuted each other from the beginning of time, and will peck, swear, fly, preach at and lye in wait for each other till the end of time. With best regards to Mr B— yours my dear Madam very sincerely –

Sydney Smith

32. MRS. BEACH

38, South Hanover-street, 1799 Edinburgh, Scotland,
Feb. 21st, Thursday

My dear Madam

In May then you may expect to see my goodly personage with Michael at my heels, and you will find us both I dare say as we are at this moment plump and in good condition.

I am sorry to hear that poor Miss Dyke still continues so ill. The termination of her life I hope will be pleasant and serene. The opening of it has been much otherwise; Yet she seems to bear it extreemly well. I have always said that the heroism and courage of men is nothing in comparison with these qualities as they are developed in women. Women cannot face danger accompanied with noise, and smoke and hallooing; but in all kinds of serene peril, and quiet horrors they have infinitely more philosophical endurance than men. - Put a woman in a boat in a boisterous Sea, let 6 or 7 people make as much noise as they can, and she is in a state of inconceivable agony; ask the same woman in a serene Summer's Evening, when all nature is at rest to drink a cup of poison for some good which would accrue from it to her husband and Children and she will swallow it like green tea. Your character of the Swiss Philosophess* sounds well; I should like to see her; you know what a Coxcomb I am about Physiognomy.

We have had tremendous weather here. The Country is in a most dreadful state from the thaw which has now taken place; except the morning after the Flood was over I should doubt if it had ever been dirtier. On that day Mrs. Noah is said to have lost a new pair of Shoes in the mud, which she could not extricate. Her white flounce petticoat which was made by an antediluvian Milliner in the Land of Edom was dirtied from top to bottom, but as she had carried two of every kind into the Ark, this was no great evil; she changed her Clothes, and after a little muttering and Swearing took a dram of brandy which Noah had had by him for 520 years ,– and all was well. We have been to Blue Beard here. A whole row of Abomelique's* Pasteboard Guards knoct their heads against a Tower and tumbled down, and Selim generously laying aside his resentment at that moment pickt them all up again – Is not this a noble rivalry? I have drawn for £100 today – making the whole receipts including what I rec'd in Town £600. Our expences at the beginning of this month stood at £455. Will you remember me very kindly to Mr. B and all the family and believe me yours very sincerely

S. Smith

34. Mrs. Beach

38, South Hanover-street, 1799,
Monday, March 18th

My dear Madam

Kemble* the player is come down here and these wicked people are employing passion week in going to tragedies, and comedies. It is I am told extremly ludicrous to see him on the Stage; half his time is employed in prompting the other actors and correcting their motions. The other Evening he was stabbed, and he was forced to put his assassin in mind that it was time to stab him; which you will allow was rather an awkward circumstance. I sent Michael once, but had not myself the curiosity to go – When he is to be seen in town with some good co'actors, I do not wish to see him here with a troop of wretched Strollers at his heels. I should not be much disquieted if I never saw him again. You will be very much surprised that the Scotch should so totally neglect all religious worship in this week; but they do not even shut the Shops on good friday – nor is there any thing like the sound of prayer in their churches, or the smell of buns in their Pastry Cooks' windows.

Michael is extreemly well, raves about dancing and has got a drawing which he thinks very well done and is bringing home for your inspection. he has at last received a Letter from his friend Mr Talbot, which he is very generously answering immediately. I think Mr Talbot deserves to be punished with a long silence. Is your Swiss Gouvernante come to you? how do you like her? Pray where is Mrs. Williams going to? to her *chambre ornée* at Bath? I have no news to tell you from this place; preaching and dancing are the great subjects of conversation here. Michael is thought to do the steps neatly; the people say it is a great pity that I don't preach as well as he capers. Will you give my best regards to Mr B and tell him I hope soon to have the pleasure of shaking him by the hand. In the mean time my dear Madam beleive me yours most sincerely

S. Smith

41. M. H. Beach

Endorsed in pencil 1799, Sep. 22
Postmark Aberystwith

My dear Sr

I am sure you will do me the justice to say, that it has not been my habit to harrass you with trivial complaints of yr Son's conduct, and indeed as I never troubled you before upon the subject, you may believe that I should not *now* do it, unless the occasion appeared to me to be such, as fully called for your interference. Is it not my duty to correct the foibles and mistakes of your Son? and is not his duty to hear what I say to him, if not with respect and attention, at least without insolence, contempt and defiance? You have no conception, of his frivolous minuteness and particularity in every thing which concerns his dress and person; it is more than feminine and upon my venturing the other morning to make some observations about the inutility of his travelling with his own boot-jack his behaviour was so extreemly improper and disrespectful that I did not open my lips to him for two days. In all this time no sort of apology: – this morning I had a very long and serious conversation with him on the Subject and tho' he knew I intended to write to you, not a Syllable of apology. Perhaps my dear Sr a few observations from you on that politeness and respect which he owes to those to whom you delegate your authority would do him more good, than I am sorry to say any advice of mine can do. You must be very sensible if he is permitted to treat me in this manner, that my time must be not only uselessly but detrimentally employed – You expect and have an undoubted right to expect from me the strictest attention to everything which goes to make up the character of your Son as a man and a gentleman, and I am sure you will use your influence and authority to protect me from insult and injury. One single word of apology on the part of your Son would have prevented you from ever knowing what has passed between us. I was the more hurt on this occasion as Mithoffer was present during the whole of his improper behaviour. I remain my dear Sr with the greatest respect your very *sincere friend*

Sydney Smith

43. M. H. Beach

Edinburgh, P office, Wednesday, Oct. 2nd, 1799

My dear Sr

I was too well convinced of the proper Sentiments in which you have educated yr Children to doubt for a moment of the manner in which you would express yourself to Michael upon that conduct of which I complained.

Yr letter produced every effect you could have wished from it. He not only apologized to me in the most ample manner, but (which convinced me he really thought himself wrong) brought in Mithoffer before whom the affront was given to witness the apology. Of course I said every thing handsome to him on the subject, and I dare say we shall be only better friends for what has passed. I am very sorry my dear Sr to have disturbed the tranquillity of yourself and Mrs Beach, but it would have been a most injurious and mistaken complaisance, to have sacrificed the real good of your Son to the present feelings of his parents. We lost no time or distance from Sr Robert Vaughan's* to this place, but were detained by repairs to the Coach, bad roads and horses and Sunday. You should certainly go and see Sr Robert – You will be very much pleased with his place, his efforts to improve the country about him, and his great good nature and hospitality. – I think Mrs B will too, tho I know Sr Robert is no great favorite of hers, but why I cannot conceive, for I have seldom seen any man, who seems to possess more natural mildness and benevolence.

He sees from his windows Cader Idris, and Snowdon, both of

them inferior to himself in heighth and bulk. It was curious and amusing to see the worthy baronet, surrounded by 16 little men and women who reached up to the waist band of his breeches, and looked like iron rails round a monument.

We are lodging-hunting, and I hope in a few days to be settled. Michael's leg has been quite well for some time. He has quite recovered his looks and is going to bathe for some time in the Sea, which always agrees with him. I hope my little friends continue quite well – Adieu my dear Sr and beleive me with best regards to Mrs B yours very sincerely

Sydney Smith

46. MRS. BEACH

Monday ⟨Nov. 1799⟩

My dear Madam

I never think any thing is decided upon in so very cursory a conversation as we had on the subject of the minerals at William-strip – *Now* upon full reflection you determine to have them; we will execute your commands with submission and pleasure. I grieve for poor Madame de Monteny,* who captivated me a good deal during my Stay at Williamstrip. I am very glad you like Edgeworth's book.* I do not know what he says upon the subject of religion, but this much I am sure of, that to attempt to impress notions of religion upon the minds of very young children before they are capable of thinking for one moment seriously upon any thing, is to associate for the whole of subsequent life ennui, and disgust to the idea of sacred reflexion; and I am fully persuaded more injury is done here by zeal than neglect. – Ketts* book I have read, some little,* but I know the Man, and know him to be incapable of any thing above mediocrity. Every event that has taken place in the French revolution, and for a hundred Years before the french revolution, has been clearly pointed out by Some clergyman or other in the prophets, and if the Clergy industriously sought for some method of disgusting rational men with the reasoning of Theologians, this perhaps would be the real way – at least I cannot extempore think of a better. . . . I remain my dear Madam yrs most sincerely

Sydney Smith

52. MRS. BEACH

Saturday, April 11th ⟨1800⟩

My dear Madam

I have very little doubt of being married in the month of June, and it is full time to consider of some arrangement about William. It will be as near as I can guess about 3 months before I shall be able to receive William,* dating from the time of my marriage, Which I think is as little time as can be required to visit my father, and to procure and furnish a house. If this is longer than you wish W. to remain at home, I will if you please return with him to Scotland, and can contrive to be here by a month after my marriage – or less – The expence will be the same to Mr B as sending him to me near Bath with the additional expence of my journeys backwards and forwards amounting I suppose to about £80 in the whole. There cannot possibly be any Spot in England where young men can be so advantageously educated as here, and he will have the advantage of mixing with other young men, which he is not sure of in the other case. *Mrs. Smith in future* has no objection to the plan – I beg you will consider me as having *no sort of choice* upon the subject, the conveniences, and inconveniences are so *exactly* balanced that I am quite at rest. Let Mr Beach consult entirely his own inclination, and convenience – I wish to have no other guide. I hope it will not appear to you indelicate that I have alluded to the expences of the journey. I shall have with the Salary I receive from Mr B. with W. clear £600 per Annum; sufficient to live here with oeconomy, but not an income sufficiently great to bear such a deduction as £80. Was I a richer man I should not have mentioned a Syllable on the subject – tho' upon this point my way of thinking has always been this – no man engages in the task of education for pleasure but with a view to emolument, and all possibility of disappointment, and complaint is effectually done away with on both Sides by submitting to a painful conversation of ten minutes I look upon you and Mr Beach to be my friends. I am certainly yours, and if you were reduced to beggary tomorrow, I do not know any action of my life could give me so much pleasure as educating your children exactly as I would have done if you were in a state of prosperity. There is no occasion for this, and the fair way is to lay before you the state of my fortune, and to shew you how much it is necessary for you to add to it to enable me to support your Son as your Son ought to be supported.

This I *have* done and I hope you do not think I have acted improperly in so doing. I have only mentioned the plan for your convenience, not for my own; my curiosity here is quite satiated. Can you form any kind of notion as to the time William will remain with me? Michael is quite well, and I have at last persuaded him to come in time to the Lecture; for the week past he has not missed once. I will beg an answer to this and the former Letter as soon as it may be perfectly convenient to you. You talk to me my dear Madam of plants; there will be no plants here for a month to come – I see Miss Browne's* marriage – may she be as happy as I intend to be, and may I be as I should believe Mr B and you always to have been. – Farewell good Madam –

[Sydney Smith was married at Cheam on 2 July 1800 to Catherine Amelia Pybus, daughter of the deceased John Pybus, a banker in Bond St. with a house at Cheam, once a member of the Council of Madras. The marriage, which was opposed by the bride's self-important brother (Letter 166), was a very happy one, as is amply attested by extant letters both of husband and wife as well as the *Memoir* written by their daughter Saba. Michael Hicks Beach ceased to be Sydney's pupil in 1800, but his younger brother William succeeded him and lived with the newly married couple at 46 George St., Edinburgh, until they left for London in 1803. Their eldest child Saba (named fancifully from the words 'Arabia and Saba' in Psalm 72) was born in the spring of 1802, and the *Edinburgh Review* first appeared in the following October. In London they lived first at 8 Doughty St., Mecklenburgh Square, where they had a boy born in 1803, who died in infancy, and another son, Douglas, born in 1805.]

58. FRANCIS JEFFREY

Postmark: June 1801

My dear Jeffrey

After a vertigo of one fortnight in London, I am now under-
going that species of hybernation or suspended existence, called
a pleasant fortnight in the country. I behave myself quietly and
decently as becomes a Corpse, and hope to regain the rational and
immortal part of my composition about the 20th of this month.

Nothing has pleased me more in London than the conversation
of Macintosh.* I never saw so theoretical a head which contained
so much practical understanding. He has lived much among
various men with great observation, and has always tried his profound moral speculations by the experience of life. He has not
contracted in the world a lazy contempt for theorists, nor in the
closet a peevish impatience of that grossness and corruptibility
of mankind, which are ever marring the schemes of secluded
benevolence. He does not wish for the best in politics or morals,
but for the best which can be attained; and what that is, he seems
to know well. Now what I object to Scotch philosophers in
general is that they reason upon man as they would reason upon
x;* they pursue truth, without caring if it be useful truth. They
are more fond of disputing on mind and matter than on anything
which can have a reference to the real world inhabited by real
men women and children; a philosophy which descends to the
present state of things is debased in their estimation: in short a
Scotchman is apt to be a practical rogue upon sale, or a visionary
philosopher. Look amongst our friends in E, and see if there be
not some truth in this. I do not speak of great prominent literary
Characters, but of the mass of reflecting men in Scotland.

Macintosh is going to India as Lecturer; I wish to God you
could find a similar situation in that country, but not before I
leave Scotland. I think it would be more to your taste than the
Scotch bar – and yet you want nothing to be a great lawyer, and
nothing to be a great speaker, but a deeper voice, slower and more
simple utterance, more humility of face and neck, and a greater
contempt for *esprit*, than men who have so much in general attain
to.

I have not the least idea when I shall return to Edinburgh: I hope the beginning of August. There seems to be no belief in invasion, and none in plots, which are now become so ridiculous that every body laughs at them.

Read Parr's* sermon, and tell me how you like it. I think it dull, with occasional passages of Eloquence. His notes are very entertaining. You will find in them a great compliment to my brother. Excuse my ending my letter so soon. I write in great haste. Mrs. S. begs her best compts. Remember me to all friends and to little Sally Patten. Delenda est Carthago. Write a book – I exclaim of my friend as Job did of his enemy. Yrs my dear Jeffrey with great regard

                                                          Sydney Smith

63. Hon. Caroline Fox*

Burnt Island, Fifeshire,
Monday, June 14th ⟨1802⟩

I have great pleasure in informing you Mrs. S is better, the Sea air has revived her, and she has made a very considerable, and satisfactory progress in the course of the 3 or 4 days last past. We are very delightfully situated in this place – opposite to Edinburgh on the other side of the Firth, and under the high woods of Aberdour Lord Morton's property. The little Town hitherto only celebrated for the cure of herrings will I hope in future be equally so for the cure of Wives.

Our contrivances would do honor to Archimedes. The spirit of substitution is strong upon us; we have barrels for tables, tongs for bells, and ropes to tie our doors instead of Locks. Nothing ministers to us in its original and destined capacity. Every thing is vicarial and supposititious.

Our little Girl is very beautiful, and very healthy, and when she can distinguish between good and evil will set as high a value upon your good wishes as every body else does who is fortunate enough to be their object.

I have transmitted Lord Holland's very obliging and considerate offer to Mr. Allen* – who sets off tomorrow for London. –

There has been a serious riot at Aberdeen – the soldiers shooting four or 5 or 6 men for flinging dead cats in the officers faces – This makes a great noise here – tho' in England I believe this Country is held in such contempt that an universal Sawnyphony or massacre of Scotchmen would hardly create as much commotion as one of Mrs. Walker's routes.*

I wish you dear Miss Fox a very happy Summer – good Sea bathing at Tenby and much pleasant company at Bowood. In the mean time beleive me with the truest respect yrs &c.

Sydney Smith

68. FRANCIS JEFFREY

Queen-street, Edinburgh, Burnt Island, Aug. 1802

Dear Jeffrey,

With the inculpative part of *your* criticism on *mine* I very much agree; and, in particular, am so well aware of that excessive levity into which I am apt to run, that I think I shall soon correct it. I will beg the favor of you to put up Nares* review in a little packet for me and to inform your servants where it may be found tomorrow in case the Carrier asks for it, while you are not at home. The levity certainly may be corrected. Of arguments upon the subject of miracles I really do not recollect to have advanced any, but appear to have confined myself to the detection of contradictions, and inconsistencies in his argument. Upon the point of severity I beg you to recollect the facts. That Nares is in point of talents a very stupid and a very contemptible fellow no one pretends to deny. He has been hangman for these ten years to all the poor authors in England, is generally considered to be hired by Government, and has talked about Social Order till he has talked himself into 6 or £700 per annum. That there can be a fairer object for critical severity I cannot conceive; and though he be not notorious in Edinburgh, he is certainly so in London. If he that deserves execution otherwise from anybody deserves it from me in particular, I confess I cannot see why the cumulation of public and private vengeance should not fall upon his head. If you think that the violent attack may induce the generality of readers to sympathize with the sufferer rather than the executioner, in spite of the general recollection that the artificer of death is perishing by his own art, then your objections to my criticism are good for the very opposite reason to that which you have alledged; not because they are too severe, but because, by diminishing the malice of the reader, they do not attain the greatest possible maximum of severity.

As for personalities grant that the man is a proper object of punishment, and in these literary executions I do not care for justice or injustice a fig. My business is to make the archdeacon* as ridiculous as possible. The readers to whom I write will allow me some personalities and refuse me others. I could not, and would not, say the man was a bad husband or a cruel father but nobody (but the very correct few) will be offended with my laughing at his dignities in the church.

You say the readers will probably think my review long. If it is amusing, they will not; and if it is dull, I am sorry for it, – but I can write no better. I am so desirous of attacking this priest, that I cannot consent to omit this article, unless my associates consider their moral or religious character committed by it; at the same time I will with great pleasure attempt to modify it.

I am very much obliged to you for your animad-versions on my inaccuracies, and should be obliged to you also to correct them. One of the instances you mention is perhaps rather awkward than incorrect, but had better be amended. I wrote my reviews as you see them; though I certainly made these blunders not in consequence of neglect, but in spite of attention.

I have received the inclosed notice that my rent is seized by one of Ballantine's my landlord's creditors. I suppose I have nothing to do but to refuse to pay my rent when it becomes due. Have the goodness to send it back when you have read it.

I will come over if I can very soon, not to detect Scotticisms, but to enjoy the company of Scotchmen. Just now I am expecting Dugald Stewart and his spouse. Pray do not lose the paper, but send it back directly.

I have been so very bitter lately against authors, and find so much of the *infusum amarum* still remaining in my style, that I am afraid you will not think my answer to your expostulation a very gracious one. If you do think so, pray think otherwise: you cannot be too candid with me. You will very often perhaps find me too vain for correction, but never so blind to the value of a frank and manly character as not to feel real gratitude, when it consults my good by pointing out my errors.

Yrs my dr Jeffrey most sincerely
Sydney Smith

71. MRS. BEACH

Edinburgh, Jan. 1803

My dear Madam,

Your son has communicated to me the very flattering request of Mr. Beach and yourself, that I should continue here another year; and it is a matter of real regret to me that I should be compelled to decline any proposal which it would give you pleasure that I should accept. I have one child, and I expect another: it is absolutely my duty that I should make some exertion for their future support. The salary you give is liberal; I live here in ease and abundance; but a situation in this country leads to nothing. I have to begin the world, at the end of three years, at the very same point where I set out from; it would be the same at the end of ten. I should return to London, my friends and connections moulded away, my relations gone and dispersed; and myself about to begin to do at the age of forty, what I ought to have begun to do at the age of twenty-five.

That my connection with William did not end two years ago I most heartily rejoice; for after the kindness you and Mr. B. showed to me during my residence at Netherhaven, I should ever have reproached myself as the most ungrateful of human beings. That kindness I shall never forget; and I shall quit this country with a very large balance of obligation on my side, which I shall always be proud to acknowledge. But I could not hold myself justified to my wife and family if I were to sacrifice, any longer, to the love of present ease, those exertions which every man is bound to make for the improvement of his situation.

After all, my dear Madam, are you doing right in keeping William any longer from the University? Are you not listening rather to your affection than your reason? One of the great objects of education is to accustom a young man *gradually* to become his own master. If a young man of William's great good sense cannot meet the little world of a University at twenty years of age, he cannot meet the great world at any age. It is in vain to tremble at the risk; all life is a constant risk of doing wrong. To accustom men to great risks, you must expose them, when boys, to lesser risks. If you attempt to avoid all risks, you do an injury infinitely greater than any you shun.

You will, I am sure, be obliged to me for speaking my opinion thus freely; and if I understand you both aright, I am equally sure that I shall not have offended you by fairly laying open to you those motives which have induced me to decline an offer that I received with the greatest pleasure, as a proof of your continued good opinion.

Sydney Smith

75. ARCHIBALD CONSTABLE*

⟨Edinburgh. Undated: 1803, before Aug. 8th⟩

Sir,

You ask me for my opinion about the continuation of the E. Review. I have the greatest confidence in giving it you, as I find every body here (who is capable of forming an opinion upon the subject) unanimous in the idea of its success, and in the hope of its continuation. It is notorious that all the reviews are the organs either of party or of booksellers. I have no manner of doubt that an *able*, *intrepid*, and *independent* review would be as useful to the public as it would be profitable to those who are engaged in it. If you will give £200 per annum to your editor, and ten guineas a sheet, you will soon have the best review in Europe. This town, I am convinced is preferable to all others for such an undertaking, from the abundance of literary men it contains, and from the freedom which at this distance they can exercise towards the wits of the south. The gentlemen who first engaged in this review will find it too laborious for pleasure; as labour, I am sure they will not meddle with it for a less valuable offer. I remain, Sir,

Your obedt. humble sert.

Sydney Smith

P.S. I do not, by the expressions I have used above, mean to throw any censure on the trade for undertaking reviews. Every one for himself; God for all. It is fair enough that a bookseller should guide the public to his own shop. And fair enough that a critic should tell the public they are going astray.

78. FRANCIS JEFFREY

Tuxford,* ⟨Aug.⟩ 1803

My dear Jeffrey,

Your very kind letter I received at the very moment of departure. I left Edinburgh with great heaviness of heart: I knew what I was leaving, and was ignorant to what I was going. My good fortune will be very great, if I should ever again fall into the society of so many liberal, correct, and instructed men, and live with them on such terms of friendship as I have done with you, and you know whom, at Edinburgh. I cannot see what obligations you are under to me; but I have so little objection to your thinking so, that I certainly shall not attempt to undeceive you in that opinion, or in any other which is likely to make you think of me more frequently or more kindly.

I have found the country everywhere full of spirit, and you are the only male despondent I have yet met with. Every one else speaks of the subjugation of England as of the subjugation of the Minotaur, or any other history in the mythological dictionary. God bless you, my dear Jeffrey! I shall always feel a pride and happiness in calling myself, and in showing myself, your friend.

S. S.

P.S. – I beg leave to except the Tuxford waiter, who desponds exactly as you do.

[Sydney Smith lived at 8 Doughty Street from 1803 to 1806, when his income as a preacher and lecturer enabled him to move to 18 Orchard Street, Portman Square. Here he lived till he moved to Yorkshire in the summer of 1809, supporting his family by his articles in the *Edinburgh Review*, by preaching at the Berkeley Chapel in Mayfair, the Fitzroy Chapel in St. Pancras, and the Foundling Hospital, and by three extraordinarily successful courses of Lectures on Moral Philosophy at the Royal Institution in Albemarle St., which finally required the erection of galleries in the lecture-room to seat the fashionable audience of 'six to eight hundred hearers' (Horner, ap. *M*., p. 129).

He had speedily made many friends in London in legal, political, and social circles. His wit and nonsense were irresistible, his good sense, sincerity, and kindness won lasting friendships. Among many other friends were Sir James Mackintosh, 'Conversation' Sharp, the poets Rogers and Moore, Whishaw 'the Pope of Holland House'. He was introduced to Holland House by Bobus, the lifelong friend of Lord Holland since their schooldays at Eton and now connected with him by marriage. Sydney became fast friends both with the witty and charming Lord Holland, whose ardour for liberty and tolerance he shared, and with Lady Holland, his beautiful, clever, and domineering wife, who soon looked upon him as one of the attractions of her famous dinner-parties. They kept up a lively correspondence to the end of Sydney's life, of which Sydney's extant letters are only less numerous than those to his later, less lively but equally close friend, Lady Grey.

Meantime, Sydney, whose younger daughter Emily was born in 1807, felt the need of a more permanent livelihood, and, failing to obtain the lease of a proprietary chapel in London, accepted in 1806 the living of Foston-le-Clay in Yorkshire, offered by the Lord Chancellor, Erskine, at the request of Lord and Lady Holland. He was very reluctant to leave London or its neighbourhood, and, as there was no habitable parsonage at Foston, he obtained permission from Archbishop Markham, on the strength of his employment at the Foundling Hospital, to serve his parish with a curate from York, while he made every effort to exchange the living for one in the Home Counties. In 1808, however, the new Archbishop of York, Edward Vernon (afterwards Harcourt), enforcing the Clergy Residence Act of 1803, required him

to take up residence, and accordingly Sydney and his family
removed to Yorkshire at midsummer 1809.]

86. Francis Jeffrey

8, Doughty-street, Brunswick-square,

Friday ⟨Oct. 28th, 1803⟩

My dear Jeffrey,

Many thanks to you for your goodness, my little boy is thank
God recovered. I sat up with him for two nights, expecting every
moment would be his last. I will not exercise my profession of
preaching common places, to you. I acknowledge your loss* was
a heavy calamity, for I can measure what you felt by what I felt
for you. May the game of life afford you ample compensation.
My great effort was to keep up Mrs. Smith's spirits, in which I
succeeded *tolerably* well.

There never were such charming girls as those Riddels. They
are heart and soul all over, and dearer to me than the light which
visits my eyes and the ruddy drops etc. etc.*

You have raised up to yourself here, *individually*, a very *high
and solid* reputation by your writings in the E.R. You are said to
be the ablest man in Scotland, and other dainty phrases are used
about you, which show the effect you have produced. Mᶜintosh
ever anxious to bring men of merit into notice is the loudest of
your panegyrists, and the warmest of your admirers. I have now
had an opportunity of appretiating the manner in which the
review is felt, and I do assure you it has acquired a most brilliant
and extensive reputation - follow it up by all means – on the first
of every month Horner and I will meet together, and order books
for Edinburgh - this we can do from the monthly lists. In addition we will scan the french booksellers' shops, and send you
everything valuable, excepting a certain portion that we will
reserve for ourselves. We will in this division be just and candid
as we can; if you do not think us so let us know. You will have
the lists, and can order for yourselves any books, not before
ordered for you; many catalogue articles I will take to avoid the
expence of sending them backwards and forwards from E to

London: many I will send. The articles I shall review for No. 6 are Iceland, Goldbering's Travels into Africa, and Ségur upon the influence of women in Society. I shall not lose sight of the probability of procuring assistance; some I am already asking for. You will not need from me more than two sheets, I presume. Pray tell me the names of the writers of this No. M°intosh says there has been no such book upon political economy as Brougham's since the days of Adam Smith. Best regards to Mrs. J. and God bless you

S. S.

91. Francis Jeffrey

⟨April or May 1804⟩

My dear Jeffrey,

I can hardly believe my own eyes when they inform me that I am up, dressed and writing by eight o'clock in the morning; and as there is nobody near by whose perceptions I can rectify my own, the fact will probably be undecided thro' the whole of my letter. To put the question to an intellectual test, I have tried an act of memory, and endeavoured to form a distinct image of the editor of the Edinburgh Review; but he appears to me of a stature so incredibly small, that I cannot venture to say I am awake, and my mind in its healthy and vigorous state: however, you must take me as you find me. Talking of the Edinburgh Review, I hardly think the article on Dumont is much liked by those whose praise I should be most desirous you should obtain; tho' it conciliates the favour of men who are always ready to join in a declaration of war against all works of speculation and philosophical enterprise; but when I speak in dispraise of this article, I only contrast it with what you have done better; for, in spite of its errors (if any such there be), it would make the fortune of anybody else.

I certainly, my dear Jeffrey, in conjunction with the Knight of the Shaggy Eyebrows,* do protest against your increasing and unprofitable scepticism. I exhort you to restrain the violent tendency of your nature for analysis, and to cultivate synthetical propensities. What's the use of virtue? What's the use of wealth? What's the use of honor? What's a guinea but a damned yellow circle? What's a chamber-pot but an infernal hollow sphere? The whole effort of your mind is to destroy. Because others build slightly and eagerly, you employ yourself in kicking down their houses, and contract a sort of aversion for the more honorable useful and difficult task of building well yourself.

I think you ought to know Horner too well by this time to expect Malthus before you see it.

The satire against me I have not yet seen. One of the charges against me, I understand, is that I am ugly; but this is mere falsehood, and a plain proof that the gentleman never can have seen me. I certainly am the best-looking man concerned with the Review, and this John Murray has been heard to say behind my back. Pray tell the said John Murray that three ladies, apparently pregnant and much agitated, have been here to inquire his direction, calling him a base, perfidious young man.

I am extremely sorry for poor Alison:* he is a man of great delicacy, and will be hurt by the attack of this scoundrel. Dumont is certainly displeased with the review. I have no doubt but that in a little time you will be great with the Riddels from whom Mrs. Smith expects every day to hear.

I conclude hastily from the hope of a frank for you.

Yrs my dr. Jeffrey *most sincerely and affectionately*
Sydney Smith

92. HON. CAROLINE FOX

Tuesday ⟨Spring 1804⟩

My business with the Bishop of London* ended as I had supposed it would in nothing. Protestant nepotism is seldom carried so far as the same vice in catholic countries. Our friend the Greek has entirely broken with his patron the bishop, or rather the patron has broken with the greek; he is no longer the Bishop's chaplain and his hopes of future preferment are at an end. In recompence he has got rid of the trouble of the young pupils and the impertinence of their mother. I have received from him a long history of the proceeding, tending to prove he is not in fault. Nothing could be more superfluous, as it is a maxim with me that a Bishop must always be in the wrong. Pray read Thomas Brown's poems,* 2 Vols Edinburgh. He is the same Brown who wrote an answer to Dr Darwin's Zoonomia, tho' I do not mean to offer this fact as presumptive evidence of poetical ability. I have sent to Messrs Longman and Rees to receive their money for my brother, but they have not yet sent for it. We will call on Mr and Mrs M°Naughton next Sunday, a day I always appropriate for visits contiguous to my chapel - Bobus has written to Scarlett* and Sharp by the last Ships; he writes in very good spirits, and as one thoroughly satisfied with what he has done.

I have not the review by me and I cannot remember what expression at the beginning can justify your remarks on Mr. Jeffrey. I am almost certain at the time he wrote that review he had never heard of Dumont, or had heard of him without impression, and however Dumont's abilities may be privately admired he and every other Author are at their first Works to be spoken of as new men. I would differ with you about the petulance of the review if by differing I could persuade you to adopt a contrary opinion, but as you have a very awkward knack of judging for yourself I make a merit of necessity and acknowledge you are right. It is generally believed that our excellent monarch is insane, and rumored that he set off full Gallop immediately on his arrival at Windsor pursued by Dr. Simmonds,* 5 other physicians, and the Apothecary in waiting, Gold Stick, all the Canons, several dogs, Dr. Langford,* and a great number of his liege subjects too obscure for the records of history. Our best regards to Miss Vernon - I remain dr Miss Fox, very affectionately and respectfully

Yrs
Sydney Smith

98. FRANCIS JEFFREY

Doughty-street, April, 1805

My dear Jeffrey,

I should be very much obliged to you to transmit the enclosed testimonials to St. Andrew's, to pay for the degree, to send me word how much you have paid for it, and I will repay you immediately. If there is any form neglected, then send us information how to proceed. The degree itself may be sent to me also by the mail or post according to its size. Pray do not neglect this affair as the interests of a poor and respectable man depend upon it.

Mrs. Smith is very well. So is Saba, so is the Boy Douglas after a very severe tryal for his life. I thought at one time he was going off just like our last little boy, but he has rallied, and is now to all appearances safe.

My Lectures are just now at such an absurd pitch of celebrity, that I must lose a good deal of reputation before the judgement of the public settles into a just equilibrium respecting them. I am most heartily ashamed of my own fame, because I am conscious I do not deserve it, and that the moment men of sense are provoked by the clamor to look into my claims, it will be at an end.

I have just skimmed over Brougham's answer to Ld. Lauderdale. Of the question I know little. The manner is not much amiss and I am glad upon the whole he has answered him. Are the interests of the Review going on as they ought?

I am at last reconciled to my father. He was very ill, very much out of spirits, and tired to death with the quarrel the moment he discovered I ceasd to care a halfpenny about it. I made him a slight apology – just sufficient to save his pride, and have as in duty bound exposed myself for these next 7 or 8 years to all that tyranny, trouble and folly with which I have no manner of doubt at the same age I shall harass my children.

I am very glad to hear that Murray and you are to be here in the autumn and hope my evil stars will not carry me away. God bless you my dr. Jeffrey and believe me with kind regards from Mrs. S. to you both yr sincere friend

Sydney Smith

99. LADY HOLLAND

8, Doughty-street, Brunswick-square,
Tuesday ⟨May, 1805⟩

My dear Lady Holland,

I told the little Poet,* after the proper Softenings of Wine,
Dinner, Flattery, repeating his Verses, etc. etc., that a friend of
mine wished to lend him some money, and I begged him to take
it. The poet said that he had a very sacred, and serious notion of
the duties of independence, that he thought he had no right to be
burthensome to others from the mere apprehension of evil, and
that he was in no immediate want. If it was necessary, he would
ask me hereafter for the money without scruple, and that the
knowing he had such resources in reserve, was a great comfort to
him. This was very sensible and honorable, nor had he the slightest feeling of affront on the subject, but on the contrary of great
gratitude to his benefactor, whose name I did not mention, as the
money was not received; I therefore cancell yr draft, and will call
upon you, if he calls upon me. This, I presume, meets yr approbation. I had a great deal of conversation with him, and he is a
much more sensible man than I had any idea of. I have received
this morning a very kind Letter from Sir Francis Baring, almost
amounting to a promise that I am to be a professor in his new
Institution.*

I cannot conclude my Lr without telling you, that you are a
very good lady for what you have done; and that I will speak a
word for you in a very high place where I have great professional
interest. I remain, dr Lady Holland, yrs very respectfully and
sincerely

Sydney Smith

I have a project for Campbell's publishing his volume of new
poems by subscription. They are already far advanced.

100. FRANCIS JEFFREY

Postmark June 12th, 1805

My dear Jeffrey,

Many thanks to you for yr attention to my diploma. When you send me a statement of expenses I will give you a draft for the money – by statement, I mean amount. I will do for Anne Bannerman* what I can, tho' that I am afraid will be very little, as I have a mortal antipathy to solliciting subscriptions.

I conclude my lectures next Saturday. Upon the whole I think I have done myself some little good by them.

I think yr last articles in the Edinburgh Review extremely able, and by no means inferior to what you have done before.

John Allen* is come home in very high favor with Lord and Lady Holland. They say he is without exception the best-tempered man that ever lived, very honorable, and of an understanding superior to most people; in short, they do him complete justice. He is very little altered, except that he appears to have some faint notions that all the world are not quite so honorable and excellent as himself. I have the highest respect for John Allen. Vive le bon A.

I wrote to Stewart, to tell him of a report which prevailed here that the General Assembly had ordered him to drink a Scotch pint of hemlock, which he had done, discoursing about the gods to Playfair and Darcy.*

Best regards to Tim Thompson. When are we to drink copiously of warm rum and water to a late hour of the morning? When am I to see you again, and John Murray and everybody in the North whom I love and respect? God bless you. Mrs. S. sends her best regards to Mrs. J. and you. Every yrs. my dear Jeffrey with the most sincere affection and respect

Sydney Smith

101. FRANCIS JEFFREY

8, Doughty-street, Brunswick-square,
July 4th, 1805

My dear Jeffrey

I am afraid I shall not be able to do much for yr friend Miss Bannerman. I am so very modest a beggar even for myself that I find an indescribable difficulty in exercising the art mendicant for others: but I will do my best. I forget if I have thanked you for the Diploma which has been duly received, and has by this time conferred the small tythes of Rum and Black Virgins* on the Reverend Gentleman to whom it is consigned. My whole family is well and we all leave London 15th July to spend a month at M. H. Beach Esq M.P. Williamstrip Park Fairford Glocestershire – and from thence to my father's till the beginning of October. My direction however will be to Mr. Beach till that period, a piece of information of which I hope you will have the goodness to avail yourself. You ask me about my prospects. I think I shall long remain as I am. I have no powerful friends. I belong to no party, I do not cant, I abuse canting everywhere, I am not conciliating, and I have not talents enough to force my way without these laudable and illaudable auxiliaries. This is ⟨as⟩ true a picture of my situation as I can give you. In the mean time I lead not an unhappy life, much otherwise, and am thankful for my share of good. I will be very honest with you and confess I do not read the Edinburgh review so diligently as I ought, but whenever I do look into it or into that part of it which you produce I find the same acuteness, profundity and justness of observation which has stamped upon it the high character it universally bears in this Town. Will you desire Murray to send to Henning* for one of my medallions and to bring it with him in a little box wrapt in Cotton – first paying for it. I am happy to find we shall meet at Mr. Beach's where Horner intends to bring Murray. Request of Murray to omit all mention of 1st. and 2nd. causes at Mr. Beach's, they have no connection with agricultural affairs. My kindest regards to him, Tomson* and all my old friends.

Ever yrs my dear Jeffrey with the truest affection

Sydney Smith

Our best regards to Mrs. J.

103. SIR JAMES MACKINTOSH,
Recorder, Bombay

October 1st, 1805

My dear M^cintosh

I do not know that I have made any new acquaintance since your departure, a description of whom could in any degree be interesting to you. With Lady Holland I believe you are acquainted; I am lately become so.* She is very handsome, very clever, and I think very agreeable. She has taken hugely to the Edinburgh Reviewers, particularly to little John Horner – whose reputation as well as Brougham's are so high for political oeconomy that they are fêted everywhere; and as in addition to their knowledge they are young and muscular, I have no doubt they will soon be called in to the personal assistance of the vicious part of the female nobility. Lord Holland is quite delightful; I hardly know a talent, or a virtue that he has not little or big. The Devil could not put him out of temper. I really never saw such a man. In addition to this, think of his possessing Holland House and that he reposes every evening on that beautiful structure of flesh and blood Lady H.

My history amounts to nothing – Je suis curé, je le serai toujours; but as there must be hewers of wood, and drawers of water in every community, so also in the Church there must be makers of Sermons and baptizers, and burriers* of the dead. The sweet privilege of doing nothing cannot be enjoyed by all – the Will of God be done.

I admire your excessive activity for knowledge and wish to God I could bring myself to any degree of your zeal; but you read in voluptatem, I in vitam; books are your object, they are my instrument for dining and supping – could I effect this without them, I should prefer almost any gratification to the improvement of my mind. You will think this affectation; it is not, but candor. I shall always miss your society very much, I have a very great regard for you. It will give me the sincerest pleasure to hear of your return and I remain my dr Mcintosh with kind love to yr Lady, Yrs most affectionately

Sydney Smith

104. FRANCIS JEFFREY

Tuesday, Oct. 29th, 1805

My dear Jeffrey,

Will you be so good as to pay Margaret Mckenzie for me ten pounds immediately, to let me know as immediately what I am in yr debt for this and the Diploma, and with an immediacy not less immediate you shall receive from me a draft for the money. I mean Miss Mckenzie the girl of feeling.*

I hear with great sorrow from Elmsley that a very antichristian article has crept into the last no. of the E.R., inaccurate in point of history, and dull in point of execution.* I need no other proof that the Review was left in other hands than yrs, because you must be thoroughly aware that the rumor of infidelity decides not only the reputation but the existence of the Review. I am extremely sorry too on my own account because those who wish it to have been written by me, will say it was so.

Tell me upon your solemn honor and word whether you think that crooked poetess* whose subscription papers you sent to me would do for a governess to Sr James Mcintosh's children at Bombay. Her ugliness and deformity are advantages as they would prevent her from marrying. Can she read without Scotch accent? Is she good tempered? Pray let Horner see her if you think there is any probability she will do; but let him see her under the influence of yr presence, or he will impregnate her. There is a fecundity in his very look; his smiles are seminal.

I hear there has been a meeting between you and your patient Southey and that he was tolerably civil to his chirurgeon.*

Do not disappoint us of yr company in the spring in this great city, and bring with you Timotheus accustomed to midnight carousal and soul-inspiring alcohol. Brown is like the laws of the Medes and Persians, he changeth not; a greater proneness to mutability would however have been much a better thing for them both; for I have no doubt but that the laws often have been and that the Doctor is hugely mistaken. Magnitude to you my dr Jeffrey must be such an intoxicating idea that I have no doubt you would rather be gigantic in yr errors than immense in no respect whatsoever. However comfort yourself that yr good qualities are far beyond the common size, for which reason originally, but now from long habit

I am yr affectionate friend

S. Smith

105. DR. REEVE

8, Doughty-street, Brunswick-square,
Monday, Oct. 29th ⟨1805⟩*

My dear Sr

I suggested everything I could to Bernard,* told him that you had made 3 distinct efforts to come home and had been robbed as many times by armed Chaplains of the Austrian Army; that Dr. De Roches had been wounded in the right glutean,* and you yourself thrown into a smart Tertian by pure grief and anxiety. The Committee will not *bind themselves* to make a new engagement with you, but I have no doubt you will secure yr situation upon yr return. I will in the mean time do all I can to get you inserted in the list for Spring 1797* which comes out I think about May 1796.

I would advise you not to fling away this occasion, which is no despicable one, for a physician; because he must be a devilish clumsy gentleman if in lecturing upon the moral and physical nature of man he cannot take an opportunity of saying that he lives at No. 6, Chancery-lane, and that few people are equal to him in the cure of fevers. As for the improvement you get my dr doctor in travelling abroad credat Judaeus. You have seen a skull of a singular formation at Dr. Baumgarten's, and seen a toe in Suabia that astonished you; but what in the name of Dr. Gregory can you see in Germany of a therapeutic nature which you cannot see better in Scotland or here? You will do yourself more real good by superintending the gutts of one woman of quality in London than by drinking tea with all the German Professors that ever existed.

All these events in Germany* have not astonished me: I allowed Bonaparte 28 days to knock both the armies *clunes super caput* (as the vulgar have it), to conclude a peace, make a speech to the Senate and illuminate Paris; he is as rapid and as terrible as the lightning of God; would he were as transient. Ah my dear doctor you are of a profession which will endure for ever; no revolution will put an end to Synochus and Synocha; but what will become of the spoils *we* gather from the earth? those cocks of ripe farina, on which the holy bough is placed – the tithes. Adieu God bless you. I will watch over yr interests and if anything occurs write to you again.

Yrs ever
S. Smith

P.S. I think, upon reflection, you had better write a lr to the Committee, stating the impossibility of your coming home, tho you strongly wish it and begging to be put on the list for spring, 1807. Add also that you will employ the intervening time in collecting materials for yr lectures. Send it to me, never mind postage.

106. FRANCIS JEFFREY

January 30th, 1806

My dear Jeffrey,

The change in administration (tho' I am not ordinarily a great politician) has made me extremely happy both because I believe the War will not be protracted longer than honor and safety require, and because the Law and the Church will be refreshed by the elevation of men of Whig principles under which appellation I find as I see more of the World all the truly honest and able men (who are of any party at all) ranging themselves. I cannot describe to you how disgusted I am by the set of canting rascals who have crept into all kinds of power during the profligate reign of Mr. Pitt, who patronised hypocrisy, folly, fraud and anything else which contributed to his power – peace to his ashes and from them, but whatever feelings and proprieties it violates I must say he was one of the most luminous eloquent blunderers with which any people was ever afflicted. For 15 years I have found my income dwindling away under his eloquence, and regularly in every Session of Parliament he has charmed every classical feeling and stript me of every guinea I possess. At the close of every brilliant display an expedition failed or a Kingdom fell, and by the time that his Style had gained the summit of perfection Europe was degraded to the lowest abyss of Misery. God send us a stammerer, a tongueless man, let Moses come for this heaven-born Aaron has failed. Horner is well and the best of all the Grecians. I agree most heartily in all the good you say of him and only quarrel with you for not saying enough. Give my kind regards to Brown, I am extremely obliged by his Letter and will answer it immediately. Archy Allison* is a charming fellow, his courtesy and affability like the Loaves and fishes might easily ⟨be⟩ divided among 5,000 of his Countrymen and many fragments left, he is an excellent Man and improves by drink. Let me intreat you to come up. I desiderate you grievously. I am sure romping with Saba will do you good. Richardson* is come here, I will ⟨show⟩ him what civility is in my power but he has pitched his camp at a great distance and I give no dinners. Remember me very kindly to the Stewarts and tell him on his death bed he will be tormented by the injustice he has done to Hartley. Hallam* is an excellent man, but of a very inferior calibre to our Edinburgh Set. I am afraid you have made a blunder in admitting his Knight, but I will tell you more about it when I have seen it. Knight's book has attracted amazing attention here. Mrs. S. has received yr Lr and will answer very soon.

> Ever yrs my dear friend with the truest affection
> Sydney Smith

109. DR. ANDREWES*

Winter 1806-7

Dear Sir,

If I do not hear from you to the contrary, I will call upon you after morning service on Sunday. I forgot to mention in my letter to you that Mr. Bernard gave me leave to make any use I please of his name in the way of reference. I beg you to recollect that the question before you for your decision, is a choice between fanaticism and the worship of the Church of England in your parish; one or the other must exist. If I doubted of any of the doctrines of the Church of England, if I were possessed of any foolish and absurd tenets of my own, I should immediately be qualified by law to open the chapel: I hope you will not disqualify me merely because I am a firm and zealous advocate in the same cause with yourself, for this would be to give a bounty on dissent and heresy. It would be a very different question if I asked you to let me open a new place of worship; but I merely ask you to change that worship from the present method, of which you completely disapprove, to that which you completely approve and eminently practise.

Excuse the trouble I give you; but when a poor clergyman sees an honest and respectable method of improving his situation in life, you cannot wonder at his anxiety. You will make me a very happy man, if you consent to my request.

With great respect, &c., &c.,

Sydney Smith

116. LADY HOLLAND

July 14th, 1807

My dear Lady Holland,

Mr. Allen has mentioned to me the Letters of a Mr. Plymley,* which I have obtained from the adjacent market-town, and read with some entertainment. My conjecture lies between three persons – Sir Samuel Romilly, Sir Arthur Pigott, or Mr. Horner, for the name of Plymley is evidently fictitious! I shall be very happy to hear your conjectures on this subject on Saturday, when I hope you will let me dine at Holland House, but I must sleep in town that night. I shall come to dinner unless I hear to the contrary, and will then answer Lord Holland's letter – Remaining my dr Lady Holland ever yrs very affectionately

S. S.

124. FRANCIS JEFFREY

January, 1808

My dear Jeffrey,

I have as yet read very few articles in the Edinburgh Review, having lent it to a sick countess, who only wished to read it because a few copies only had arrived in London.

I like very much the review of Davy, think the review of Espriella much too severe, and am extremely vexed by the review of Hoyle's Exodus.* The levities it contains will I am sure give very great offence; and they are ponderous and vulgar as well as indiscreet. Such sort of things destroy all the good effect which the liberality and knowledge of the Edinburgh Review is calculated to produce, and give to fools as great a power over you as you have over them. Besides the general regret which I feel from errors of this nature, I cannot help feeling that they press harder upon me than upon anybody – by giving to the Review a character which makes it perilous to a clergyman in particular to be concerned in it. I am sure you will excuse me for expressing my feelings upon this subject, and I know you have friendship enough for me to be more upon your guard in future against a style of writing which is not only mischievous to me in particular but mischievous to the whole undertaking, and without the slightest compensation of present amusement. The author I know; and when he told me the article upon which he had been employed, I foresaw the manner in which he would treat it. Upon this subject Brougham entirely agrees with me.

I am glad you like the Methodists.* Of the Scotch market you are a better judge than I am, but you may depend upon it it will give great satisfaction here; I mean, of course, the nature of the attack, not the manner in which it is executed. All attacks upon the Methodists are very popular with steady men of very moderate understandings, the description of men among whom the bitterest enemies of the E.R. are to be found.

I do not understand what you can mean by levity of quotation. I attack these men because they have foolish notions of religion. The more absurd the passage, the more necessary it should be displayed – the more urgent the reason for making the attack at all.

I am decidedly of opinion that the Booksellers should be left entirely to fix their own price, to the purchaser, and that you should compell them to give a great deal more than they do – at least 20 guineas a sheet. As you live on the spot you take out the payment half in money, half in hommage and fraudulent smiles.

I am thinking of writing a sheet this time about the Missions* to India and elsewhere; in short, a sort of exposé of the present state of Protestant missions, which I will do very gravely and without giving you any opportunity of turning against me the observations I have made against you in this Letter. Pray let me know in your next Mr. M.'s terms,* where he lives, and what family he has; and present my kind remembrances if you please to Mrs. M. Little Saba is recovering from a long illness; the rest all well and unite in the most sincere regards to you.

Sydney Smith

Pray write me a line to say if this subject be vacant.

134. LADY HOLLAND

June 29th, 1808

My dear Lady Holland,

You said yesterday that Ld. Holland had some notion of asking the Chancellor for some small living for me, not a pleasant thing to do at any time, much less so of course when the request is made to a man of opposite politics for a person who has taken as decided a part as I have done – and who am the supposed author of a publication in which the Chancellor himself is so frequently laughed at. If it is done, it will therefore be a great favor conferred by him (however insignificant the living) and he will have a right so to consider it. Now tho' Yorkshire is a great evil, it is possible from local disadvantages a less remote situation might be a greater evil, and it is therefore *possible* that I might be compelled to decline that which was asked not without pain and given not without reluctance, and in this case I should appear to be a capricious coxcomb who had not the decency to make up his own mind before he had engaged weighty men, and good friends to be solicitous in his behalf. For these reasons I should feel more easy if such an application were not made. If I can by activity in which I am not deficient find any trifling chancery living where I *know* I could live, here the unpleasant event which I before mentioned can have no place or there would be no indelicacy to ask of individuals a living of trifling, or no value.

I will make no apology for writing to you so often about myself and my own concerns, and I am sure you and Lord Holland will think I have taken the reasonable view of the subject. If by exchange, or in addition, I can get any thing *tolerable* in the South, I shall esteem myself very fortunate; if not, my situation there is not destitute of many advantages, and I must content myself as well as I can. Do not give yourself the trouble to answer this as I shall see you so soon.

I hope you were not robbed, nor even whistled at, for whistling (as I learn from a friend of ours) is not without danger; indeed as the wind of a Cannon Ball often kills, so I suppose the whistle of a robber can stop.

> Ever yours my dear Lady Holland most sincerely
> Sydney Smith

Will you be so good as to let the enclosed go to the 2dy post.

135. DR. REEVE (Norwich)

Bishop's Lydiard,* Taunton, Aug. 11th, 1808

My dear Sir,

I thank you very kindly for your invitation, and for your recollection of me. I sincerely wish that the little time I can get away from London would admit of my making such a visit: nothing would give me greater pleasure. You mention many inducements: I can want no other than the pleasure of paying my respects to you and to Mrs. Opie.*

The Bishop* is incomparable. He should *touch* for bigotry and absurdity! He is a kind of man who would do his duty in all situations at every hazard: in Spain he would have headed his diocese against the French; at Marseilles he would have struggled against the plague; in Flanders he would have been a Fénelon. He does honour to the times in which he lives, and more good to

Christianity than all the sermons of his brethren would do, if they were to live a thousand years. As you will probably be his physician when he is a very old man, bolster him up with nourishing meats, my dear doctor, invigorate him with medicated possets. Search for life in drugs and herbs, and keep him as a comely spectacle to the rising priesthood. You have a great charge!

Sydney Smith

137. LADY HOLLAND

Howick,* Sept. 29th, 1808

Dear Lady Holland,

   I left Brougham at Lord Roslyns* at the Drums.* I have set him the name of the *Drum Major*. I found a great number of philosophers in Edinburgh in an high state of obscurity and metaphysics. The Itch this year has been extremely severe and the Professors and others were just recovering the outer or scarf skin as I left the place. Poor Dugald Stewart is extremely alarmed by the repeated assurances I made that he was the author of Plymley's Letters – generally so considered to be. I have been staying here two days on my return, two days on my journey to Edinburgh. An excellent man, Lord Grey, and pleasant to be seen in the bosom of his family. I approve very highly also of his Lady. Early next week I hope to dine with you, and remain, my dear Lady Holland, ever most affectionately yrs

Sydney Smith

138. LADY HOLLAND

⟨London, prob. Oct. 6th, 1808⟩

Dear Lady Holland,

   I take the liberty to send you two brace of grouse, curious, because killed by a Scotch metaphysician; in other and better language they are mere ideas, shot by other ideas, out of a pure intellectual notion called a gun. yrs ever very truely

Sydney Smith

I will do myself the pleasure of dining with you on Saturday next - tomorrow evening I am engaged. The modification of matter called Grouse which accompanies this note is not in the common apprehension of Edinburgh considered to be dependant upon a first cause, but to have existed from All Eternity. Allen will explain.

140. LADY HOLLAND

18 Orchard Street, Portman Square,
Oct. 24th, 1808

My dear Lady Holland,

No sooner was your back turned than I took advantage of your absence to give up Harefield, and settle in Yorkshire. I never liked the Harefield scheme – bad society – no land – no house, no salary – dear as London, neither in London, nor out of it, not accessible as a native – not interesting as a stranger – but the fear of you before my eyes prevented me from saying so.

My lot is now cast and my heritage fixed – most probably. But you may chuse to make me a Bishop, in which case I shall return to Town in the tenth or 15th Year of the Hegira with great shouting and glory. If you do make me a Bishop I think I shall never do you discredit; for I believe that it is out of the power of lawn and velvet, and the crisp hair of dead men fashioned into a wig, to make me a dishonest man; but if you do not, I am perfectly content, and shall be ever grateful to the last hour of my life to you, and Lord Holland. I leave London the 25th of March next.

Poor little Vernon* is recovering. We are all well. I called at H.H. upon Lady Affleck:* the children were looking in the most perfect health. Mrs. Sydney and I are to go over and spend a day with Lady Affleck very soon. Everything was in perfect order.

Brougham is not returned but is still beating the *drum* in Scotland: the Mufti* in high leg about the Spaniards, Horner so extremely serious about the human face, that I am forced to compose my face half a street off before I meet him.

Our next King of Clubs is on Saturday, where you and your

expedition will be talked over at some length. I presume you have received a thundering letter from Lord Grey.

You will see in the next Edinburgh Review* two articles of mine, – one on the Catholics, the other on the Curates Bill, – neither of which, I think, you will read.

I feel sometimes melancholy at the idea of quitting London, – the warm precincts of the cheerful day;* but it is the will of God, and my destiny, and I am sure I shall gain by it wealth, knowledge, and happiness. My very kind regards to Lord Holland and Allen. I remain my dear Lady Holland ever most affectionately yrs

Sydney Smith

142. FRANCIS JEFFREY

York, Nov. 20th, 1808

My dear Jeffrey,

It is a very long time since I have answered your letter, but I have been choked by the cares of the world. I came down here for a couple of days, to look at 2 places which were to be let, and have been detained here in pursuit of them for 10 or 12 days. The place I am aiming at is only a mile and an half from York; a convenient house and garden with 12 acres of land. This will do for me very well while I am building at Thornton,* where I shall in all human probability spend the rest of my days. I am by no means grieved at quitting London; sorry to lose the society of my friends, but wishing for more quiet, more leisure, less expence, and more space for my children. I am extremely pleased with what I have seen of York.

About the University of Oxford I doubt; but you shall have it, if I can possibly find time for it. I am publishing 50 sermons* at present, which take up some considerable share of my attention: much more, I fear, than they will that of any other person.

I am very glad that the chances of life have brought us 200 miles nearer together. It is really a fortunate circumstance, that in quitting London where I have pushed so many roots, I should be brought again within the reach of the bed from which I was transplanted.

I return to town next Friday, and leave it for good on Lady-day. Mrs. Sydney is delighted with her rustication. She has suffered all the evils of London, and enjoyed none of its goods. I hope Mr. Morehead likes his young gunpowder pupil.* I think from his appearance he must be mild and amiable.

Yrs my dear Jeffrey ever most truely,

Sydney Smith

143. FRANCIS JEFFREY

⟨November or December, 1808⟩

My dear Jeffrey

Nobody knows better than myself the accute pain of the Tooth-ache, and an hollow Tooth (which from the Style of your Letter I perceive yours to have been) is infinitely more painful than any other. The Edinburgh review is a literary Scheme which I am surely not bound to pursue longer than I like, or to feel for with more warmth than the moment supplies me with. Your sub-sistence does not depend upon it, but it is your amusement. I wish it well as I do the Game of Fives or billiards if you pursue them, but I cannot see why I am bound in friendship to think and speak of such games with enthusiasm. The Edinburgh review is useful, but it surely is not the only way in which you and I can do good. I am so far from considering the continuation of the E.R. to be a good to either of us that I am not sure it would not be wise in us, and advantageous to us, to put an end to it tomorrow. I heard from you and from many other Quarters that you was resolved there should be no more politics in the review, – *party* politics omitted in your first Letter you have added in your explanation and this little word makes all the difference. I put to you then the very probable consequence of irritating Brougham: supposing your resolution to have been what your language implied it to be, and under that supposition I reminded you how the review set out, and my ignorance of any change in its plan and arrangement. I am sorry this has offended you, but I really cannot take any blame to myself for the hint, and my love of Justice is such that under a similar mistake I cannot promise that I may not again be tempted to make to you a similar remonstrance.

I cannot think that I have underrated the importance of the Edinburgh confederacy, or the new review,* which you seemed in your last to consider as of such consequence and which appear to me to be of none at all. If the review would have gone on without them, it will in my humble opinion go on just as well in spite of them. You are angry with me for not being alarmed at perils which I cannot comprehend.

I have not deserted you, nor had I the smallest intention of doing so, tho' it was not in my power to do the universities. Still however I am hesitating very much in my own mind about my future conduct with respect to the Review; when I have made up my mind you shall immediately know what that mind is. You I am sure will do me the justice to suppose that I am not making myself of consequence, but really reflecting upon a subject of importance to my future plans and future reputation. I shall be obliged to you to alter this review* as little as is consistent with Safety, and Grammar. I forget whether I have told you the Scrape you have got me into by the alterations in Perceval's curate Bill;* you have put into my mouth the most extraordinary assertions respecting English benefices which ever were heard ...

[The rest of the MS. is missing.]

145. LORD GREY

18, Orchard-street, Portman-square,
Dec. 21st, 1808

Dear Lord Grey,

Many thanks for your kind letter. I shall write to Lord Ponsonby who I am sure will comply with my request if he can. Lord Lauderdale is full.*

Brougham and I are going next week to stay a day or two with a Mr. Richard Brinsley Sheridan,* where we are to meet your friend Mrs. Wilmot* whom I am very curious to see.

Dr. Vaughan's brother* is just come over who says the Spaniards are quite sure of succeeding, and that it is impossible to conquer them. I mean to have him examined next week by Wishaw, Brougham, and other Whigs.

I am just publishing 50 discourses which I shall take the liberty to send to Lady Grey, conceiving that in so remote a part of England theology is not to be had so pure as here. I remain dr. Ld. Grey very sincerely yrs

Sydney Smith

146. LADY HOLLAND

⟨After Christmas, 1808⟩*

Why my dear Lady Holland do you not come home? It is all over, it has been all over this month; except in the Holland family there has not been a man of sense for some weeks who has thought otherwise. Are you fond of funerals? Do you love to follow a nation to their grave? What else can you see or do by remaining abroad? If the Spaniards would murder the nobility and clergy there might be some chance. Linendrapers and shoe-makers might save Spain, – in the hands of Dukes, and Bishops it is infallibly gone.

Our friend Brougham has been bolting out of the course again in the Edinburgh Review. It is extremely difficult to keep him right. He should always remain between 2 tame elephants, Abercrombie and Wishaw, who might beat him with their tusks,* when he behaved in an unwhiglike manner. Little John Horner is in the corner ill, and has been so for some time.

I have bought a book about drilling beans, and a greyhound puppey for the Malton meeting. It is thought I shall be an eminent rural character. I am delighted with Don Juan's* zeal and with his ardor for miracles; but Spain seems to be beyond the power of miracles. Do not listen to anything that is written to you about a change of administration. There may be a change from one scoundrel to another, but there is not the slightest chance for the Whigs.

The very worst possible accounts from Ireland. I shall be astonished if they do not begin to make some stir. They will not rebell just now, but they will threaten. . . .

Kindest regards to Lord H and Allen; ever yours most truely and affectionately

[No signature]

147. Lady Holland

January 10th, 1809

My dear Lady Holland,

Many thanks for two fine Gallicia hams; but as for boiling them in wine, I am not as yet high enough in the Church for that; so they must do the best they can in water.

Everybody attacks you and Lord Holland for not coming home. Lord Bruce* even stopped me in the street and opened a battery upon you. I approved your conduct and said you was determined to see blood drawn and to draw it yourself; at which he turned as pale as ashes, as if he would not see blood drawn, to save the Queen and all her scrofulous progeny.

You know Mr. Luttrell* is prisoner in Fez, and put to stone cutting. Great scandal about Jeffrey and the Dutchess of Gordon.* He is a very amorous little gentleman, and her disposition is not I fancy wholly dissimilar; it is probable therefore they will build a nest.

Wordsworth* vows personal vengeance upon Jeffrey for his last critique, and blood will flow.

You have no idea of the consternation which the Sieur Brougham's attack upon the titled orders has produced:* the Review not only discontinued by many people but returned to the Bookseller from the very first volume: the library shelves fumigated, &c.

The new review of Ellis, and Canning is advertised, and begins next month. In the next number of the Edinburgh Review you will see an attack of mine upon the Society for the Suppression of Vice; tell me how you like it.

We have admitted a Mr. Baring,* importer and writer, into the King of Clubs, upon the express promise that he lends £50 to any member of the Club when applied to. I proposed this amendment to his introduction, which was agreed to without a dissenting voice.

I wish you would speak to Romilly* about the levity and impropriety of his conversation, he is become an absolute Rake, and Ward* and I talk of leaving the Club if a more chaste line of dialogue is not adhered to.

Mufti* has been ill, but the rumor of a Tory detected in a job has restored him. Horner is in the tenth week of his confinement – a liver case. He was desired to read amusing books: upon searching his library it appeared he had no amusing books, – the nearest to any work of that description being *The India Trader's Complete Guide*.

I cannot tell you how much I miss you and Holland; for besides the pleasure I have in your company, I have contracted a real regard, and affection for you, – wish you to get on prosperously and wisely, want other people to like you, and should be afflicted if any real harm happened to you and yours.

[No signature]

[There had been no resident rector of Foston since the time of Charles II and the parsonage was a ruinous cottage; so Sydney rented a house at Heslington, a village some twelve miles from Foston and two from York. From here he used to drive himself and Mrs. Sydney over to Foston every Sunday to take two services. Here his last child, Windham, was born in 1813. The Archbishop allowed him to postpone actual residence in the parish for no less than four years, while he still had hopes of an exchange; but in June 1813 he began to build the new parsonage which he entered with his family in March 1814. He was his own architect and hired his own labour. The account of his proceedings makes one of the most delightful portions of *M*. (ch. vii).

Sydney lived at Foston till May 1829, as (in his own words), 'village parson, village doctor, village comforter, village magistrate, and Edinburgh Reviewer' (*M*., p. 204). He was entitled to three months' absence from his living in each year, and he availed himself of his right, spending at least a month in London every year, after paying long visits, with his family, to his friend Philips at Sedgley, and short visits to the Greys at Howick, to his old friends in Scotland, and to other friends acquired during his residence in Yorkshire. During these years he became intimate with the Greys, with the Morpeths (afterwards Carlisles), with Archbishop Harcourt and especially with his daughter Georgiana. In 1826 he spent a month in Paris, where the Hollands were staying. In January 1828 he was given a canonry at Bristol by

Lord Chancellor Lyndhurst, who also enabled him in the following year to exchange his living of Foston for that of Combe Florey near Taunton, where he took up his residence in June 1829.]

154. Lady Holland

June 24th, 1809

My dear Lady Holland,

This is the third day since I arrived at the village of Heslington, 200 miles from London. I missed the hackney-coaches for the first three or four days. but after that prepared myself for the change from the aurelia to the grub state, and dare say I shall become fat, torpid, and motionless with a very good grace.

I have laid down two rules for the country: first, not to smite the partridge; for if I fed the poor, and comforted the sick, and instructed the ignorant, yet I should do nothing worth, if I smote the partridge. If anything ever endangers the Church, it will be the strong propensity to shooting for which the clergy are remarkable. Ten thousand good shots dispersed over the country do more harm to the cause of religion than the arguments of Voltaire and Rousseau. The squire never reads, but it is not possible he can believe that religion to be genuine whose ministers destroy his game.

I mean to come to town once a year, tho' of that I suppose I shall soon be weary finding my mind growing weaker and weaker and my acquaintance gradually reduced to very much neglected aunts and cousins, to whose proffered tea I shall crawl in, a penitent and Magdalene kinsman. I shall by that time have taken myself again to shy tricks, pull about my watch-chain, and become (as I was before) your abomination.*

I am very much obliged to Allen for a long and very sensible letter upon the subject of Spain. After all the fate of Spain surely depends upon the fate of Austria. Pray tell the said Don Juan, if he comes northward to visit the authors of his existence he must make this his resting-place.

Mrs. Sydney is all rural bustle impatient for the parturition of hens and pigs; I wait patiently knowing all will come in due season. Pray give my kindest regards to Lord Holland, and believe me ever dear Lady Holland, your grateful and affectionate friend

Sydney Smith

155. FRANCIS JEFFREY

⟨Postmark July 3rd, 1809⟩

My dear Jeffrey,

I reply immediately to your letter to remove the misconception that I take any interest in this new project of Brougham's. He never said a syllable upon the subject to me in Town, but wrote to me about it here. I replied to him as I stated to you that I thought it more dignified that the Booksellers should be in our power, than that we should be in theirs; and so I do think; but I think also the subjection of which Brougham speaks is of very little consequence and I am perfectly satisfied that everything should remain as we arranged it in London. Do you and Brougham settle it between you: I am perfectly passive. My chief motive for acquiescing in Brougham's project was the fear of losing him, tho' I think we could carry on the review very well without him, if he could not be persuaded to continue. I am so perfectly satisfied with the arrangement of the review in force that I had no thought of looking into the state of profits again for these two years. I never interfered but once, which was to say that the Booksellers were not paying us nearly as much as they ought, and that the payment, when increased, should be divided among those who planned and continued to support the work. To the plain justice and common sense of this you immediately assented, and I am sure we never should have had another syllable of discussion on the subject. Do not therefore I beseech you confound me with the restless and perturbed Brougham, whose pride I suppose is become more irritable as he increases in business and is further removed from the character of a literary Scotchman.

Respecting my sermons I most sincerely beg of you to extenuate nothing. Treat me *exactly* as I deserve. Remember only what it is you are reviewing, – an oration confined by custom to 20 or 30 minutes before a congregation of all ranks and ages. Do not be afraid of abusing me if you think abuse necessary: you will find I can bare it extremely well from you.

As for the Quarterly Review,* I have not read it, nor shall I, nor ought I – where abuse is intended not for my correction but my pain. I am however very fair game. If the oxen catch a butcher, they have a right to toss and gore him.

I can only trifle in this Review. It takes me some time to think about serious subjects, not having my head full of all arguments on all subjects, like a certain friend of mine, – to whom all happiness!

Sydney Smith

I get in my hay on Monday.

158. Lady Holland

Heslington, Sept. 9th, 1809

My dear Lady Holland,

The name of the beneficed clergyman at Jamaica, the clergyman whom you have beneficed, is Bowerbank; the name of the servant Sarah Pritchard, and she lives at no. 2 Kinton Place Edgeware Road or at 34 Dorset St. Portman Square.

I hear you laugh at me for being happy in the country, and upon this I have a few words to say. In the first place whether one lives or dies I hold and always have held to be of infinitely less moment than is generally supposed; but if life is the choice then it is common sense to amuse yourself with the best you can find where you happen to be placed. I am not leading precisely the life I should chuse, but that which (all things considered, as well as I could consider them) appeared to be the most eligible. I am resolved therefore to like it and to reconcile myself to it; which is more manly than to feign myself above it, and to send up complaints by the post, of being thrown away, and being desolate and such like trash. I am prepared therefore either way. If the chances of life ever enable me to emerge, I will shew you that I have not been wholly occupied by small and sordid pursuits. If (as the greater probability is) I am come to the end of my career, I give myself quietly up to horticulture, and the annual augmentation of my family. In short, if my lot be to crawl, I will crawl contentedly; if to fly, I will fly with alacrity; but as long as I can possibly avoid it I will never be unhappy.

I have read the Review, and like the review of Rose exceedingly. How can anybody dislike it? Parliamentary Reform exceedingly good with some objections; Miss Edgeworth overpraised; Strabo by Payne Knight excellent; the Bakerian Lecture very good; Lord Sheffield dull and hot. I am glad you liked Parr.* It is wrong to say in so unexplained a phrase that Hanging is cheap, but it answers the objection to Capital Punishment that the Labor of the Pendulous is lost to Society, - whereas it is notorious that Government lose large sums by the Labor of their convicts.

I am very sorry to find you have been ill; for one virtue and excellence which depends upon principle, there are five hundred which proceed from the body; it is the great cause of moral good and evil, and the meanest Apothecary can teach wisdom and magnanimity better than Seneca.

I am about to open the subject of classical learning in the Review, from which by some accident or other it has hitherto abstained. It will give great offence, and therefore be more fit for this journal, the genius of which seems to consist in stroking the animal the contrary way to which the hair lies.

I dare say it cost you much to part with Charles;* but in the present state of the world it is better to bring up our young ones to war than to peace. I burn gunpowder every day under the nostrils of my little boy, and talk to him often of fighting to put him out of conceit with civil sciences, and prepare him for the evil times which are coming. God bless you dear Lady Holland.

Ever respectfully and affectionately your sincere friend

Sydney Smith

166. JOHN ALLEN

York, Nov. 22nd, 1809

Dear Allen,

I am much obliged to you for your book,* to which I see but one objection, and that is, that there will be an end of Spain before the Cortes can be summoned or the slightest of your provisions carried into execution, – admirable rules for diet to a patient in the article of death. I shall read it however, as an Eutopia* from your romantic brain.

I beg my congratulations to the Lord and Lady of the Castle on the event which your postscript announces to me for the first time.* Be it your care my dear Allen to make this child perfect in the Catechism and other Church exercises. Let it learn Principles from Dumont, Sharpe shall teach it ease and nature, Lauderdale* wit, my own Pybus* shall inspire his Muse, and you* shall show him the way to heaven.

As for the Opposition, if they give up the Catholics, I think their character is ruined. Ireland is much endangered, and the King will kick them out again after he has degraded them. A politician should be as flexible in little things as he is inflexible in great. The probable postponement of such a measure at such times for 10 years, – how is it possible for any honest public man to take office at such a price? I have eaten and drank so often with Ward and Brougham that I shall say nothing about them, except to express my astonishment at the absence of the latter from Holland House. I have no doubt but that the country would rather submit to Massena than Whitbread.* If the King were to give the opposition carte blanche tomorrow, I cannot see how they could form an administration in the house of commons. I have not *promised*, as you say, to write a pamphlet called Common Sense, in the spring; it is of very little or no consequence whether I do write it, or not; but I have by no means made up my mind to do it.

We have a report here that the measles and hooping-cough have got amongst the new administration; it is quite foolish to make such young people ministers.

God bless you my dear Allen – an event I cordially wish for, tho' I cannot say I have any great hope it will ever take place.

Yours most truely,
Sydney Smith

I will send you in return for your pamphlet a sermon against horse-racing and coursing, judiciously preached before the Archbishop and the sporting clergy of Malton.

175. LADY HOLLAND

January 27th, 1810

My dear Lady Holland,

I purpose, unless that purpose is interrupted by my coming up to see Cecil, to be in town a month before and a month after Easter and to spend my Easter at Bath with my father. A thousand thanks to you for your kindness. I need not say I shall spend as much time with you as from our mutual engagements will be agreeable to you and possible to me. Some of the best and happiest days of my life I have spent under your roof, and tho' there may be in some houses, particularly in those of our eminent prelates, a stronger disposition to pious exercises and as it were devout lucubrations, I do not believe all Europe can produce as much knowledge, wit and worth as passes in and out of your door under the nose of Thomas the porter. It will give me more pleasure to see you and Holland again than either I will say or you believe.

I always thought Lord Grenville would give up the Catholics, and I think Earl Grey right about the veto. I cannot say how much I like the said Earl – a fine nature, a just and vigorous understanding, a sensitive disposition, and infirm health. These are his leading traits. His excellencies are corage, discretion, and practical sense; his deficiency, a want of executive coarseness.

I trust we shall see Henry* on his way back if I am in the country. I have long intended writing him a letter and will speedily do so.

Poor Charles!* pray remind him of my existence, of my good

wishes towards him, of our common love of laughter, and our common awkwardness in riding.

I am very glad Brougham is in Parliament. He will pretend to be indifferent about it, which I believe as I should believe Miss Brougham his sister pretending indifference as to her nuptials with some tall and ruddy disbeliever of these climates.

Many thanks to John Allen for his letter in answer to my first imputation of the horrid crime of Protestantism having crept into the King of Clubs. He is forced at last to reduce himself to Lord Holland, Romilly, the atrocious soul of Cato,* and that complex bundle of ideas which is popularly called *Allen*. As for Romilly, he had no merit in not changing. *Principes** are eternal, and totally independent of events. Benthamism existed before time and space, and goes on by immutable rules, like freezing and thawing. To give up the Catholics, would be to confound the seventeenth pain with the eighteenth.*

In short, God bless you my dear Lady Holland; for I should go on scribbling this nonsense all night, as I should talking it, if I were near you. Very sincerely and affectionately yours

Sydney Smith

Mrs. Sydney begs her kind regards. I come up alone. Parsons wives never leave home in the spring - ducklings to be watched - a critical time. Pray remember me to Ld. Lauderdale if you see him, do not let him forget me.

178. Lady Holland

⟨Probably March–April 1810⟩

Dear Lady Holland,

It is barely possible I may come to your recollection before you set down to dinner: and therefore I write to account for my absence. You invited me to dine with you on this day a week past, and in consequence I have refused to dine with the Marquis of Stafford,* and again with Lord Crewe;* but as you said nothing to me about it this morning, and said I should see you at the Opera, I presumed you had forgotten it and did not come for fear of another *surprise*. The consequence of your forgetfulness of me has been that I am now dining with a *Maiden Aunt*, and that dinner will be over before you have read this. When the happiness of your fellow creatures is at stake you should really be more careful.

Yrs &c.
Sydney Smith

179. LADY HOLLAND

⟨Probably March–April, 1810⟩*

Dear Lady Holland,

If you expect that at any period of my life I shall ever be indifferent to your forgetfulness of me, you know nothing of the very sincere, and affectionate attachment which I bear to you; forgive however that I have made this feeling in this instance troublesome to you. You shall have to complain no more of my formality, but I will enter into explanations when they are necessary. After all you have taken me more in earnest than I was, for I meant to give you only a gentle scolding, but I will scold you no more nor do any thing else unpleasant to you, and I hereby make you a present of the *ungrateful Evergreen*.

God bless you –
S S

180. *From* MRS. SYDNEY SMITH *to* FRANCIS JEFFREY*

Heslington, ⟨April⟩ 1810

My dear Mr. Jeffrey,

I have scarcely a moment in which to tell you, – what, by the bye, I ought to have done a week since, and should have done, but that I have been too ill to write a single word that I could avoid, – that Sydney comes home the 17th; and therefore, as soon as you can resolve to come to us, *tant mieux pour nous*. It will make us both sincerly happy to see you, for as long a time as you can contrive to spare us;   d I hope you will give us the satisfaction of seeing you quite well.

We have been a sad house of invalids here, but we are all cheering up at the prospect of Sydney's return. The other day, poor little Douglas was lying on the sofa very unwell, while Saba and I were at dinner; and I said, 'Well, dear little Chuffy, I don't know what is the matter with us both, but we seem very good-for-nothing!' 'Why, mamma,' said Saba, '*I'll* tell you what the matter is: you are so melancholy and so dull because papa is away; he is so merry, that he makes us all gay. A family doesn't prosper, I see, without a papa!' I am much inclined to be of her opinion: and suspecting that the observation would please him quite as well as that of any of his London flatterers, I despatched it to him the next day.

Yours very sincerely
Catherine Amelia Smith

195. LORD GREY

January 2nd, 1811

Dear Lord Grey,

I congratulate you very sincerely upon the safety of Lady Grey; and I beg you will convey also my kind congratulations to her. I think now you will not be ashamed to speak with your enemies in the gate. 'Happy is the man who hath his quiver full of them. He shall not be ashamed to speak with his enemies in the gate.'

I have just been reading Allen's account* of your Administration. Very well done, for the cautious and decorous style; but it is really quite shameful that a good stout answer has not been written to your calumniators. The good points of that Administration were the Slave Trade, the Army, the Auditors Bill, Newport's Corn Bill, Romilly's Bankrupt Bill, the attempt at Peace, and the effort made for the Catholics. The disadvantages under which the Administration laboured were, the ruin of Europe – the distress of England – and the hatred of King and people. The faults they committed were, not coming to a thorough understanding with the King about the Catholics – the making a Treasurer an auditor,* and a Judge a politician – protecting the King's money from decimation – and increasing the number of foreign troops.

Balancing the good and evil I am sure there has been no such honest and enlightened Administration since the time of Lord Chatham. God send it a speedy return, but alas the deity will do no such thing.

Ever my dear Lord yrs with the most sincere respect and regard,

Sydney Smith

200. LADY HOLLAND

York, January 24th, 1811

Dear Lady Holland,

I send you this day a very odd present two Legs of that Scotch mutton of which you approved so much in the summer, killed the day before yesterday and 3 years old. Mrs. Smith said you would think it very odd, but I said you would not think it very odd from me. Lady Caroline Lamb says you are to be Regentess of the United Kingdoms, and I see every day in the papers a meeting between the Regent, and Lord Holland, gracious reception, etc. etc. I shall rejoice sincerely if any Halcyon days are coming to the poor Whigs, but the Sovereign has a deplorable knack of recovering. . . .

The drawing-room in Pall Mall must have been an entertaining scene for some weeks past: the crowds below waiting for facts upon Allen, and acquaintances of 1806 calling above. Lord Lauderdale* has not I hear had his clothes off for 6 weeks but has set up from sheer vigor of character. Pray remember me very kindly to him: I cannot say how much I like him.

I hope to see your Ladyship early in April, by which time the tumult will be hushed, and you will be either in full power, or in perfect weakness. God bless you dear Lady Holland: our kind regards to all. yrs very affectionately

Sydney Smith

I will have Lord Lauderdale Privy Seal with the patronage for Scotland. I hope he has given up all thoughts of going to the East Indies.

202. LADY HOLLAND

February, 1811

My dear Lady Holland,

I was terribly afraid at first that the Prince had gone over to the other party; but the King's improved condition leaves a hope to me that his conduct has been dictated by prudence, and the best idea he can form of filial piety from books and chaplains; for that any man in those high regions of life cares for his father, is what I cannot easily believe. That he will gain great popularity from his conduct, I have no doubt: perhaps he may deserve it, but I see thro' a Yorkshire glass darkly.

I am exceedingly glad Lord Holland has taken up the business of libels;* the punishments of late appear to me most atrocious. If libels against the public are very bad, they become sedition or treason, new crimes, and may be punished as such; but as long as they are only libels such punishments as have been lately inflicted are preposterous and seem to proceed from that hatred which feeble, and decorous persons always feel against those who disturb the repose of their minds, call their opinions in question, and compel them to think and reason. There should be a maximum of imprisonment for libel. No man should be imprisoned for more than a year for any information for libel filed by the Attorney-General. Libels are not so mischievous in a free country as Mr. Justice Grose* in his very bad lectures would make them out. Who would have mutinied for Cobbett's libel? or who would have risen up against the German soldiers? And how easily might he have been answered. He deserved some punishment; but to shut a man up in a jail for two years for such an offence is most atrocious. Pray make Lord Holland speak well, and eloquently on this subject.

I begin to suspect that my little Boy will turn out extremely clever. He strikes my fancy very much, and I think I should be rather more fastidious than even a stranger would be upon this subject. However in revenge I dare to say he will have all possible vices, run me into debt and make my life unhappy. All sons do so: there are a few instances to the contrary but they are very rare.

Thank God little Vernon recovered. It would have been a truely miserable welcome to his father and mother had the event taken another turn. I shall be glad to come to Town for a little time which I propose to do in April. By that time I presume you will be returned to Holland House. God bless you dear Lady Holland. Ever most sincerely and affectionately yrs

S. S.

205. LADY HOLLAND

81, Jermyn-street, May 23rd, 1811

How very odd, dear Lady Holl* to ask me to dine with you on Sunday, the 9th, when I am coming to stay with you from the 5th to the 12th. It is like giving a gentleman an assignation for Wednesday when you are going to marry him on the Sunday preceding – an attempt to combine the stimulus of gallantry with the security of connubial relations. I do not propose to be guilty of the slightest infidelity to you while I am at H H except you dine in town; and then it will not be infidelity, but spirited recrimination.

Ever the sincere and affectionate friend of Lady Holland,

Sydney Smith

I believe no two dissenting ministers in London will rejoice at Lord Sidmouth's defeat* more than Lord Holland and myself.

212. J. A. MURRAY

Heslington, Dec. 6th, 1811

My dear Murray,

I cannot say how much mortified I am not to have reached Edinburgh; nothing should have prevented me but fraternity, and to that I was forced to yeild.* I went to Lord Grey with young Vernon the Archbishop's son, a very clever young man, genus Whig, species Whiggista mitior, of which species I consider Lord Lansdown to be at the head, as the Lords Holland and

Grey are of the Whiggista truculentus anactophonus. I heard no news at Howick, Lord Grey sincerely expects a change, and a radical change. I taxed him with saying so from policy, but he assured me it was his real opinion, perhaps it was.

Many thanks to you for your kind offer of accomodation. I should certainly have quartered myself either upon you, or Jeffrey had I been able to come; you will not now believe me when I say I will come to Edinburgh, but I *will* – most assuredly and make a much longer stay than I could have made this year.

I am reading Locke in my old age never having read him in my youth, a fine satisfactory sort of a fellow, but very long winded. You do not know perhaps that among my thousand and one projects is to be numbered a new metaphysical language, a bold fancy for any man not born in Scotland. Physic Metaphysics Gardening Atheism* and Jobbing are the privileges of the North – by the bye have you ever remarked that very singular verse in the Psalms:– 'promotion cometh neither from the East, nor the West, nor yet from the South'?

Why is Jeffrey so long in the bringing forth. I am afraid it is a Breech case, pray desire Thomson to attend with his forceps and extract the next Number.

Everybody here is expiring with colds except me, who by dint of early rising keep free of any calamity of body and mind. We shall quit this place for Bath either the end of Jany or February, and stay two or 3 months. I rather quarrel with you for not sending me some Edinburgh politics. I have a very sincere attachment to Scotland, and am very much interested by Scotch news. 5 of the most agreeable years of my life were spent there, and there I have found many friendships which I am sure will last as long as I live. Adieu dear Murray. Mrs. S. sends her kind regards. Pray write to me – ever your sincere friend

Sydney Smith

214. LADY HOLLAND

Heslington, Jan. 7th, 1812

My dear Lady Holland

I send (led by inclination, and bound by Charter) my annual Ham of which I beg your acceptance, accept with it also my ever grateful recollection of your, and Lord Hollands kindness to me.

We are all perfectly well and about to quit this place for a visit of a month to Manchester and two Months to Bath. Mrs S. will set off about the 24th and I at the end of the Month. I shall stay as little as I can help at Bath. I congratulate you on having, or having had, Charles* with you, knowing that you love him very much, and that he is very agreeable.

I have heard no political News for a long time, I presume there has been none to hear. You are very often good enough to refresh my Solitude with Rumor's agitations. I confess myself quite astonished at the Princes reserve; whatever he intends to do, I thought would have been well known, even to those who nightly renew the Splendor of his Lamps at Carleton house Gates, and been matter of talk, and notoriety to the Parish Watchmen. Uncertainty does not imply reserve; he may change his mind week by week, and still tell his present mind to everybody.

We were flattered at Lord Grey's with a report that the public revenue was deficient but having heard nothing about it for 3 months, nor seen anything of it in the papers—I am afraid there can be no truth in it.

We are about to have a meeting at York respecting the Education of the poor in the principles of Tithe paying, etc. etc.* Your friend Robert Markham* the Spiritual is the principal instigator. I am sorry I shall be absent or I should certainly make a Speech; at all events I will subscribe my money – but it will never do. That the Church should make itself useful, and bestir itself to diffuse Secular knowledge among the poor and continue to do so for any length of time is scarcely credible. I believe it is only a plan to prevent the little Boys from learning at Lancasters, and that a sort of Sham Multiplication Table will be introduced, teaching them all wrong, and rendering the real acquirement impossible. There should be a lay Committee to investigate from time to time whether the Spelling Books provided by the Clergy are real Spelling Books, just as the Magistrates search for false weights and measures. We all unite in kindest Regards to Lord Holland and yourself and I remain ever dear Lady Holland Yrs with the most sincere attachment and affection –

Sydney Smith

The Ham weighing 23½ lbs. set off on the 6th Jany and arrives at the Bull and Mouth, Bull and Mouth St,* Sunday or Monday next.

222. LORD HOLLAND

August, 1812

Dear Lord Holland,

I can buy you some sheep by means of the agent I always employ for myself; but then there is a history to tell. I live only from hand to mouth (as the common people say), and for weeks together I am not master of ten pounds, nor do I know where to get as much; therefore you must give me a power of drawing on your bankers for any sum not exceeding £90, which will more than cover every possible expence, tho' I hope they will be bought much more advantageously. You will I am sure excuse my frankness; but it may very probably happen when the time comes for buying the sheep that I am entirely without money. I will write to Johnson; but I think the better way will be, to send them at once to Holland House.

On the circuit I saw a good deal of Brougham. He purposely introduced the subject of Holland House, declared solemnly that he was utterly ignorant of the cause which had estranged him from it, that he lamented it exceedingly, and stipulated that I was to introduce him in a joking manner as a new acquaintance when I came to Town. I do not pretend to understand Brougham, but this he said very seriously, and he is so great a card, and so agreeable a person, that perhaps you will allow a *locus penitentiae*. God bless you.

S. S.

225. LORD HOLLAND

Heslington, Oct. 26th, 1812

I do not know a better judge of character than you, nor is there any man for whose various excellencies of understanding and character I have an higher admiration; but for sheep, for that particular animal, by whose destruction mutton is obtained, you must excuse me, in that department of knowledge pardon me for saying that you betray the most profound, and ludicrous ignorance. You are a statesman, a scholar, and a wit, but no butcher. Be assured that a better lot at the price were never sent from the North, and turn as deaf an ear to Johnson as he turns to you. They will by August 1813 weigh 15 lb. a quarter, 6 lb. or 8 lb. of inside fat, and the wool and skin will be worth half a crown. You may put 8 sheep to an acre upon your land, and this for half a year will be equal to 16 per annum. Calculate this profit and bind the laxity of your views by the rigors of arithmetic. You are indeed a fortunate man to have a friend in the North who understands grazing so well, and I now suspect you placed me here for the express purpose. It is not unamusing to see you deciding upon the nationality of sheep. When an human creature is lean, lousy, and logical we know him to be a Scotchman, but how does this apply to sheep? or what are your criteria? The meaning of Scotch mutton is *old*, *small* mutton fed on poor pastures – These requisites attended to the register of birth is idle. Lastly without joke, if the sheep are bad I am very sorry. I employed a very intelligent honest cattle dealer to buy them, and we both did our best, and as such in your good nature I am sure you take it.

As for Bobus he is a County in himself and out of my Jurisdiction. He has hitherto in public matters acted as a very honest man, I hope and trust he will persevere to the end. I am extremely sorry to hear poor Lady Holl has been so ill; pray give my kind love to her.

I am very busy in building my Cemetery at Foston, but I will be a merry corpse and kick against worms, and corruption as long as I can. Poor Brougham,* Poor Romilly, Poor Horner, Poor Curran, Poor Tierney, Poor old England. God bless you.

S S

228. LADY HOLLAND

January 17th, 1813

My dear Lady Holland,

I have innumerable thanks to return to you for the kind solicitude you have displayed respecting my rural architecture. I have explained myself so fully to Allen upon the convenience, and necessity of this measure that I will not bore you any more with the subject; but I must add a word upon the Archbishop's conversation with Abercrombie.* Is it not a little singular, that his Excellence,* in all the various conversations I have had with him on this subject; in the promise I had made him to build; in the complaints I have frequently made to him on the hardship and expence of building; when I laid before him my plans, should never have given me the most distant hint directly, or indirectly that such a process could be in honor dispensed with? Is it not a little singular that he should have reserved this friendly charge of supererogation till I had burnt my bricks, bought my timber, and got into a situation in which it was more prudent to advance, than to recede? The Archbishop is a friendly good man; but such is not the manner of laymen. It would be a bad comfort to an Indian widow, who was half-burnt, if the head Bramin were to call out to her, 'Remember, *it is your own act and deed*; I never ordered you to burn yourself, and I must take the liberty of telling you that you are a fool for your pains'. 'No, good Sr., but you knew that it was a common custom of our religion; that it was expected of me. I conversed with you upon it; you saw me bringing the faggots, and have reserved this opinion of the superfluity of the act till I am half roasted, and till death is better than life'.

I am truely concerned my dear Lady Holland that you are so unwell. I thought it had long since passed away, – your illness, but it appears to hang upon you. I must come, and prescribe for you myself. I have great knowledge, and zeal, and have been of great service to sick ladies.

We have had meetings here of the clergy upon the subject of the Catholic petition, but none in *my district*; if there is, I shall certainly give my solitary voice in favor of religious liberty, and shall probably be tossed in a blanket for my pains.

Conceive the horror of 14 men hung* yesterday morning; and yet it is difficult to blame the judges for it, tho' it would be some relief to be able to blame them. The murderers of Horsefall were all Methodists; one of them I believe a preacher.

I hope you will take a ramble to the North this year. You want a tour, nothing does you so much good. Come and alarm the village, as you did before. Your coming has produced the same impression as the march of Alexander or Bacchus over India, and will be as long remembered in the traditions of the innocent natives. They still believe Antonio* to have been an ape. Pray accept a Yorkshire ham, which set off yesterday directed to Lord Holland, St. James's-square pr. Hartley's waggon which comes to the Bull and Mouth; it weighs 20 lbs. I mention these particulars because when a thing is sent it may as well be received, and not be changed. Kind love and regards from all here, dear Lady Holland. I remain ever most sincerely and affectionately yrs

Sydney Smith

231. ROBERT SMITH

March 17th, 1813

My dear Bobus,

It seems to me a long time since I heard from you. Pray write to me, and if you are vexed, or uneasy, or dispirited, do not be too proud to say so.

I have heard about you from various good judges, all of whom concur in the statement made to me from Holland House; that the coach appeared to be made of admirable materials, and that its breaking down was a mere accident, for which it is impossible to account.* I see you have spoken again, but your speech is only given in my three days' paper, and that very concisely. If you said what you had to say without a fresh attack of nervousness, this is all I care about. If the body does not play you these tricks, I have no fear of the mind. By the bye, you will laugh at me, but I am convinced a working senator should lead a life like an athlete. I wish you would let me send you a horse, and that you would ride every morning ten or fifteen miles before breakfast, and fling yourself into a profuse perspiration. No man ever stopped in a speech, that had perspired copiously that day. Do you disdain the assistance of notes?

I am going on prosperously with my buildings, but I am not yet out of sight of land. We most earnestly hope nothing will prevent you this year from coming down into Yorkshire. I have learnt to ride backwards and forwards to my living since I saw you, by which means I do not sleep away from home; – and I have found so good a manager of my accounts, that one day a week is sufficient for me to give up to my buildings.

When you have done anything that pleases yourself, write me word; it will give me the most unfeigned pleasure. Whether you turn out a consumate orator or not, will neither increase nor diminish my admiration for your talents or my respect for your character; – but when a man is strong, it is pleasant to make that strength respected; – and you will be happier for it, if you can do so (as I have no doubt you will soon).

My very kind love to Caroline and the children, and believe me ever your affectionate brother,

Sydney Smith

233. ROBERT SMITH

Heslington, York, May 10th, 1813

My dear Bobus,

Maria* writes Mrs. Sydney word that you are not quite so stout as you used to be. Pray take care of yourself. Let us contrive to last out for the same or nearly the same time: weary will be the latter half of my pilgrimage, if you leave me in the lurch!* By the bye, I wish Mrs. Smith and you would promise to inform me if you are ever seriously ill. I should come up to you at a moment's warning, and should be very unhappy if the opportunity were not given me of doing so.

I was very much pleased with Canning's additions to Grattan's Bill;* they are very wise, because they give satisfaction to the great mass of fools, of whom the public is composed, and who really believe there is danger in conceding so much to the Catholics.

I cannot help detailing to you a remark of Douglas's, which in Scotland would be heard as of high metaphysical promise. Emily was asking why one flower was blue, and another pink, and another yellow. 'Why, in short,' said Douglas, 'it is their *nature*; and when we say that, what do we mean? It is only another word for *mystery*; *it only means that we know nothing at all about the matter*.' This observation from a child eight years old is not common.

We are threatened with a visit from the excellent Greek, I understand, who is conducting his young warrior to the north.* How contemptible our modern way of arming must appear to him! He will doubtless speak to the Colonel about the fighting in Homer, and the mode of it.

God bless you, dear Bobus! Love to your dear children.

Sydney Smith

234. J. A. MURRAY

Heslington, July 12th, 1813

My dear Murray,

I understand you are one of the Commissioners for managing the Edinburgh Review, in the absence of our small-bodied, great-minded leader.* He has made to me a very affecting appeal for assistance, and for such as I can afford shall not make it in vain; the difficulty is to find a book, and I will review any two of the following – Clarkson's Life of Penn, Buchanan's Colonial Establishment, Thompson's Travels in Sweden, Graham's Residence in India, or Horsley's Speeches. Have the goodness if you please, to tell me *which* of these I shall take, and at what time I shall send them, giving me all the time you can, as I really am distressed for that article. My situation is as follows: – I am engaged in agriculture without the slightest knowledge of the art; I am building a house without an architect, and educating a son without patience. Nothing short of my sincere affection for Jeffrey, and pity for his transatlantic loves, should have induced me to draw my goose quill. Jeffrey knows elegant women when he sees them.*

As I know you love a bit of London scandal learn that Lady Caroline Lamb stabbed herself at Lady Ilchester's Ball for the love of Lord Byron, as it is supposed. What a charming thing to be a Poet. I preached for many years in London and was rather popular, but never heard of a Lady doing herself the smallest mischief on my account.

If ever you feel moved to pack up your books and make me a long Visit, we shall be delighted to see you, and I will tell you very fairly whether our house is free or not from engagements. My new Mansion springs up apace, and there I shall really have a pretty place to receive you in and a pleasant Country to shew you. Remember me very kindly to all friends, and beleive me my dear Murray ever most sincerely yrs

Sydney Smith

237. LADY HOLLAND

Heslington, Sept. 17th, 1813

Dear Lady Holland,

Few events are of so little consequence as the fecundity of a cleryman's wife; still your kind disposition towards us justifies me in letting you know that Mrs. Sydney and her new born son are both extremely well. His name will be Grafton,* and I shall bring him up as a Methodist and a Tory.

Ever my dear Lady Holl affectionately yrs,

Sydney Smith

243. LADY HOLLAND

Heslington, Jan. 20th, 1814

My dear Lady Holland,

I heard with great concern of Lord Holland's illness. Pray say everything that is kind on my part, and when he gets better I seriously wish you would confine him to two glasses of wine. A pint of wine seems to be temperance, but it is not Temperance, and the accumulation of this quantity of wine brings on fits of the gout. All people above the condition of laborers are ruined by excess of stimulus and nourishment, Clergy included. I never yet saw any Gentleman who ate and drank as little as was reasonable.

My boy's name is Windham, and Wishaw is your co-ajutor. I am much obliged by the kind expressions you use towards him. I wish you had said a word of your own health, and that a good word. I have not read Miss Edgeworth's novel* nor have I much opinion of her powers of execution saving and excepting Irish characters. Every thing else I have read of hers I thought very indifferent, even her Tale called *Eunice*.* If she has put into her Novels people who fed her and her odious father, she is not Trustworthy.

I see your protegé Ward is gone abroad with Lord Castlereagh. I should think this must amount to another turn in politics. I am afraid you will be going abroad again hungry from long abstinence. When everything is quite quiet and I can get some money I shall do the same myself. Paris will be my object and there I shall remain for some months. This is a project I have long set my heart upon and which I think will be within my compass.

God bless you dear Lady Holl. Ever most affectionately yrs

Sydney Smith

244. JOHN ALLEN

Saturday, March 10th,* 1814

Dear Allen,

I cannot at all enter into your feelings about the Bourbons, nor can I attend to so remote an evil as the encoragement of superstitious attachment to kings, when the present evil of a military Monarchy, or of thirty years more of war, is before my eyes. I want to get rid of this great disturber of human happiness, and I scarcely know any price too great to effect it. If you were sailing from Alicant to Aleppo in a storm, and if (after the sailors had held up the image of a Saint and prayed to it) the storm were to abate, you would be more sorry for the encoragement of superstition than rejoiced for the preservation of your life, – and so would every other man born, and bred in Edinburgh.

My view of the matter would be much shorter and coarser; I should be so glad to find myself alive that I should not care a farthing if the storm had generated a thousand new, and revived as many old Saints. How can any man stop in the midst of the stupendous joy of getting rid of Buonaparte, and prophesy the little piddling evils that will result from restoring the Bourbons? Nor am I quite certain that I don't wish Paris burnt and France laid waste by Cossacks for revenge, and for security. The most important of all objects is the independence of Europe: it has been twice very nearly destroyed by the French; it is menaced from no other quarter; and the people must be identified with their sovereign. There is no help for it; it will teach them in future to hang kings who set up for conquerors. I will not believe that the Bourbons have no party in France. My only knowledge of politics is from the York paper; yet nothing shall convince me that the people are not heartily tired of Buonaparte, and ardently wish for the cessation of the conscription; that is, for the Bourbons.

I shall be in my house by the 25th of March, in spite of all the evils that are prophesied against me. I have had eleven fires burning night and day for these two months past and my walls tried by frost or in rainy weather are as dry as Drummond.*

I am glad to hear that this intention of raising a statue to Playfair and Stewart is now reported to have been only a joke. This is *wut*, not *wit*; by way of pleasantry the oddest conceit I ever heard of; but you gentlemen of the North are, you know, a little singular in your conceptions of the Lepid. I quoted to Whishaw the behaviour of Paul and Barnabas, under similar circumstances, as mentioned in the Acts; I wonder if Stewart and Playfair would have behaved with as much modesty had this joke dropped down into a matter of fact.

We are all very well: tho' Douglas alarmed us the other night with the croup. I darted into him all the mineral, and vegetable resources of the shops, cravatted his throat with blisters, and fringed it with leaches, excited now the Peristaltic, now the Antiperisaltic motion like the *Strophe* and the *Antistrophe* of the

Tragedies, and set him in 5 or 6 hours to play at marbles, breathing gently and inaudibly; as did Lord Robert Spencer in antient times at Woolbedding,* when in the dead of the night thro' the long passage etc etc –

How is Lord Holland? How is my Lady? Pray give my kindest regards, and believe me my dear Allen most sincerely yrs

Sydney Smith

248. LADY HOLLAND

June 25th, 1814

My dear Lady Holland,

I set off on Tuesday morning, and reached home Wednesday night by 10 o'clock, finding everybody very well, and delighting them not a little next day by the display of your French presents; but of this Mrs S will speak herself.

I liked London better than ever I liked it before, and simply I believe from water-drinking. Without this London is stupefaction, and inflammation. It is not the love of wine, but thoughtlessness and unconscious imitation: other men poke out their hands for the revolving wine, and one does the same without thinking of it.

If Allen stays a day in York why should he not come over here? Consider this if you please and arrange accordingly.

I am uneasy dear Lady Holland at your going abroad. Consider what a thing it is to be well. If I were you, I would not stir from Holland House for 2 years; and then as many jolts, and frights as you please, which at present you are not equal to. I should think you less to blame if the world had anything new to shew you; but you have seen the Parthian, the Mede, the Elamite and the dweller in Mesopotamia; no variety of garment can surprise you, and the roads upon the earth are as well known to you as the wrinkles in Rogers' face.

Be wise my dear Lady and re-establish your health in that gilded room* which furnishes better and pleasanter society than all the wheels in the world can whirl you to, and God bless you as I do, I his minister and yours very affectionately

S. S.

249. FRANCIS JEFFREY

Postmark Dec. 30th, 1814

My dear Jeffrey,

I am much obliged to you for the Review,* and shall exercise the privilege of an old friend in making some observations upon it. I have not read the review of Wordsworth, because the subject is to me so very uninteresting; but may I ask was it worth while to take any more notice of a man respecting whom the public opinion is completely made up? and do not such repeated attacks upon the man wear in some little degree the shape of persecution?

Without understanding anything of the subject, I was much pleased with the 'Cassegrainian Telescope',* as it seemed modest, moderate in rebuke, and to have the air of wisdom, and erudition. The account of Scotch husbandry is somewhat cox-comical, and has the fault of digressing too much into political economy, but I should guess it to be written by a very good farmer – I mean, by a man thoroughly acquainted with the method in which the art is carried on. I delight in the Jacobinism of the Carnotist;* it is virtuous and honorable to do justice to such a man. I should guess that the travels of the Frenchman in England are those of your friend, and relation Mr Simon.*

With respect to what you say of your occasional feelings of disgust at your office of editor and half-formed intentions of giving it up, I think you should be slow to give up so much emolument, now that you are married, and may have a family; but if you can get as great an income by your profession and the two cannot be combined, I would rather see you a great lawyer than a witty journalist. There can be no doubt which is the most honorable, and lucrative situation and not much doubt which is the most useful.

It will give us the greatest pleasure to see you in the spring, or, if not, then in your excursion to France. I like my new house very much; it is very comfortable, and after finishing it, I would not pay sixpence to alter it; but the expence of it will keep me a very poor man, a close prisoner here for my life, and render the education of my children a difficult exertion for me. My situation is one of great solitude, but I preserve myself in a state of cheerfulness, and tolerable content, and have a propensity to amuse myself with trifles. I hope I shall write something before I grow old, but I am not certain whether I am sufficiently industrious. I shall never apologize to you for egoism; I think very few men in writing to their friends have enough of it. If Horner were to break fifteen of his ribs, or marry, or resolve to settle in America, he would never mention it to his friends; but would write with the most sincere kindness from Kentucky to inquire for your welfare, leaving you to marvell as you chose at the post-mark, and to speculate whether it was Kentucky or Kensington.

I think very highly of 'Waverley', and was inclined to suspect in reading it that it was written by Miss Scott of Ancram.*

I am truely glad to read of your pleasure from your little girl and your chateau.* The haunts of Happiness are varied, and rather unaccountable; but I have more often seen her among little children, and home firesides, and in country houses, than anywhere else, – at least, I think so. God bless you. your sincere friend

S S.

273. LADY MARY BENNET*

Sedgeley, Jan. 6th, 1817

Dear Lady Mary Bennet,

I think it was rather bad taste on my part to speak of the Princess as a royal person, when you were lamenting her loss as an acquaintance; but I am very jealous of the monarchical feelings of this country.

I do not know whether you are acquainted with the Philips* with whom I am now staying; he is very rich, the discoverer of cotton, and an old friend of mine. I am going to preach a charity sermon next Sunday. I desire to make three or four hundred weavers cry, which it is impossible to do since the late rise in cottons.

And now, dear Lady Mary, do you want anything in the flowering cotton, or Manchester velvet, or chintz line? Remember, this is not a town where there are only a few shops, but it is the great magazine from which flow all the mercers' shops in the known world. Here tabbies and tabinets are first concocted! Here muslin – elementary, rudimental, early, primeval muslin – is meditated; broad and narrow sarsnet first see the light, and narrow and broad edging! Avail yourself, dear lady, of my being here, to prepare your conquering armour for your next campaign.

I shall be in town by the end of March, and shall have real pleasure in seeing you. I think you begin to feel at ease in my company: certainly, you were much improved in that particular the last time we met. God bless you! I admire you very much, and praise you often.

Sydney Smith

274. LORD HOLLAND

Foston, March 13th, 1817

My dear Lord Holland,

Nobody I assure you is more desirous of living at ease than I am; but I should prefer the approbation of such men as the Duke of Bedford and yourself, to the most unwieldy bishopric obtained by means you would condemn, and despise. Doubtless, when you think of that amorous and herbivorous parish,* and compare it with my agricultural benefice, you will say, 'Better is the dinner of herbs where *love* is, than the stalled ox,' etc. etc. Be this as it may, my best thanks are due to you for your kind exertions in my favour; but you and Lady Holland are full of kindness to me on all occasions. You know how sincerely I am attached to you both.

I entirely agree to, and sympathize with, your opposition to the suspension.* Nothing can be more childish and mischievous. Christianity in danger of being written down by doggrel thymes – England about to be divided into little parcels, like a chessboard— The flower and chivalry of the realm flying before one armed apothecary – How can old Mother Grenville and Mother Fitzwilliam swallow such trash as this?

I say nothing of the great and miserable loss we have all sustained. He will always live in our recollection; and it will be useful to us in all the great occasions of life to reflect how Horner would act and think in them if God had suffered him to live.* My kind love to Lady Holl. Ever my dear Lord Holland most truely and affectionately yrs,

Sydney Smith

278. LADY HOLLAND

Scarborough, July 31st, 1817

My dear Lady Holland,

I write to you from Scarborough, with a clear view from my window of the Hague and Amsterdam. We are waiting the arrival of the Bobii who will not be here for 10 days. Not a soul in the place.

I saw Brougham at York, at the circuit. He may as well keep away; the attornies expect in a lawyer the constancy of a turtle dove.

Mr. Shuttleworth* is with you. Pray make interest for his nomination of Windham to Winchester. Some friends of mine have beforespoken to him on the subject and I do not think he is averse to it, but you are omnipotent. All the persons tried here for rioting and sedition have been acquitted. I have got back all my letters from Leonard Horner. He offered and I accepted them as well for myself as for Mrs. Sydney. Mine were of a description that are intended for immediate combustion. It is hardly a fair practise to keep letters. It ought not to be done if the correspondent does not like it, and that nobody does like it is clear, for it would put an end to any correspondence, or render it not worth keeping up. They still talk of publishing a collection of letters for which I am very sorry. They can publish nothing at all equal to his reputation and the expectation of the public.

It is very curious to consider in what manner Horner gained in so extraordinary a manner the affection of such a number of persons of both sexes all ages parties and ranks in society; for he was not remarkably good-tempered, nor particularly lively and agreeable; and an inflexible politician on the unpopular side.

The causes are, his high character for probity, honor, and talents; his fine countenance; his character contrasted with that of his rival Brougham; the benevolent interest he took in the concerns of all his friends; his simple and gentlemanlike manners; his untimely death.

I hope you are not going to stay beyond October, I mean not going to winter abroad, for I always suspect you of long absences, and do not like to trust you across the seas. Pray keep me in favor, and do not get tired of me. We all send our kind love and regards to you, and I remain dear Lady Holland ever very affectionately yrs.

Sydney Smith

280. E. Davenport

Foston, Sept. 1817

Dear Davenport,

You have no idea what a number of handsome things were said of you when your six partridges were consumed today. Wit, iterature, and polished manners were ascribed to you – some good quality for each bird. You never met with a more favorable jury. I conclude the *éloge* with my best thanks for your kind and flattering attention. We all, however, objected to your equipage; longevity is incompatible with driving two horses at length. Man is frequently cut off even in buggies; an inch to the right or the left may send you to the Davenports of ages past, and put half Cheshire in mourning.

Ever most truly yours
Sydney Smith

281. Lady Mary Bennet

Foston, ⟨Sept.,⟩ 1817

Dear Lady Mary,

There never was better venison, or venison treated with more respect and attention. Chillingham is a place of the greatest merit.

I envy Brougham his trip to Paris. There is nothing (except

the pleasure of seeing you) I long for so much as to see Paris, and I pray my life may be spared for this great purpose, or rather these great purposes. Easter will do for the first, as I shall be in town about that time. My brother and his family quit us on Monday for Bowood. A house emptied of its guests is always melancholy for the the first three or four days. Their loss will be supplied by Sir Humphry and Lady Davy, who are about to pay us a visit next week.

I have not framed your drawing yet, because I want another to accompany it, and then they shall both go up together. I do not know whether this is *exigeant* or not; but I have so great an idea of your fertility in these matters, that I consider a drawing to be no more to you than an epic poem to Coleridge, or a prison and police bill to some of your relations.

Sydney Smith

285. John Whishaw

January 7th, 1818

My dear Whishaw,

We have been here* for about a fortnight, and stay till the 21st. The company who come here are chiefly *Philippical*, as there is an immense colony of that name in these parts; they seem all good-natured worthy people, and many of them in the *Whig* line. In these days, too, every lady reads a little; and there is more variety and information in every class than there was fifty years ago. About the year 1740, a manufacturer of *long ells* or *twilled fustians* must have been rather a coarse-grained fellow. It is not among gentlemen of that description I would at present look for all that is delightful in manner and conversation, but they certainly run 'finer' than they did, and are (to use their own phrase) a *superior article*.

The acquittal of Hone gave me sincere pleasure, because I believe it proceeded in some measure from the horror and disgust which excessive punishments for libel have excited; and if jurymen take this mode of expressing their disgust, judges will be more moderate. It is a rebuke also upon the very offensive and scandalous zeal of Lord Ellenborough, and it teaches juries their strength and importance. In short, Church and King in moderation are very good things, but we have too much of both. I presume by this time your grief at the death of the Princess is somewhat abated. Death in the midst of youth is always melancholy, but I cannot think it of the smallest political importance.

I dread a popular King, because they are always popular from some low and pernicious art, and anything which weakens the power of the crown seems to be a good.

I am very glad the Hollands have sent Henry from home; he is a very unusual boy, and he wanted to be exposed a little more to the open air of the world.

Poor Mackintosh,* I am heartily sorry for him, but his situation at Hertford will suit him very well (pelting and contusions always excepted). He should stipulate for *pebble money*, as it is there technically termed, or an annual pension in case he is disabled by the pelting of the students. By the bye, might it not be advisable for the professors to learn the use of the sling (*balearis habena*)? – it would give them a great advantage over the students.

We are all perfectly well, with the usual January exceptions of colds, sore throats, rheumatism, and hoarseness. I shall be in town in March and make some stay, but pray write to me before if you have any leisure.

Ever your sincere friend,
Sydney Smith

288. LORD HOLLAND

Foston, Feb. 28th, 1818

Dear Lord Holland

The Birthday of my eldest Boy Douglas (now thirteen) renews my sage desire to get him to India and reminds me of your kind promise to interest Baring in his behalf. There is not perhaps in the circle of human Events a more striking contrast than the facility with which a Clergyman begets a Child, and the difficulty with which he educates him – a difficulty by no means lessened if there hangs about the priest the odor of opposition politics.

I do not wish you to do any thing unpleasant or painful to yourself, but if you can without any sacrifice obtain such a favor from Baring you will as you have often done before make me happy. It is better to lose sight of a Child than to retain him near you in poverty, obscurity and dependance.

Fortune I beleive has done for me all she ever means to do, and I have no better prospect for Douglas than that concerning which I am writing to you.

I was truely happy to hear of your increase of fortune, and I hope to see you in the full enjoyment of it in the course of the Summer – Ever most truely and gratefully Yrs

Sydney Smith

291. LADY HOLLAND

March, 1818

My dear Lady Holland,

Mrs. Sydney, and the children do not come to Town this year, or they would have great pleasure in making you a visit; they beg to be kindly remembered. You may depend upon it I will not make any mischief between Mr. Tierney* and my friend Philips. I well know that the former (however he may indulge in a little quizzing with you) has the highest admiration of Philips's enlarged views of constitutional questions, and I believe they mutually rehearse speeches to each other in that Marco-Tullian garden at Philips's house. I am truely glad to find that Tierney is better from those nitrous baths. Can so much nitrous acid get into the human frame without producing some moral and intellectual effects as well as physical? If you watch I think you will find changes.

You have done an excellent deed in securing a seat for poor Mackintosh, in whose praise I most cordially concur; he is a very great and a very delightful man, and with a few bad qualities added to his character would have acted a very conspicuous part in life. Yet after all he is rather Academic than Forensic; a professorship at Hertford is well imagined and if he can keep clear of contusions at the Annual Peltings, all will be well. The season for Lapidating the Professors is now at hand, keep him quiet at Holland House till all is over.

If I could envy any man for successful ill nature I should envy Lord Byron for his skill in satyrical nomenclature. Botherby* is peculiarly appropriate.

Castle Howard moves to London today, great is the moving thereof. Remember me very kindly to Lord Morpeth; he has only one fault, he has not the fear of Malthus before his eyes.

I have no doubt you will decide for the best about Ampthill. I shall if you give me any encouragement make it my road to the North. I hope Henry is perfectly recovered from his ague; he is a tender plant, but a very fine clever boy. Nothing can exceed the evils of this spring, all agricultural opeartions are at least a month behindhand; the earth that ought to be as hard as a biscuit is as soft as dough. We live here in great seclusion but happily, and comfortably. My life is cut up into little patches; I am Schoolmaster farmer doctor parson justice etc, etc. Bobus is not to be diverted from his solitude. I presume he will not go into Parliament again; then of course the evil will become worse – Whatever faults Bobus has, he has them in fee, his tenure is freehold, they are not to be touched or changed. This is true also of his virtues, which God be praised are many. So I remain always dear Lady Holland very affectionately yrs

Sydney Smith

295. Lady Davy

Holland House, May, 1818

.   .   .   .   .   .

You are of an ardent mind, and overlook the difficulties and embarrassments of life. Luttrell, before I taught him better, imagined muffins grew! He was wholly ignorant of all the intermediate processes of sowing, reaping, grinding, kneading, and baking. Now you require a *prompt* answer; but mark the difficulties; your note comes to Weymouth-street, where I am *not*; then by the post to Holland House, where, as I am not a marquis, and have no servant, it is tossed on the porter's table; and when found and answered, will creep into the post late this evening, if the postman is no more drunk than common.

Pray allow for these distressing embarrassments, with which human intercourse is afflicted; and believe how happy I shall be to wait on you the 22nd, being always, my dear Lady Davy, sincerely yours,

Sydney Smith

307. LADY HOLLAND

Foston, Oct. 11th, 1818
my direction is for the future Foston, York.

My dear Lady Holland,

Allen asked when Douglas and I came to the South; but I had no thoughts of coming, and Douglas has been at Westminster some time; fought his first battle, came off victorious, and is completely established. Instead of the south, I am turning my face northwards to see Lord Grey and Jeffrey. John Murray and I are to meet at the best of all possible châteaux.

Some surprise is excited by your staying so long at Ampthill; but Rogers I find has been sent for as a sort of condiment or pickle, and Luttrell has been also in your epergne.

I am sorry we cannot agree about Walter Scott. My test of a book written to amuse is amusement; but I am rather rash and ought not to say I am amused, before I have inquired whether Sharp and Mackintosh are so. Wishaw's plan is the best: he gives no opinion for the first week, but confines himself merely to chuckling and elevating his chin; in the meantime he drives diligently about to the fixed critical stations, breakfasts in Mark-lane hears from Hertford College and by Saturday night is as bold as a lion; and is as decisive as a court of justice.

Brougham's pamphlet* accidentally happens to be very dull. It is not of much importance but there was no absolute necessity for its being so. Wit and declamation would be misplaced, but a clever man may be bright and flowing while he is argumentative and prudent. He makes out a great case in general: and nobody would accuse Lord Londsale and the Bishop of undue precipitation if they were to make some sort of reply to the charge of particular delinquencies levelled against them. Why they should suffer themselves to be considered as Schoolboy Ogres while they have any reply to make I cannot conceive.

The Morpeths are gone to the Duke of Devonshire's, and superfine work there will be, and much whispering; so that a blind man should sit there, and believe they are all gone to bed, though the room is full of the most brilliant society. As for me I like a little noise and nature, and Rogers much chagrined, and a large party very merry, and happy.

I hope dear Lady Holland you have not forgotten me and that I am not out of favor. If I am you will be never the less in favor with me. I can live upon recollections, though they are by no means the best sort of diet. We are all well. I hope Holland has escaped the gout. I have no gout of my own and would take a fit for him with the greatest pleasure if Providence would allow it. God bless you dear Lady Holl. I am ever with great attachment and affection yrs

Sydney Smith

315. LADY MARY BENNET

Saville-row, Dec. 1818

My dear Lady Mary,

I was much amused with your thinking that you had discovered me in the Edinburgh Review; if you look at it again, you will find reason to alter your opinion.

I have brought all my children up to town; and they are, as you may suppose, not a little entertained and delighted. It is the first time they have ever seen four people together, except on remarkably fine days at the parish church. There seems to be nobody in town, nor will there be, I presume, before the meeting of Parliament.

I am writing to you at two o'clock in the morning, having heard of a clergyman who brought himself down from twenty-six to sixteen stone in six months, by lessening his sleep. When he began, he was so fat that he could not walk, and now he walks every day up one of the highest hills in the country, and remains in perfect health. I shall be so thin when you see me, that you may trundle me about like a mop. God bless you!

Sydney Smith

318. LADY GREY

Tuesday, Jan. 12th, 1819

Dear Lady Grey

Nothing has happened in London since I wrote to you last. I hear you are sending one of your Boys to Sea which must make you nervous as you have had no practice in parting with your Boys. I think he must be in the new North West Expedition which they are going to send out. The Admiralty (that is to say Barrow)* are dissatisfied with the Conduct of the Captains of the late Expedition. The Seconds in command agree with Barrow, and are to command in this second undertaking. Lord Erskine is very ill at Oatlands.* I am inclined to think this Rumor of his Expedition to Gretna Green is true; at least it has long been said that such was his intention; the only explanation is that he is old, and loves tranquility and the Lady is determined he shall not enjoy it till her terms are acceded to. . . .

I have no shyness with strangers, and care not where, and with whom I dine. Today I dined with Sir Henry Torrens,* the Duke of York's secretary, and found him a very gentlemanlike civilized person, with what would pass in the army for a good understanding. I was very well pleased with all I saw, for he has 6 elegant pretty children and a very comfortable villa at Fulham; his rooms were well lighted, warmed in the most agreeable luxurious manner with Russian stoves, and his dinner excellent. Everything was perfectly comfortable. What is the use of fish or venison, when the backbone is 6 degrees below the freezing-point? Of all miserable habitations an English house in very hot or very cold weather is the worst.

My little boy, whom you were so good as to inquire about, is quite well, and returned to Westminster. He likes the school, and seems to be doing very well in it, has fought two or 3 battles victoriously, and is at the head of his class.

I hope Lord Grey liked Burdett's letter to Cobbett. It is excellent, and will do that consummate villain some mischief; he is still a great deal read.

I passed four hours yesterday with my children in the British Museum. It is now put upon the best possible footing, and exhibited courteously and publickly to all. The visitors when I was there were principally maid-servants. 50,000 people saw it last year. My kindest regards if you please to my young friends and to the excellent Lord of Howick.

Ever dear Lady Grey most truely.

327. LADY HOLLAND

Foston, April 20th, 1819

My dear Lady Holland,

We have taken the Liberty to send you two Hams in token of your Seignorage over Foston and its inhabitants. They are I understand of domestic manufacture and we shall feel exalted above the neighboring Clergy if they are approved of at Holland House. I heard of your negotiation with Miss Berry. I am settled at last into liking the Miss Berrys, and shall never change any more. They have both better understandings, and much more sense than from their unquiet manner they seem to have, which manner is not unlike that of seafowl before a storm. As for mixt parties I think you never look happy there.

I have been lame for some time by a fall from my horse. He had behaved so well and so quietly that I doubled his allowance of corn and in return he kicked me over his head in the most ignominious, and contemptuous manner. This should be a warning to you against raising servants' wages. I am recovering fast tho' sorely bruised; fifteen stone weight does not fall from sixteen hands high with impunity.

Hallam's style does not appear to me so bad as it has been represented; indeed I am ashamed to say I rather think it a good style.* He is a bold man and great names do not deter him from finding fault; he began with Pindar, and who has any right to complain after that? The characteristic excellencies of the work seem to be fidelity, accuracy, good sense, a love of Virtue and a zeal for Liberty.

We are all very well and have subsided very well into country clergymen and clergy women. I am going to review Galiani's Correspondence, and to write an article upon Tithes – a subject I believe untouched among the many important articles which have been discussed in the Edinburgh Review. I had a letter yesterday from poor Jeffrey who is in considerable alarm about an only child, a misery he experienced in his former marriage.

You seem to have a very pleasant party at Ampthill – your two body Poets* and some of your best friends. My kind regards to them all and particularly to Lady Georgiana* and to the very agreeable and volatile Henry and my excellent friend Charles. God bless you dear Lady Holland. Always your very affectionate friend

Sydney Smith

333. Archibald Constable

York, June 28th, 1819

Dear Sir,

I am truly obliged by your kindness in sending me the last novel* of Walter Scott. It would be profanation to call him Mr. Walter Scott. I should as soon say Mr. Shakespeare or Mr. Fielding. Sir William and Lady Ashton are excellent, and highly dramatic. Drumthwacket is very well done; parts of Caleb are excellent. Some of the dialogues between Bucklaw and Craigengelt are as good as can be, and both these characters very well imagined. *As the author has left off writing*, I shall not again be disturbed so much in my ordinary occupations. When I get hold of one of these novels, turnips, sermons, and justice-business are all forgotten.

Your sincere well-wisher
Sydney Smith

337. FRANCIS JEFFREY

Foston, Aug. 7th, 1819

My dear Jeffrey,

You must consider that Edinburgh is a very grave place, and that you live with Philosophers – who are very intolerant of nonsense. I write for the London, not for the Scotch market, and perhaps more people read my nonsense than your sense. The complaint was loud and universal of the extreme dulness and *lengthiness* of the Edinburgh Review. Too much I admit would not do of my style; but the proportion in which it exists enlivens the Review if you appeal to the whole public, and not to the 8 or 10 grave Scotchmen with whom you live. I am a very ignorant, frivolous, half-inch person; but, such as I am, I am sure I have done your Review good, and *contributed* to bring it into notice. Such as I am, I shall be, and cannot promise to alter; such is my opinion of the effect of my articles. I differ from you entirely about Lieutenant Heude. To do such things very often would be absurd; to punish a man every now and then for writing a frivolous book is wise and proper; and you would find, if you lived in England, that the review of Heude is talked of and quoted for its fun and impertinence, – when graver, and abler articles are thumbed over, and passed bye. Almost anybody of the sensible men who write for the Review would have written a much wiser, and more profound article than I have done upon the Game Laws; but I am quite certain nobody would obtain more readers for his essay upon such a subject and I am equally certain that the principles are right, and that there is no lack of sense in it.

So I judge myself but after all the practical appeal is to you. If you think my assistance of no value, I am too just a man to be angry with you upon that account; but while I write, I must write in my own way. All that I meant to do with Lord Selkirk's case was to state it. I am afraid my dear Jeffrey that it is quite impossible for me to be at Brougham's but I will meet you at Phillips at Manchester, any time from the 27th of September for the whole month of October.

I am extremely sorry for Moore's misfortune,* but only know generally that he has met with misfortune. God bless you.

Your sincere friend,
Sydney Smith

It is not impossible I may come to Brougham's for a very few days. Write me word of the *precise day* you will be there.

338. The Farmer's Magazine*

August, 1819

Sir,

It has been my lot to have passed the greater part of my life in cities. – About six or seven years ago, I was placed in the country, in a situation where I was under the necessity of becoming a farmer; and, amongst the many expensive blunders I have made, I warn those who may find themselves in similar situations, against *Scotch Sheep* and *Oxen for ploughing*. I had heard a great deal of the fine flavour of Scotch mutton, and it was one of the great luxuries I promised myself in farming. A luxury certainly it is; but the price paid for it is such, that I would rather give up the use of animal food altogether, than obtain it by such a system of cares and anxieties. Ten times a day my men were called off from their work to hunt the Scotch sheep out of my own or my neighbour's wheat. They crawled through hedges where I should have thought a rabbit could hardly have found admission; and, where crawling would not do, they had recourse to leaping. Five or six times they all assembled, and set out on their return to the North. My bailiff took a place in the mail, pursued, and overtook them half way to Newcastle. Then it was quite impossible to get them fat. They consumed my turnips in winter, and my clover in the summer, without any apparent addition to their weight; 10 or 12 per cent. always died of the rot; and more would have perished in the same manner, if they had not been prematurely eaten out of the way.

My ploughing oxen were an equal subject of vexation. They had a constant purging upon them, which it was impossible to stop. They ate more than twice as much as the same number of horses. They did half as much work as the same number of horses. They could not bear hot weather, nor wet weather, nor go well down hill. It took five men to shoe an ox. They ran against my gate-posts, lay down in the cart whenever they were tired, and ran away at the sight of a stranger.

I have now got into a good breed of English sheep, and useful cart-horses, and am doing very well. I make this statement to guard young gentlemen farmers against listening to the pernicious nonsense of brother gentlemen, for whose advice I am at least poorer by 300l, or 400l.

Yours etc.

Z

342. LADY GEORGIANA MORPETH

Foston, Sept. 5th, 1819

Dear Lady Georgiana,

Everybody is haunted with spectres and apparitions of sorrow, and the imaginary griefs of life are greater than the real. Your rank in life rather exposes you the more to these attacks. Whatever the English zenith may be, the horizon is almost always of a sombre colour. . . . I like in you very much that you are a religious woman, because, though I have an infinite hatred and contempt for the nonsense which often passes under, and disgraces the name of religion, I am very much pleased when I see anybody religious for hope and comfort, not for insolence and interest. About the nature of your complaint, I hope and trust you are wrong; if you are right, I shall pity you as much as I please, and shew that I do so as much as you please. Your praise and approbation are very grateful to Mrs. Sydney and Saba; as for me, I will promise never to quiz you, that is, only a very little, and to your face, and in a low voice, and not before strangers; and for the rest, you will always find me a discreet neighbour and a sincere friend.

Sydney Smith

345. LADY GEORGIANA MORPETH

Autumn, 1819

Dear Lady Georgiana,

Excuse my making a short reply to your politics. If a very important privilege in a free government appears to have been fragrantly violated, and if such violation is approved by the administration, it is high time that the people should meet together, express their sense of the apparent wrong, and call for inquiry. If I were a politician, and found the people remiss in meeting on such occasions, I would be the first to rouse them. If they met of their own accord, I should think it the most important of all duties to be amongst them, that I might enlighten their ignorance, repress their presumption, and direct their energy to laudable purposes.

For these reasons I think Lord Fitzwilliam* has acted like a virtuous and honourable man. I am no more surprised at his dismissal than you are. It is a blow aimed at the manly love of reasonable liberty, the natural recompense which a profligate prince requires from those to whom he delegates his power. As for your confidence in the times, I hope it is as well founded as it is agreeable; but if the revenue continues to decay, and commerce and manufactures do not soon revive, I think you will not find the sufferers and the enjoyers to remain upon the same friendly terms which you kindly suppose them to be upon at present. When I state my opinion about the meetings of the people, of course I acknowledge that honest and enlightened men may arrive at conclusions entirely opposite. I would punish neither line of conduct, but if either, then I would dismiss lord-lieutenants who had *not* called meetings.

Ever, dear Lady Georgiana, very truly yours

Sydney Smith

347. LADY HOLLAND

⟨November, 1819⟩

My dear Lady Holland,

I had expected this sad event* since Wishaw informed me of the relapse. I received the intelligence of it this morning – frequent enquiries I thought would only give trouble without doing any good. You know me well enough to know that I have the most sincere interest in every important event which befalls Lord Holland and you. The World is full of all sorts of sorrows and miseries – and I think it is better never to have been born – but when evils have happened turn away your mind from them as soon as you can to everything of good which remains. Most people grieve as if grief were a duty or a pleasure, but all who can controul it should controul it – and remember that these renovations of sorrows are almost the charter and condition under which life is held. God Almighty bless you dear Lady Holland. I would have cut off one of my hands to have saved your little Playfellow - but we must submit. My kindest regards to Lord Holland and Allen.

Sydney Smith

348. LORD GREY

Foston, York, Dec. 3rd, 1819

My dear Lord Grey,

I am truely concerned to see you in the papers talking of your health as you are reported to have done. God grant you may be more deceived in that than you are in the state of the country. Pray tell me how you are when you can find leisure to do so.

I entirely agree with you that mere force alone without some attempts at conciliation will not do. Readers are fourfold in number compared with what they were before the beginning of the French war; and demagogues will of course address to them every species of disaffection. As the violence of restraint increases there will be private presses as there are private stills. Juries will acquit, being themselves Jacobins. It is possible for able men to do a great deal of mischief in libels, which it is extremely difficult to punish as libels; and the worst of it all is that a considerable portion of what these rascals say is so very true. Their remedies are worse than their evils; but when they state to the people how they are bought and sold and the abuses entailed upon the country by so corrupted a Parliament it is not easy to answer them, or to hang them. What I want to see the State do is to lessen in these sad times some of their numerous enemies. Why not do something for the Catholics and scratch them off the list? Then come the Protestant Dissenters. Then of measures, – a mitigation of the game-laws – commutation of tithes – granting to such towns as Birmingham and Manchester the seats in Parliament taken from the rottenness of Cornwall – revision of the Penal Code – sale of the Crown lands – sacrifice of the Droits of Admiralty against a new war; – anything that would show the Government to the people in some other attitude than that of taxing, punishing, and restraining. I believe what Tierney said to be strictly true that the House of Commons is falling into contempt with the people. Democracy has many more friends among tradesmen and persons of that class of life than is known or supposed commonly. I believe the feeling is most rapidly increasing and that Parliament in two or three years' time will meet under much greater circumstances of terror than those under which it is at present assembled.

From these speculations I slide by a gentle transition to Lady Grey: how is she? how is Lord Howick? Are you at your ease about the young man? If ever you will send him or any other of your sons upon a visit to me it will give me great pleasure to see them. They shall hear no Tory sentiments and Howick will appear the centre of gaiety and animation compared to Foston. I am delighted with the part Lord Lansdowne has taken: he seems to have made a most admirable speech; but after all I believe we shall all go *ad veteris Nicolai tristia regna, Pitt ubi combustum Dundasque videbimus omnes.*

Ever yours dear Lord Grey most sincerely,
Sydney Smith

356. LADY GEORGIANA MORPETH

Foston, Feb. 16th, 1820

Dear Lady Georgiana,

. . . Nobody has suffered more from low spirits than I have done – so I feel for you. 1st. Live as well as you dare. 2nd. Go into the shower-bath with a small quantity of water at a temperature low enough to give you a slight sensation of cold, 75° or 80°. 3rd. Amusing books. 4th. Short views of human life – not further than dinner or tea. 5th. Be as busy as you can. 6th. See as much as you can of those friends who respect and like you. 7th. And of those acquaintances who amuse you. 8. Make no secret of low spirits to your friends, but talk of them freely – they are always worse for dignified concealment. 9th. Attend to the effects tea and coffee produce upon you. 10th. Compare your lot with that of other people. 11th. Don't expect too much from human life – a sorry business at the best. 12th. Avoid poetry, dramatic representations (except comedy), music, serious novels, melancholy sentimental people, and everything likely to excite feeling or emotion not ending in active benevolence. 13th *Do good*, and endeavour to please everybody of every degree. 14th. Be as much as you can in the open air without fatigue. 15th. Make the room where you commonly sit, gay and pleasant. 16th. Struggle by little and little against idleness. 17th. Don't be too severe upon yourself, or underrate yourself, but do yourself justice. 18th. Keep good blazing fires. 19th. Be firm and constant in the exercise of rational religion. 20th. Believe me, dear Lady Georgiana,

Very truly yours,
Sydney Smith

362. FRANCIS JEFFREY

April, 1820

My dear Jeffrey,

For the number next but one, I have engaged to write an article on Ireland, which shall contain all the information I can collect, detailed as well as I know how to detail it.

The Unitarians think the doctrine of the Trinity to be a

profanation of the Scriptures; you compel them to marry in your churches, or rather, I should say, we compel them to marry in our churches; and when the male and female Dissenter are kneeling before the altar, much is said to them by the priest, of this, to them, abhorred doctrine. They are about to petition Parliament that their marriages may be put upon the same footing as those of Catholics and Quakers. The principles of religious liberty which I have learnt (perhaps under you) make me their friend in the question; and if you approve, I will write an article upon it. Upon the receipt of your letter in the affirmative, I will write to the dissenting king, William Smith,* for information. Pray have the goodness to answer by return of post, or as soon after as you can, if it is but a word; as despatch in these matters, and in my inaccessible situation, is important.

Sydney Smith

367. LORD HOLLAND

Foston, York, June 1st, 1820

My dear Lord Holland,

I return you my sincere thanks for your letter and for the exertions in my behalf, which you have made with your accustomed friendship, and kindness.

The Chancellor is quite right about political sermons, and in this I have erred; but I have a right to preach on general principles of toleration and the fault is not mine if the congregation apply my doctrines to passing events. But I will preach no more upon political subjects; I have not done so for many years, from a conviction it was unfair. You gave me great pleasure by what you said to the Chancellor of my honesty, and independance. I sincerely believe I shall deserve the character at your hands as long as I live. To say that I am sure I shall deserve it, would be as absurd as if a lady were to express an absolute certainty of her future virtue. In good qualities that are to endure for so many years, we can only *hope* for their continuance.

The incumbent is proceeding by slow stages to Buxton. I wish him so well, that under other circumstances I should often write to know how he was going on; at present I must appear unfriendly, to avoid appearing hypocritical. I have spent at least four thousand pounds upon this place; for you must remember I had not only an house but farm-buildings to make; and there had been no resident clergyman for 150 years. I have also played my part in the usual manner, as doctor, justice, road-maker, pacifier, preacher, farmer, neighbor, and diner-out. If I can mend my small fortunes I shall be very glad; if I cannot, I shall not be very sorry. In either case I shall remain your attached and grateful friend,

Sydney Smith

368. Douglas Smith,
King's Scholar at Westminster College

Foston Rectory, Summer, 1820

My dear Douglas,

Concerning this Mr. ——, I would not have you put any trust in him, for he is not trustworthy; but so live with him as if one day or other he were to be your enemy. With such a character as his, this is a necessary precaution.

In the time you can give to English reading you should consider what it is most needful to have, what it is most shameful to want, – shirts and stockings, before frills and collars. Such is the history of your own country, to be studied in Hume, then in Rapin's History of England, with Tindal's Continuation. Hume takes you to the end of James the Second, Rapin and Tindal will carry you to the end of Anne. Then, Coxe's 'Life of Sir Robert Walpole,' and the 'Duke of Marlborough;' and these read with attention to dates and geography. Then, the history of the other three or four enlightened nations in Europe. For the English poets, I will let you off at present with Milton, Dryden, Pope, and Shakspeare; and remember, always in books keep the best company. Don't read a line of Ovid till you have mastered Virgil; nor a line of Thomson till you have exhausted Pope; nor of Massinger, till you are familiar with Shakspeare.

I am glad you liked your box and its contents. Think of us as we think of you; and send us the most acceptable of all presents, – the information that you are improving in all particulars.

The greatest of all human mysteries are the Westminster holidays. If you can get a peep behind the curtain, pray let us know immediately the day of your coming home.

We have had about three or four ounces of rain here, that is all. I heard of your being wet through in London, and envied you very much. The whole of this parish is pulverized from long and excessive drought. Our whole property depends upon the tranquillity of the winds: if it blow before it rains, we shall all be up in the air in the shape of dust, and shall be *transparished* we know not where.

God bless you, my dear boy! I hope we shall soon meet at Lydiard. Your affectionate father,

Sydney Smith

374. J. A. Murray

Foston, York, Sept. 3rd, 1820

My dear Murray,

Many thanks for your kindness in inquiring about your old friends. I am very well, doubling in size every year, and becoming more and more fit for the butcher. Mrs. Sydney is much as she was.

I seldom leave home (except on my annual visit to London), and this principally because I cannot afford it. My income remains the same, my family increases in expense. My constitutional gaiety comes to my aid in all the difficulties of life; and the recollection that, having embraced the character of an honest man and a friend to rational liberty, I have no business to repine at that mediocrity of fortune which I *knew* to be its consequence.

Mrs. —— is a very amiable young woman, inferior in beauty to Lady Charlotte Campbell,* and not so remarkable as Madame de Staël for the vigour of her understanding. Her husband appears to be everything that is amiable and respectable.

The Queen is contemptible; she will be found guilty, and sent out of the country with a small allowance, and in six months be utterly forgotten. So it will, I think, end; but still I think Lord Liverpool very blamable in not having put a complete negative upon the whole thing. It would have been better for the country, and exposed his party to less risk than they have been already exposed to in this business. The Whigs certainly would have refused to meddle with the divorce.

I am sorry to read in your letter such an account of Scotland. Do you imagine the disaffection to proceed from anything but want of employment? or, at least, that full employment, interspersed with a little hanging, will not gradually extinguish the bad spirit?

I have just read 'The Abbot'; it is far above common novels, but of very inferior execution to his others, and hardly worth reading. He has exhausted the subject of Scotland, and worn out the few characters that the early periods of Scotch history could supply him with. Meg Merrilies appears afresh in every novel.

I wish you had told me something about yourself. Are you well? rich? happy? Do you digest? Have you any thoughts of marrying? My whole parish is to be sold for £50,000; pray buy it, quit your profession, and turn Yorkshire squire. We should be a model for squires and parsons. God bless you! All the family unite in kind regards. Shall we ever see you again?

S. S.

376. J. G. Lambton

Philippi Manchester, ⟨late⟩ Oct. 1820

My dear Sir,

I left Foston on the 27th, with my family, on a visit to Marcus Tullius Philips, from whence I write thanking you for your kindness in proposing that Lady Louisa and yourself should pay us a visit at Foston, and assuring you that it would have given Mrs. Sydney and myself the greatest pleasure to have seen you. . . . I was glad to extort from Lady Grey a confession that the climate of Devonshire is superior to that of Northumberland, and that Lady Grey was better. I now consider that my prediction to

Lady Grey is in a train of being accomplished – that she will live till past eighty, and die intensely fond of cribbage and piquette. Everything here is prosperous beyond example. Philips doubles his capital twice a week; we talk much of cotton, more of the fine arts, as he has lately returned from Italy, and purchased some pictures which were sent out from Piccadilly on purpose to intercept him. If Lady Louisa wants anything in the calico line – happy to serve her.

> Yours, my dear Sir,
> most truly,
> Sydney Smith

377. LADY MARY BENNET

Sedgeley, Oct. 1820

My dear Lady Mary,

I cannot shut my eyes, because, if I open them, I shall see what is disagreeable to the Court. I have no more doubt of the Queen's guilt than I have of your goodness and excellence. But do not, on that account, do me the injustice of supposing that I am deficient in factious feelings and principles, or that I am stricken by the palsy of candour. I sincerely wish the Queen may be acquitted, and the Bill and its authors may be thrown out. Whether justice be done to the Royal plaintiff is of no consequence: indeed he has no right to ask for justice on such points. I must, however, preserve my common sense and my factious principles distinct; and believe the Queen to be a very slippery person at the moment I rejoice at the general conviction of her innocence.

I am, as you see, near Manchester. While here, I shall study the field of Peterloo.

You will be sorry to hear the trade and manufactures of these counties are materially mended, and are mending. I would not mention this to you, if you were not a good Whig; but I know you will not mention it to anybody. The secret, I much fear, will get out before the meeting of Parliament. There seems to be a fatality which pursues us. When, oh when, shall we be really ruined?

Pray send me some treasonable news about the Queen. Will the people rise? Will the greater part of the House of Lords be thrown into the Thames? Will short work be made of the Bishops? If you know, tell me; and don't leave me in this odious state of innocence, when you can give me so much guilty information, and make me as wickedly instructed as yourself. And if you know that the Bishops are to be massacred, write by return of post.

Do you know how poor ——* is handled in the Quarterly Review? It bears the mark of ——; I hope it is not his, for the sake of his character. Let me be duller than Sternhold and Hopkins, if I am to prove my wit at the expense of my friends! and in print too! God bless you!

Sydney Smith

383. LADY MARY BENNET

Foston, Dec. 20th, 1820

My dear Lady Mary,

In the first place I went to Lord Grey's, and stayed with them three or four days; from thence I went to Edinburgh, where I had not been for ten years. I found a noble passage into the town, and new since my time; two beautiful English chapels, two of the handsomest library-rooms in Great Britain, and a wonderful increase of shoes and stockings, streets and houses. When I lived there, very few maids had shoes and stockings, but plodded about the house with feet as big as a family Bible, and legs as large as portmanteaus. I stayed with Jeffrey. My time was spent with the Whig leaders of the Scotch bar, a set of very honest, clever men, each possessing thirty-two different sorts of wine. My old friends were glad to see me; some had turned Methodists – some had lost their teeth – some had grown very rich – some very fat – some were dying – and, alas! alas! many were dead; but the world is a coarse enough place, so I talked away, comforted some, praised others, kissed some old ladies, and passed a very riotous week.

From Edinburgh I went to Dunbar, – Lord Lauderdale's, – a

comfortable house, with a noble sea-view. I was struck with the great good-nature and vivacity of his daughters.

From thence to Lambton. And here I ask, what use of wealth so luxurious and delightful as to light your house with gas? What folly, to have a diamond necklace or a Correggio, and not to light your house with gas! The splendour and glory of Lambton Hall make all other houses mean. How pitiful to submit to a farthing-candle existence, when science puts such intense gratification within your reach! Dear lady, spend all your fortune in a gas-apparatus. Better to eat dry bread by the splendor of gas than to dine on wild beef* with wax candles; and so goodbye, dear lady –

Sydney Smith

387. FRANCIS JEFFREY

February 2nd, 1821

My dear Jeffrey

I have read Southey,* and think it so fair and reasonable a book, that I have little or nothing to say about it; so that I follow your advice, and abandon it to any one who may undertake it. What I should say, if I undertook it, would be very unfavourable to Methodism, which you object to, though upon what grounds I know not. Of course Methodists, when attacked, cry out, 'Infidel! Atheist!' – these are the weapons with which all fanatics and bigots fight; but should we be intimidated by this, if we do not deserve it? And does it follow that any examination of the faults of Dissenters is a panegyric upon the Church of England? But these are idle questions, as I do not mean to review it. I have written an article upon Dissenters' marriages, which I will send the moment I get some books from town. On other points I am stopped for books.

I purpose sending you a short article upon the savage and illegal practice of setting spring-guns and traps for poachers.

God bless you! Your sincere friend,
Sydney Smith

388. LADY GREY

February 9th, 1821

My dear Lady Grey,

There proceeds from York this day an Iron Back, and you must attend to the enclosed drawing: this will destroy Smoke, that is prevent you from being annoyed by Smoking Chimneys.

I have promised you another receipt for lemon juice which is that you must keep always in the house Citric acid, and 10 Drams of it to 1 pint of water a little warm makes lemon juice. You may buy Citric acid at any Druggist, but had better buy it at Apothecaries Hall – The French Essence of lemon peel which you may buy either at the Chemist, or Confectioners gives the flavor of Lemon Peel; 1 or 2 Drops are sufficient for 8 oz of Lemon Juice – and now I have taught you to do without Yeast or Lemons, or Smoky Chimneys. So much for the common affairs of Life.

I hope Lord Grey and you like the new novel:* I think it very good, and entertaining, though far inferior to those novels where the Scene is laid in Scotland.

There is an end for ever of all idea of Whiggs coming into power; the Kingdom is in the hands of an Oligarchy, who see what a good thing they have got of it, and are too cunning, and too well aware of the Tameability of Mankind to give it up. Lord Castlereagh smiles when Tierney prophecies resistance; his Lordship knows very well that he has got the people under, for ninety nine purposes out of an hundred, and that he can keep them where he has got them – Of all ingenious instruments of despotism I must commend a popular Assembly, where the majority are paid and hired, and a few bold and able men by their brave Speeches make the people believe they are free. Lord Lauderdale has sent me two pamphlets and 230 Lb of Salt Fish –

I hear you have taken an house in Stratford-place. The houses there are very good – You will be much more accessible than heretofore, – a few yards in London dissolve or cement a friendship. Lady Augusta Greville is going to marry Lord Aylesford.* – The Morpeths are in tribulation; Lord Morpeth is in a lingering Gout which depresses him in body, and mind. All the Children have the Measles.

I have not made up my mind when I come to Town, I think it must be so as to spend the month of May there, – by which time Elizabeth and Georgiana will I suppose be married.*

I think you will like Lady Georgiana's* daughters, they are really charming; The 3rd will into the bargain be a beauty. I hope the dr Lady Grey is better; kindest regards to my Lord and to you all

ever your sincere friend
Sydney Smith

390. MRS. MEYNELL

Foston, Feb. 12th, 1821

Dear Mrs. Meynell,

I was very glad to receive your letter, and to find you were well and prosperous.

The articles written by me in the Edinburgh Review are, that upon Ireland, and that upon Oxley's 'Survey of Botany Bay.'

The Archbishop of York makes me a very good neighbour, and is always glad to see me.

I agree with you that there is an end for ever of the Whigs coming into power. The country belongs to the Duke of Rutland, Lord Lonsdale, the Duke of Newcastle, and about twenty other holders of boroughs. They are our masters! If any little opportunity presents itself, we will hang them, but most probably there will be no such opportunity; it always is twenty to one against the people. There is nothing (if you will believe the Opposition) so difficult as to bully a whole people; whereas, in fact, there is nothing so easy, as the great artist Lord Castlereagh so well knows.

Let me beg of you to take more care of those beautiful geraniums, and not let the pigs in upon them. Geranium-fed bacon is of a beautiful colour; but it takes so many plants to fatten one pig, that such a system can never answer. I cannot conceive who put it into your head. God bless you –

Sydney Smith

393. FRANCIS JEFFREY

R. Smith Esq., Lydiard, Taunton, Somersetshire
Aug. 7th, 1821

My dear Jeffrey,

I have travelled all across the country with my family to see my father now 82 years of age. I wish at such an age you and all like you, may have as much enjoyment of life; more you can hardly have at any age. My father is one of the very few people I have ever seen improved by age. He is become careless, indulgent, and anacreontic.

I shall proceed to write a review of Scarlett's Poor Bill, and of Keppel Craven's Tour* according to the license you granted me, not for the No. about to come out, but for the No. after that. The review of the first will be very short, and that of the 2nd not long. Length indeed is not what you have to accuse me of. The above-mentioned articles, with perhaps *Wilks's Sufferings of the Protestants in the South of France*,* and the Life of Suard, will constitute my contribution for the number after the next, i.e. the 71st. The £12 due to me may be transmitted when you send me what will be due to me for the 70th No.

The wretchedness of the poor in this part of the country is very afflicting. The men are working for one shilling per day all the year round; and if a man have only 3 children he receives no relief from the parish, so that 5 human beings are supported for little more than 10d a day. They are evidently a dwindling, and decaying race; nor should I be the least surprised if a plague in the shape of typhus fever broke out here. The country is exquisitely beautiful, the people fully as far advanced in the arts of life as in the Heptarchy.

Do me the favor to remember me kindly to all my friends, and to number me amongst those who are sincerely and affectionately attached to you.

Sydney Smith

I beg my kind regards to Mrs. Jeffrey, and the little tyrant who rules the family. We shall be at Foston about the 10 or 12 of September.

406. MRS. MEYNELL

London, May 10th, 1822

Dear Mrs. Meynell,

I have got into all my London feelings, which come on the moment I pass Hyde Park Corner. I am languid, unfriendly, heartless, selfish, sarcastic, and insolent. Forgive me, thou inhabitant of the plains, child of nature, rural woman, agricultural female! Remember what you were in Hill-Street, and pardon the vices inevitable in the greatest of cities.

They take me here for an ancient country clergyman, and think I cannot see!! . . . How little they know your sincere and affectionate friend

Sydney Smith

409. ARCHIBALD CONSTABLE

Foston, June 21st, 1822

Dear Sir,

Many thanks for Nigel; a far better novel than The Pirate, though not of the highest order of Scott's novels. It is the first novel in which there is no Meg Merrilies. There is, however, a Dominie Sampson in the horologer. The first volume is admirable. Nothing can be better than the apprentices, the shop of old Heriot, the state of the city. James is quite excellent wherever he appears. I do not dislike Alsatia. The miser's daughter is very good; so is the murder. The story execrable; the gentlemanlike, light, witty conversation always (as in all his novels) very bad. Horrors or humour are his forte. He must avoid running into length – great part of the second volume very long and tiresome; but upon the whole the novel will do – keeps up the reputation of the author; and does not impair the very noble and honourable estate which he has in his brains.

I hope you are better, that you are leaving it to your deputies to increase your wealth, and making it your care and the care of your doctors to amend your health.

Your sincere well-wisher
Sydney Smith

418. MRS. MEYNELL

Foston, Feb. 18th, 1823

My dear Mrs. Meynell,

You are quite right about happiness. I would always lay a wager in favour of its being found among persons who spend their time dully rather than in gaiety. Gaiety – English gaiety – is seldom come at lawfully; friendship, or propriety, or principle, are sacrificed to obtain it; we cannot produce it without more effort than it is worth; our destination is to look vacant, and to sit silent.

My articles in the last number are, the attack on the Bishop of Peterborough, and on Small Pox. If you do not know what to think of the first, take my word that it is merited. Of the last you may think what you please, provided you vaccinate Master and Miss Meynell.

I am afraid we shall go to war: I am sorry for it. I see every day in the world a thousand acts of oppression which I should like to resent, but I cannot afford to play the Quixote. Why are the English to be the sole vindicators of the human race? Ask Mr. Meynell how many persons there are within fifteen miles of him who deserve to be horse-whipped, and who would be very much improved by such a process. But every man knows he must keep down his feelings, and endure the spectacle of triumphant folly and tyranny.

Adieu, my dear old friend. I shall be very glad to see you again, and to witness that happiness which is your lot and your *due*; two circumstances not always united. God bless you!

Sydney Smith

431. LADY HOLLAND

October 19th, 1823

You have made my little boy very happy dear Lady Holland and through him his parents. He seems to have been popular at Lady Affleck's, and I am sure must have done well under his charming and amiable governess Mary.*

We have been making some visits and came last from M. A. Taylor.* Mrs. Taylor and I begin to be better acquainted, and she improves. I hope *I* do; though, as I profess to live with open doors and windows, I am seen (by those who think it worth while to look at me) as well in 5 minutes as in 5 years. I have just received your last note or would have answered it before.

Ever my dear Lady Holland most affectionately and gratefully yours

Sydney Smith

I distinguished myself a good deal at M. Taylor's in dressing sallads; pray tell Luttrell this. I have thought a good deal about sallads, and will talk over the subject with you and Mr. Luttrell when I have the pleasure to find you together.

446. John Allen

Thursday, April 28th, 1825

Many thanks my dear Allen for your kind congratulations.* It is indeed a very agreeable event – and puts me at my ease for the present. I shall not be in Town till Tuesday – pray say so to Lord and Lady H thanking them for their kind invitation. We have had a little fight about the Catholics – you will see what passed in the York paper. I feel ashamed of meddling with such nonsense but the Protestants must not have it all their own way. To get an Archdeacon* and the son of an Archbishop* to appeal in favor of the Catholics is worth while.

Ever yrs
S. Smith

Thursday

Saturday *next* Brougham and I call Allenday. Brougham is getting amazing business here.

447. LADY GREY

20, Saville-row, Bond-street
⟨?May–June, 1825⟩*

My dear Lady Grey,

The most helpless of all beings is a poor parson, of an evening,
in London in wet weather, without a carriage. The characteristic
of London is that you never go where you wish, nor do what you
wish, and that you always wish to be somewhere else than where
you are.

most truely yrs
Sydney Smith

454. LADY HOLLAND

Foston, York, Nov. 4th, 1825

My dear Lady Holland,

The General report here is that Mary is to marry the King of
Prussia. I call it rather an ambitious than an happy match.* It
will neither please Lord Holland nor Allen, or Wishaw.

Lord and Lady Carlisle are gone to Town about their house.
They have resolved to live at Castle Howard, but to live with
economy and retrenchment. They are well seconded by Lock*
who is discharging the Venerable domestics (consummate
Scoundrels) of the antient regime.

I stayed a Week with Brougham – a pretty place, sensible
mother, bad house, Scotch house-keeping – Brougham very
pleasant – Macintosh was there very much improved in health;
from thence I went to Howard of Corby* a Catholic, then to
Orde,* who lives in a/very beautiful inaccessible place at the end
of the World – very comfortably. I have also paid a Visit to Lord
Fitzwilliam and am astonished never to have heard before of the
magnificence of Wentworth house, twice as great a front as Castle
Howard. The good old lord was there, who was very kind to me;
as was also (due allowance made for his hard anabaptist nature)
Lord Milton* who with his family made the whole of our party.
Lord Morpeth came for one day. I was going to Wortley, but he
was at Newmarket occupied with Horses and *Ryders.** I have

sent fourteen resolutions to Bishop Doyle* to be signed by all the Irish Catholic Prelates and circulated universally. The Substance of them is a denial of those Errors commonly imputed to the Catholics and more and more believed for want of proper contradiction. He writes me word it shall be done.

We are all well except my eldest Son Douglas who has been long ill, but is recovering. I hope you are doing well, and that you amuse yourself. Little Moore passed through York the other day and tendered himself to me; but I was from home. I rejoice at the Success of his book.* God bless you dear Lady Holland kind regards and affection to all.

Sydney Smith

[In fulfilment of a long-cherished wish, S. paid a visit to Paris in April 1826 on the invitation of the Hollands who were living there from the previous September until June. He was enabled to do this by being given the living of Londesborough by the Duke of Devonshire to hold until his nephew, William George Howard (1808–89), came of age to hold it, sc. 1832. The church was in charge of a curate, and S. drove over from Foston 'two or three times a year' to take the service (R., p. 246–9, *M.*, p. 253).]

467. Mrs. Sydney Smith

April 19th, 1826

Dearest Kate,

I saw Lord and Lady Holland yesterday. She is become an old woman and getting red in the face, he is weak and ill. The new Doctor Turner seems to be a simple unaffected man. There was at dinner a Dutch Baron, a french Lady, Charles, Henry, and Miss Fox, and Miss Vernon, everything much the same as at Holland House. In the evening she sent me home. I called upon the Duke of Bedford, who took me for Sr Sydney Smith* and refused me; I met him after in the street. I have not yet seen Mrs. Greathead, she lives out of Town.

I have bought a coat-of-arms for 6s which will hereafter be the coat-of-arms of the family. This letter is sealed with it.*

Paris is very badly lighted at nights, and the want of a trottoir is a great evil. The equipages are much less splendid and less numerous. The Champs Elysees are very poor and bad; but for the two towns in spite of these inconveniences believe me there is not the smallest possibility of a comparison; Regent-street is a perfect misery, compared to the fine parts of Paris.

I met General Ramsey in the street who threatens to call upon me for which I am sorry – I want my time to myself. I called upon the Embassador. Nobody at home. She sent me a note Lady Granville I mean, inviting me to her box at the Comedie Francaise to see Mademoiselle Mars;* unfortunately I did not get her note till I came from dinner. The Column in the Place Vendome is one of the most magnificent things in Paris; it is the series of the victories of Buonaparte.

I called upon Dumont who says that our hospitality to his friends has made us very popular at Geneva, and that Chauvet gave a very entertaining account of us.

Lord Grey has written to announce the marriage of Lady Elizabeth with Mr. Bulteel,* and they say, but I heard nothing of it in London, that Lord Dudley is to marry a daughter of Mr. Bea*

I think in general that the display of the shops here is finer than in London.

Miss Vernon will stay long enough to execute your commission.

Of course my opinions from my imperfect information are likely to change every day, but at present I am inclined to think that I ought to have gone, and that we will go to the Boulevards. Lady Affleck is very unwell.

There are no table-cloths in the coffee-houses, this annoys me; at least none for breakfast; and the want of W.C. is one of the most crying evils in Paris.

I am very well, though still a little heated with the journey. God bless you all.

Sydney Smith

I have written regularly every day.

470. MRS. SYDNEY SMITH

Paris, April 22, 1826

Dearest Kate,

The slaughtering cattle in the streets of a great town is so odious and offensive, that Buonaparte constructed in 5 or 6 quarters of the outskirts of the Town great abbatoires where all the butchers are compelled to kill their meat. I saw one of these yesterday morning the Abbatoir of Mont Martre; they kill there every week 600 oxen, 4000 sheep and 2000 calves. There are 6 others. It is a very useful institution but a sight not worth seeing.

From Mont Martre there is a noble panorama of Paris. From thence I went to the Assembly of Deputies, a dark, disagreeable hall. I was placed so far from them that I could not hear. They got up and read their speeches, and read them like very bad parsons. I dined at 7 o'clock;* Miss Fox carried me there. The company consisted of Lord and Lady Granville, Lady Hardy,* Sir Charles Hardy's lady, Mr. and Mrs. Ellis,* Lady Caroline Wortley,* Mr. Sneyd,* Mr. Abercrombie,* two or three attachés; and in the afternoon came a profusion of French duchesses, in general very good-looking, well-dressed people, with more form and ceremony than belongs to English duchesses. The house was less splendid than I expected, though I fancy I did not see the state apartments. There is an assembly there this morning, to see the greenhouses and gardens, where I am invited. You know my botanic skill - it will be called into action this morning; but first I am going dejeuner a la fourchette with the Duke de Broglie. I met at Lord Granville with Mr. and Lady Mary Stanley,* Lord Lauderdale's daighter, and I renewed my acquaintance with Crevecœur young Craddock;* there is something in him but he does not know how little it is; he is much admired as a Beauty. Mary Fox is very much admired and appears to be always surrounded with Beauxs, but I hear nothing of anything serious. Lord Holland is a little better today, his improvement has been effected I believe by keeping him away from company. The weather has been beautiful, this is the sixth or 7th day in which I have been able to go out for every minute without the least interruption.

I am agreeably surprised by the water of Paris being so good. It is the purified water of the Seine, and so with the best water and with tea infinitely better than London tea I breakfast well. I found Lady Granville very civil, but I am not captivated by her. God bless you all

S S

I have written every day.

472. MRS. SYDNEY SMITH

April 26th, 1826

Dearest Kate,

I went yesterday into a great upholsterers shop. Nothing can exceed the magnificence and beauty of the furniture, it is also about 20 or 30 pr ct. cheaper than our furniture. They have also a way of making their plate look much brighter and better. Their papers are most beautiful so that I think I shall bring over some.

I went to the Jardin des plantes. Nothing can exceed the beauty and comfort of this Institution. It is a great collection of natural History. There is an immense botanical garden with every shrub and flower in the world which will live out of doors, immense Green and Hot Houses, fine walks, picturesque grounds, an immense quantity of wild animals not cooped up but living at their ease in well secured inclosures. Cabinets of natural History, anatomy mineralogy and lectures open to the public without paying anything. From thence I went to the Sal Petriere where are 7000 people poor, mad and incurable. It seems to be governed in the very best manner. The French are a very methodical people and have great talents for arrangement.

From thence I went to the Halle aux Vins where I saw nothing but 12 or 14 acres of wine in casks. Then, to the Institute (Royal Society) where there is nothing to see, and then to Buonaparte's elephantine plaister. Buonaparte had a project of making an immense Elephant in bronze carrying a large Tower on his back full of water, with a staircase in one of his legs. It was to have been placed on the site of the Bastile. It is at least 30 or 40 feet high and is really a very noble object. It is only as I have observed before the plaister model, he did not remain long enough to finish the Bronze.

I dined with Lord Bath, nobody there of any consequence, and in the evening went to the French Theatre to see Mademoiselle Mars, the great French actress. Her forte is comedy, she seems to excel in such parts as Mrs. Jordan* excelled in and has her sweetness of voice; she is very old and ugly; excels also in genteel comedy as Miss Farren* did. I certainly think her a very considerable actress. In the evening after the Comedy I went to Lady Holland's where was Humboldt* the great traveller, a lively pleasant talkative man. Lord Holland is better. Miss Vernon goes Monday or Wednesday, I do not know which nor does she. Mr Greathead returned my visit; this is all I have seen of him, he appears to be a pompous foolish man. I shall leave Paris Tuesday senight. God bless you all

S S

473. MRS. SYDNEY SMITH

Thursday, April 27th, 1826

Dearest Kate,

Yesterday was a very bad draggling day, and Paris is not pleasant at such time. I went to the King's Library, containing 400,000 volumes; they are lent out, even the MS, and I am afraid sometimes lost and stolen. It is an enormous library, but nothing to strike the eye. I then saw the Palais de Prince de Conde which is not worth seeing.

I dined with Lord Holland who is better. The famous Cuvier* was there, and in the evening came Prince Talleyrand* who renewed his acquaintance with me and enquired very kindly for my brother. I mean to call upon him. The French manners are quite opposite to ours: the stranger is introduced and he calls upon the native who never calls upon him first. This is very singular and I think contrary to reason.

In the evening I went to Lady Granville's ball; nothing can be more superb. It is by all accounts the first house at Paris, and it is generally admitted that Lady Granville is the great Lady of

Paris. I met there crowds of English. Madame de Bourke,* the wife of the late Danish Embassador renewed her acquaintance with me. I met there Mrs. Greathead who mumbled something about dinner, and received from me a responsive mumble. I believe they are very poor and that a dinner is a serious consideration to them. He is always speculating and in spite of what he has already suffered cannot keep himself quiet. The prettiest girl in the room was Miss Rumbold, the daughter* of Sr Sydney Smith.

My pamphlet* is very much liked here. Lord Holland and Miss Fox are enchanted with it. I am very sorry I did not bring over some copies. I have half a mind to send for some even now. I have not had a line from anybody since I have been here. Charles and Henry wanted to give me a dinner at some celebrated Tavern here in conjunction with some other young men, but I declined it. I have no fancy to dine with young men, and above all none to have a dinner given me; besides it seemed to imply an obligation on me to be agreeable which is sure to make me other wise.

I have bought nothing here except a Coat of Arms for 6s.

The French Government are behaving very foolishly, flinging themselves into the arms of the Jesuits, making processions through the streets, of 1200 priests with the King and Royal Family at the head of them, disgusting the people, and laying the foundations of another revolution, which seems to me (if this man lives) to be inevitable. God bless you all.

S. S.

I have written every day.

474. Mrs. Sydney Smith

Friday, April 28th, 1826

Dearest Kate,

Yesterday was a miserable day it rained torrents from morning to night. I employed the morning in visiting in an hackney coach. It is curious to see in what little apartments a French Savant lives; you find him at his books covered with snuff, with a little dog who bites your legs.

I had no invitation to dinner and dined by myself at a coffee-house. I dined upon a Demi Macreau à la Maitre d'Hotel, Bif Steak à l'Anglaise, des Harricaux blanches à la Maitre d'Hotel, Fromage de Neuf Chatel, Demi Bouteille de Vin de Bordeaux ordinaire – all good and well chosen. I improve in my knowledge of Paris cookery.* There were four English ladies dining in the public coffee-house, very well-bred women. After dinner I accomplished getting some tea at home; for you must observe at some Hotels you eat in the house, at others you dine out or every thing is sent from a Restaurant; mine is of the latter description. After tea I was engaged in an admirable speech of the Duke de Broglie and was as tired with it as one always is with admirable productions, when I received an invitation from Mrs. Hurt Sitwell to go with her and her son to the Opera. I went, and was pleased with the gaiety of the house; there is no ballet, and at present no good singer. I am astonished that with so small an house they can pay the great singers and rival the London opera, which is about 4 times as big. The house was full of English who talk loud and seem to care little for other people; this is their characteristic, and a very brutal and barbarous distinction it is. After the Opera I went to drink tea with Mrs. Sitwell, and so ended my day.

This morning it is snowing. I am going to breakfast with the Duke de Broglie. I have unfortunately left behind me my thick shoes which are as necessary for walking on the sharp stones of Paris as they are ill calculated for the clean and flat pavements of London. I shall certainly not exceed 3 weeks from the day of entering Paris. I shall probably quit it the 9th of May, and be in London as soon as I can get there from that time. God bless you all.

S S

487. JOHN ALLEN

Foston, Nov. 9th, 1826

Dear Allen,

Pray tell me something about Lord and Lady Holland as it is several centuries since I have seen them. I heard of Lady Holland on a sofa. I thought she had done with sofas. How are you – are

you quite well? I was in the same house in Cheshire with Vane*
but he was too ill to see me; extreme depression of spirits seems
to be his complaint, an evil of which I have a full comprehension.
Mrs. Taylor appears to be really alarmed about him.

Have you finished your squabbles with Lingard?* The
Catholics are outrageous with you, and I have heard some of the
most violent express a doubt whether you are quite an orthodox
member of the Church of England.

You will be amused with John Murray's marriage. It was concocted at Mr. Philips under the auspices of Mrs. Sydney and
myself. The lady* has £60,000, is a considerable Greek Scholar,
a Senior Wrangler in Mathematics and the most perfect Instru-
mental Musician I ever heard. Ten days finished the matter;
indeed she has no time to lose since she is 39. I never saw two
longer fatter Lovers, for she is as big as Murray. They looked
enormous as they were making love in the plantations. She is so
fond of Murray that she pretends to love porridge, cold weather
and metaphysics. Seriously speaking it is a very good marriage,
and acting under the direction of medical men, with perseverance
and the use of stimulating diet there may be an heir to the house
of Henderland.

I never saw Lord Carlisle looking so well; is not happiness good
for the gout? I think that remedy is at work upon him. I cannot
say how agreeable their neighborhood is to me.

I am very glad to find that Mcintosh is really at work upon his
History; it will immortalize him and make Ampthill* classical
from recollections.

I think of going to Edinburgh in the spring with my family on
a visit to Jeffrey who was with us this summer Bag and Baggage.
Health and respect my dear Allen, prosperity to the Church, and
power to the Clergy.

ever yrs
Sydney Smith

We have seen a good deal of old Whishaw this summer; he is
as pleasant as he is wise and honest; he has character enough to
make him well received if he was dull and wit enough to make
him popular if he was a rogue.

505. MESSRS. HUNT AND CLARKE,
Booksellers, York St., Covent Gard.

Foston, June 30th, 1827

Gentlemen,

I have received from you within these few months some very polite and liberal presents of new publications, and though I was sorry you put yourselves to any expense on my acct, yet I was flattered by this mark of respect and goodwill from gentlemen to whom I am personally unknown.

I am quite sure however that you overlooked the purpose and tendency of a work called Elizabeth Evanshaw,* or that you wd not have sent it to a clergyman of the Established Church, or to a clergyman of any church. I see also advertised at your house a translation of Voltaire's 'Philosophical Dictionary'. I hope you will have the goodness to excuse me, and not to attribute what I say to an impertinent, but to a friendly disposition. Let us pass over all higher considerations and look at this point only in a worldly view, as connected with your interests. Is it wise to give to your house the character of Publishers of *Infidel Books*? The English people are a very religious people, and those who are not religious hate the active dissemination of irreligion. The zealots of irreligion are few and insignificant and confined principally to London. You have not a chance of eminence and success in pursuing such a line, and I advise you prudently and quietly to back out of it.

I hate the insolence, persecution and intolerance which so often pass under the name of religion, and (as you know) I have fought against them; *but I have an unaffected horror of irreligion and impiety; and every principle of suspicion and fear wd be excited in me by a man who professed himself an infidel.*

I write this from respect to you. It is quite a private communication, and I am sure you are too wise and too enlightened to take it in evil part. I shall read all the works and will tell you my opinion of them from time to time.

I was very much pleased with the 'Two* Months in Ireland', but did not read the poetical part; the prosaic division of the work is very good.

I remain, Gentlemen, yours faithfully,
Sydney Smith

508. LORD HOLLAND

Scarborough, Aug. 21st, 1827

My dear Lord Holland

In due time and at a Convenient Season pray say a Word about me to Lord Goodriche.* Others will do the same. It may be that I may get some preferment before the administration is swallowed up in the Gulf of Toryism. Whether I do or not, I shall always be the same, and like the patent flannel at 7/0 p yard will never shrink in heat nor Cold.

When the Chancellor* imagined he was politically moribund he offered me very kindly a Living of £800 per Ann in Lincolnshire, which I went to see; but it was above Value, out of distance and if resided on would have required an outlay of £3000.* Nothing can exceed the kindness and friendship of Cleopatra.* If I had sailed with her down the Cydnus (a navigation which to tell you the truth would have been very agreeable to me) She could not have been more kind. I find she has been to Holland House.

Little Wilberforce* is here, and we are great friends. He looks like a little Spirit running about without a body, or in a kind of undress with only half a body. Mrs. Sydney has received great benefit from Scarbro'. My eldest Son Douglas has a regular fit of the Gout and a bad one. It is certainly a mistake and was intended for me.

All that I said of Brougham to the Chancellor was that he was very irritable and had bitten several people dangerously who were taking the Ormskirk Medicine* and bathing in the Sea; but that the only safe plan was to have the part cut out – or Cauterized.

I have written nothing in the last Review and shall write nothing in the next. I hope your Gout is better, and that you will be coming into the North this year. I hear that the North has come to you, and the Cold and damp is universal.

I beg my kind and affectionate regards to Lady Holl and am ever my dear Lord Holland your sincere friend

Sydney Smith

My father is dead, and has left me £10,000 –

509. LADY GREY

20, Savile-row, Sept. 13th, 1827

My dear Lady Grey,

What is so utterly insignificant as whom the daughter of a poor parson marries? but not so to kind natures and old friends. My youngest daughter is to marry Mr. Hibbert of the North Circuit, son of George Hibbert* the Indian Merchant, a sensible high-minded young man who will eventually be well off. Give them your blessing and believe me very sincerely and affectionately yrs

Sydney Smith

513. LADY HOLLAND

⟨Foston,⟩ Nov. 18th, 1827

My dear Lady Holland

This living I mentioned to the Chancellor* 6 months since, and I shall be *surprised* if he does not give it to me; but as it is a week since I have written to *him*, and *her* and have received no answer I begin to have serious doubts. However I have done all I can do; when I know more of good or bad I am sure you will not think it an intrusion if I send you word. I am truely sorry you give so indifferent an account of Yourself. Let me ascribe it to this infernal Month of November, against which no Spirits are proof.

We are bustling all day long about this Stupid Wedding. I am tired of flounces. What are Mrs. Sydney and I to do when Saba is married? I must give up Foston and take lodgings in Regent St. You see my younger Brother Courtenay* is turned out of Office in India, for refusing the Surety of the E Indian Company. Truely the Smiths are a Stiff-necked Generation and yet they have all got rich but me. Courtenay they say has £150000 - and keeps only a Cat. The Last Letter I had from him which was in 1782* he confessed that his Money was gathering very fast. - We have had here Captain Howard* the Indian Son; he stayed with us 3 or 4 days and the Verdict of the Ladies as well as my own was unanimous and strong in his favor. There are in him the

Elements of a clever acute and agreeable man and his manners will be hereafter very gentlemanlike. I think him at some little discount at the Castle, but so he stands with us.

We are all going to spend next Week at Bishopthorpe. The Archbishop has offered to marry Emily which I have accepted with becoming gratitude –

Early next Month my home will become a perfect Hibbert Warren. Pray present my respectful Compts to the best and most honorable of human Dukes,* and beleive me ever your affectionate friend

Sydney Smith

521. LADY HOLLAND

Lower College Green, Bristol,
Nov. 5th, 1828

My dear Lady Holland

I hope you are better and Lord Holland also. I envy you your *Sejour* at Brighton which is in my imagination (for I never saw it) the gayest city in England, if any thing at all *can* be gay in England.

I have been on the Eve of changing Foston, but was prevented by certain Circumstances. A living is now vacant, Halberton in Devonshire, near Tiverton. I must try to change Foston for something tenable with Halberton, or Halberton for something tenable with Foston. This is easier said than done.

Today I have preached an honest Sermon – (5th November) before the Mayor and Corporation in the Cathedral, the most protestant Corporation in England. They stared with all their Eyes. I know your taste for Sermons is languid, but I must extract one passage for Lord Holland to show that I am still as honest a man as when he first thought me a proper object for his patronage.

'I hope in this condemnation of the Catholic religion in which I sincerely join their worst Enemies, I shall not be so far mistaken as to have it supposed that I would convey the slightest approbation of any Laws which disqualify and incapacitate any class of men for Civil offices on account of religious opinions. I consider all such Laws as fatal, and lamentable mistakes in Legislation. They are the mistakes of troubled times, and half barbarous ages. All Europe is gradually emerging from their influence. This Country has lately made a noble and successful Effort for their abolition. In proportion as this Example is followed I firmly believe the Enemies of Church and state will be lessened and the foundations of peace, order and happiness will receive additional Strength. I cannot discuss the uses and abuses of this day without touching upon the errors of the Catholic faith from which we have escaped; but I should be beyond measure concerned if a condemnation of Theological Errors were construed into an approbation of laws so deeply marked by the Spirit of Intolerance –'.

I am going on Tuesday into Devonshire to look at this Living; then I shall come back and stay a little at Longleat,* then come to London, where I hope to see you. I have been reading the Duke of Rovigo* – a fool, a Villain, and dull as it is possible for any book to be about Buonaparte.

Lord Bathurst's place* is ugly, his family and himself always agreeable. I hear Lord John is to marry a daughter of the beautiful Hardy.* She is a robust and energetic young woman. God send it may agree with John. I hope he will be fed up highly at Holland House before the Event, and plumped out: – and let us indulge an hope dear Lady Holland that some patriotic Babies some Anti Corporation and Test Infants may come of it. I told that beautiful Mother that I had invented a new word for *Tendresse*, and should adopt instead of it *Hardy esse*. John may use the expression if he pleases. Accept my hommage dear Lady

and believe me always very affectionately yrs

Sydney Smith

I have just received a long letter from your friend Dr. Maltby,* an excellent man and a great fool.

522. E. J. LITTLETON

Lower College Green, Bristol,
Nov. 7th, 1828

My dear Littleton,*

Many thanks for your game, and for your entertaining and interesting letter from Ireland. I direct to your country place, not knowing exactly where you will be, and presuming Mrs. Littleton will know. Putting all things together, I think that something will be done. The letter from the three foolish noblemen,* the failure of Penenden-heath* to excite a general and tumultuous feeling, are all very favourable. I share in your admiration of Lord Anglesey's* administration; I have reason to believe Ministers are a little dissatisfied with his disposition to oratory, which is thought undignified and rash in a Vice-King.

At Bristol, on the 5 of November, I gave the Mayor and Corporation (the most Protestant Mayor and Corporation in England) such a dose of toleration as shall last them for many a year. A deputation of *pro-Popery* papers waited on me today to print, but I declined. I told the Corporation, at the end of my Sermon, that beautiful Rabbinical story quoted by Jeremy Taylor,* 'As Abraham was sitting at the door of his tent', etc. etc., which by the bye, would make a charming and useful placard against the bigoted.

Be assured I shall make a discreet use of the intelligence you give me, and compromise you in nothing.

Remember me, if you please, to Wilmot Horton* when you write: I like him very much, and take a sincere interest in his welfare.

Ever yours, dear Littleton, very sincerely
Sydney Smith

523. LADY GREY

Lower College Green, Bristol,
Nov. 8th, ⟨1828⟩

My dear Lady Grey

A Rumor all over Yorkshire of one of the Lady Greys marriage to Mr. Wood – I never believed it.*

I stayed two days with the Bathursts who were (as they always are) very agreeable.

Heavenly Weather, and a very fine Climate at Bristol, a town remarkable for Burglary, and Turtle; Every body's Stomach is full of green fat, every bodies house is broken open; all this comes of not hanging people. It is seven years since any one was hung here. How can 100,000 people live together in peace upon such terms? I hear good accounts of Lord Grey. I wish you joy on the Rev. and Honble Grey's living.* I am aware of the political awkwardness but considering his health and family it is a piece of good fortune.

I have settled in my own mind that Lord Grey is to go to Ireland to carry the Catholic Question, and to take me with him as Chaplain –

The Duke of Rovigo* is a Scoundrel, a fool and the dullest of all writers upon a Subject where it is so difficult to be dull. The Corporation of Bristol (talking of dullness reminds me of them) is the most protestant Corporation in this very protestant kingdom. They come to the Cathedral in great State every 5th of November. I preached before them; I need not tell you they had it not all their own Way.

I will send the Sermon to your London Residence. I only require you to read the Story at the end, – it is beautiful.

The Text is that very fine, and intelligible Verse in the Psalms – 'or ever your Pots are hot with Thorns' etc. I have taken a liking to the Duke of Wellington's foreign politics. – I mean his disposition to keep us at profound peace and to leave other nations to scramble for Liberty as we have done without interfering with them. I am a very bad foreign politician, but this pleases me. I live here in profound solitude in a large Gothic room, waited upon by an old Woman. I am profoundly Ennuied – horrid

Suffering – to wish to talk, and to have nobody to talk to. Cupping does no good, Calomel equally useless. Soliloquy unavailing. Heaven have mercy upon the guests the first place I dine at in London. Only think of Lord John Russell marrying Lady Hardy's daughter – heaven send it may agree with him. I am going to pay a visit to Lady Bath. If you will vouchsafe me a Line pray direct here. I hope to be in London beginning of December for a few days – I am threatened with change of Livings and all sorts of miseries. Always my dear Lady Grey with sincere affection and respect

yrs
Sydney Smith

Mrs. S and family are in Yorkshire.

524. J. A. MURRAY

November 28th, 1828

My dear Murray,

Noble weather! I received some grouse in the summer, and upon the direction was marked W. M. This I construed to be William Murray, and wrote to thank him. This he must have taken as a foolish quiz, or as a petition for game. Pray explain and put this right.

The Kent Meeting* has, I think, failed as an example. This, and the three foolish noblemen's letters, will do good. The failure of the Kent precedent I consider as of the utmost importance. The Duke keeps his secret. I certainly believe he meditates some improvement. I rather like his foreign politics, in opposition to the belligerent Quixotism of Canning. He has the strongest disposition to keep this country in profound peace, to let other nations scramble for freedom as they can, without making ourselves the liberty-mongers of all Europe; a very seductive trade, but too ruinous and expensive.

How is Jeffrey's throat? –

> That throat, so vex'd by cackle and by cup,
> Where wine descends, and endless words come up.

Much injured organ! Constant is thy toil;
Spits turn to do thee harm, and coppers boil:
Passion and punch, and toasted cheese and paste,
And all that's said and swallow'd, lay thee waste!

I have given notice to my tenant here, and mean to pass the winters at Bristol. I hope, as soon as you can afford it, you will give up the law. Why bore yourself with any profession, if you are rich enough to do without it? Ever yours, dear Murray,

Sydney Smith

525. LADY HOLLAND

December, 1828

Many thanks my dear Lady Holland for your kind anxiety respecting my health. I not only was never better, but never half so well: indeed I find that I have been very ill all my life without knowing it. Let me state some of the goods arising from abstaining from all fermented liquors. 1st sweet sleep; having never known what sleep was I sleep like a baby or a ploughboy. If I wake, no needless terror, no black views of life, but pleasing hope and pleasing recollection: Holland House, past and to come. If I dream, it is not of lyons and tygers, but of Love* – and Tithes. 2ndly I can take longer walks and make greater exertions without fatigue. My understanding is improved, and I comprehend Political Economy. I see better without wine and spectacles than when I use both. Only one evil ensues from it: I am in such extravagant spirits that I must loose blood, or look out for some one who will bore and depress me. Pray leave off wine – the stomach quite at rest; no heartburn, no pain, nor distension.

Lady Lyndhurst says the Hollands are very kind to her. I have done nothing as yet respecting any exchange of livings; perhaps I may not be able to effect it. Everybody here in the highest health. Bobus is more like a wrestler in the Olympic games than a victim of the gout. I hope you liked Morpeth's speech; his excellent father was very nervous about it. I am glad George* is become so bold. How often have I conjured him to study indiscretion, and to do the rashest things that he could possibly imagine. With what sermons and with what earnest regard I have warned him against prudence and moderation. I begin to think I have not labored in vain.

I disappear from the civilized world on Thursday. Pray for me but don't let Allen do so.

529. LORD GREY

5, New Cavendish-street, Portland-place
Wednesday, ⟨April 15th, 1829⟩

My dear Lord Grey

My poor boy died this morning at an early hour. I am sure such kind and such old friends as Lady G. and yourself will feel for my Situation, but take no notice of me, and God bless you all
Sydney Smith

[For the last sixteen years of his life Sydney Smith was rector of Combe Florey. His father had died in 1827, leaving him £10,000. In September 1831 Lord Grey appointed him to a canonry of St. Paul's, worth £2,000 a year. For the next four years he lived, when in residence, sometimes with Bobus in Saville Row or with his daughter Emily and her husband Nathaniel Hibbert in Weymouth St., sometimes in hired apartments: but in January 1836 he bought the lease of 33 Charles Street, Berkeley Square; and in October 1839, having inherited some £50,000 from his brother Courtenay who died intestate, he bought a larger house at 56 Green Street, Grosvenor Square, where he died on 22 February 1845.

He threw himself with characteristic vigour and directness into the duties and opportunities of his canonry, with special attention to the upkeep of the cathedral and to the exercise of patronage. He plunged effectively into the controversy over the Ecclesiastical Commission in 1837 and over the Ballot in 1839. His preaching attracted large congregations, and his company was in perpetual request at breakfast and dinner parties and at the country houses of friends, such as Lord Lansdowne, the Ashburtons, the Harcourts, while his rectory at Combe Florey was rarely without visitors for any length of time. Contemporary letters and memoirs contain innumerable references not only, as of course, to his wit and irresistible drollery, but to his forthright sincerity, clear judgement, and untiring sympathy and kindness. His own letters bear unconscious testimony to all these qualities. The predominance of letters to women is a common characteristic of the best letter-writers, partly because women for many generations had so much more time and taste for letter-writing than their menfolk, and partly because men of lively minds and feelings have always tended to make the most of the sympathy and vivacity of intelligent women. But Sydney Smith was also thoroughly a man's man, as his host of friends proclaims. And if there is comparatively little expression in his letters of his more intimate home-affections, there is abundant evidence of his devotion to family life in his daughter's *Memoir*, in Mrs. Sydney's letter to Jeffrey in this collection (Letter 180), and in the following artless sentences from the unpublished 'Narrative for my grandchildren' written after her husband's death.

'There never before *was*, and never again *will be* another Sydney!!'

'And now, dear children, I have done!! After passing nearly $\frac{1}{2}$ a century with *such* a man, I am alone without one protecting hand that I can feel *belongs* to me! and whose feelings go along with mine!!'

'I do not believe that anyone filling only a subordinate rank in life ever past thro' it more universally beloved, more sought after for his brilliancy and wit, his honourable bearing, his masterly talents, his truth, his honesty!']

533. LADY GREY

Combe Florey, July 13th, 1829

My dear Lady Grey

I should be very glad to hear that Lord Howick* is recovered, and that you have past through the London campaign, if not with glory at least without defeat – and doctors bills. I am extremely pleased with Combe Florey, and pronounce it to be a very pretty place in a very beautiful country. The house I shall make decently convenient. I have 60 acres of good land round it. The habit of the country is to give dinners, and not to sleep out; this I shall avoid. My neighbors look very much like other people's neighbors; their remarks are generally of a meteorological nature.

I was glad to see my Lord presiding at the Democratical College:* he would do it in the very best manner the thing could be done. . . .

My spirits are very much improved, but I have now and then sharp pangs of grief. I did not know I had cared so much for anybody, but the habit of providing for human beings, and watching over them for so many years generates a fund of affection of the magnitude of which I was not aware.

The god Hymen favors the Carlisles; Euclid leads Blanche to the altar – a strange choice for him as she has not an angle about her.* I am truely glad for all their sakes as I have an hearty affection for, and a sincere gratitude towards them.

Though living in a very improved climate, we have had fires in every room in the house. It is a bad and an unhappy year. It grieves me to think when you go to the North that I shall be 500 miles from Howick. I should like to be very near Howick. It is now near 30 years since I made acquaintance and then friendship with its inhabitants. You must all come and see this valley of flowers when you come to visit Lady Elizabeth in the West. It is a most parsonic parsonage, like the parsonages described in novels.

God bless you, dear Lady Grey. Write me a line when you have any time to spare to tell me of the welfare of all your family. Your affectionate friend

Sydney Smith

541. LADY GREY

Combe Florey, Taunton, Sept. 6th, 1829

My dear Lady Grey

The Harvest here is got in without any rain – I mean the

Wheat Harvest – The Cyder is such an enormous Crop that it is sold at 10s pr Hogshead; So that an human Creature may lose his reason for an halfpenny.

I continue to be delighted with the Country. My parsonage will be perfection. Pray come and see it your first Visit to Lady Elizabeth.

I am going tomorrow to Bowood, and the first week in October to Lord Morley's. Lord Grey's friend Lady Lyndhurst was to have come this Week, but she is detained* by an *accident* at Walmer Castle, and keeps her room. The only Visitor I have had here is Mr. Jeffrey, who I believe (though he richly deserves that good fortune) is scarcely known to Lord Grey and yourself; a man of rare talent and unbending integrity, who has been honest even in Scotland, which is as if he were temperate and active at Capua.

Talking of honest men, I beg to be remembered to Lord Howick, on whom I lay great Stress. From his understanding, Rank, and Corage he will be an important personage in the days to come. Pat him on the back, and tell him that the safety and welfare of a country depends in great measure upon men like himself –

Pray tell us of some good books to send for from the Subscription Library. I would tell *you* if I had looked at any other book than the Builders price Book –

I hear Lord Holland is out of Spirits at parting with his two Sons* (no wonder). Henry *will* go, Charles *must* go. Henry they say has quite lost his English Soul, and has a Soul of Macaroni, or Sour Kraut.

Tremendous reports of a great friend of Yours!!!!!* I am sure you are sorry, and every body must be sorry for him, and also for her so charming a person, and so excellent a man. If error was inevitable, was there any lack of youthful and Vicious nobility? – Why a low and unknown person? but the subject is really painful.

Eternal Rain. – Mr Jeffrey wanted to persuade me that Myrtles grew out of doors in Scotland: upon Cross Examination it turned out that they were prickly and that many had been destroyed by the family Donkey. They are opposing poor Sr Thomas Lethbridge for the County of Somerset. I mean to vote and do every

thing I can for him. It is right to encorage such Apostates.* God
bless you dear Lady; my kind regards to my Lord and Lady G.

> Your sincere and affectionate friend
> Sydney Smith

542. LADY HOLLAND

Combe Florey, Sept. 19th, 1829

My dear Lady Holland,

After 30 years of kindness it was not necessary to apologize for
not replying to my light and nonsensical effusions which really
required no answer. I had heard (and was sincerely concerned to
hear) of your illness at Bowood where I was for a few days. I
would make such a run, but I am solemnly pledged to run in an
opposite direction. I am going to the Morleys, where I was first
bound to meet the Chancellor, and Lady Lyndhurst. Nothing can
be more insane than to make such engagements in my present
state. I consider that every day's absence from home costs me £10
in the villainy of carpenters and bricklayers; for as I am my own
architect Clerk of the Works, you may easily imagine what is done
when I am absent. I continue to be delighted with my house and
place.

The Duke of Wellington has given I think the first signs I ever
remarked of weakness in prosecuting for libels; not for libels
which regard a particular fact, as that for which the Chancellor
has prosecuted, but for general abuse.* It is now proved he can
feel, which was not before thought to be the case – I thought he
was covered with tortoise shell. Mrs. Sydney and Saba are
flourishing. I lament heartily for Charles and Henry. I am keeping all Foxes in England; not a soul of them should stir out of
the Island if I were Master – unless in my company.

Sir Thomas Lethbridge the last of those who came over from
Lambeth to the Pope will be ejected for the County. I am sorry
for the King, and for all his subjects upon whom the evils of age
are falling.

I told Vernon* if he would persevere he would have a little
girl at last. I might have said if he did not take care he would have

20 little girls. What is there to prevent him from having a family sufficient to exasperate the placid Malthus? I met your neighbours Mr. and Mrs. Calcott* at Bowood – reasonable, good-natured, enlightened people. I was also much pleased with Lady Louisa,* Lord Lansdowne's daughter very clever and very amiable. I could not make out Kerry.* Luttrell came over for a day from whence I know not, but I thought not from good pastures; at least, he had not his usual soup-and-pattie look; there was a forced smile upon his countenance which seemed to indicate plain roast and boiled and a sort of apple-pudding depression as if he had been staying with a clergyman.

God bless you dear Lady Holland. Kindest regards to all.

553. J. A. Murray

Combe Florey, Dec. 14th, 1829

Dear John Murray,

My house is assuming the forms of maturity, and a very capital house it will be for a parsonage, – far better than that at Foston. Your threats of coming to see us give us great pleasure. When will you come? Let it be for a good long stay. Pray remember me kindly to Mrs. Murray, and tell her that the only fault I find in her is an excessive attachment to bishops and tithes; an amiable passion, but which may be pushed too far.

I cannot say the pleasure it gives me that my old and dear friend Jeffrey is in the road to preferment.* I shall not be easy till he is fairly on the Bench. His robes, God knows, will cost him little; one buck rabbit will clothe him to the heels.

I have been paying some aristocratic visits to Lord Bath and Lord Bathurst. Lady Bath is a very agreeable, conversible woman. Lord and Lady Bathurst, and Lady Georgiana,* are charming. Nothing can exceed the beauty of this country, – forty and fifty miles together of fertility and interesting scenery. I hardly think I have any news to tell you. The Duke of Bedford has given in his adhesion to the Duke of Wellington, as have all the Tories, except four. Read 'Les Mémoires d'une Femme de Qualité sur Louis XVIII.' It is by Madame du Cayla,* and extremely interesting.

I was not at all pleased with the article in the Edinburgh Review on the Westminster Review,* and thought the Scotchmen had the worst of it. How foolish and profligate, to show that the principle of general utility has no foundation, that it is often opposed to the interests of the individual! If this be not true, there is an end of all reasoning and all morals: and if any man asks, why am I to do what is generally useful? he should not be reasoned with, but called rogue, rascal, etc., and the mob should be excited to break his windows.

God bless you, dear Murray!

Sydney Smith

555. J. A. Murray

Clifton, Jan. 3rd, 1830

My dear Murray,

I have not heard the particulars of Jeffrey becoming Lord Advocate, but I know enough to know they rebound to your honour. Your conspiracy at Brougham Hall must have been very interesting. Principally Edinburgh Reviewers! How very singular! The Review began in high places (garrets), and ends in them.

There is an end of insurrection; I had made up my mind to make an heroic stand, till the danger became real and proximate, and then I should have been discreet and capitulating.

I can hardly picture to myself the rage and consternation of the Scotch Tories at this change, and at the liberality which is bursting out in every part of Scotland, where no lava and volcanic matter were suspected. I love liberty, but hope it can be so managed that I shall have soft beds, good dinners, fine linen, etc., for the rest of my life. I am too old to fight or to suffer. God bless you! Love to Mrs. Murray. Ever yours,

Sydney Smith

563. LADY HOLLAND

Weston House, Chipping Norton,
Oct. 15th, 1830

My dear Lady Holland,

We are here upon a visit to Sr George Philips who has built a very magnificent house in the Holland House style but of stone – a pretty place in a very ugly country. The evils of old age, gout and prolixity of narrative, are invading the worthy and recent Baronet. The Smiths (meaning my small detachment of that memorable race) are in good health. Mrs. Sydney finds that the climate of Combe Florey agrees perfectly with her throat. Our own situation is so warm that I should do better without a coat and waistcoat at Combe Florey than with them here.

I sincerely hope that Lord Holland and you are well and enjoying the autumn, and the young Foxes. I have quite finished my house at Combe Florey: it is much more commodious, and spacious than that at Foston. You gave me some hopes you would judge of this for yourself. The sooner you begin that operation, and the more time you employ in it, the greater will be the favor done to us.

I am very glad to see Charles in the Guards. He will now remain at home; for I trust there will be no more embarkation of the Guards while I live, and that a captain of the Guards will be as ignorant of the color of blood, as the rector of a parish. We have had important events enough within the last 20 years. May all remaining events be culinary, amorous, literary, or anything but political.

Lord John Russel comes here today. His corporeal antipart, Lord Nugent,* is here. Heaven send he may not swallow John. There are, however, stomach-pumps in case of accident: and there is the encoraging precedent of Jonas which I will state to them. Bobus talks of coming to us in November; when I see him I will believe in him.

I have been reading Lady Morgan.* I had no conception she had so good an understanding, and could write so well. In trifling subjects she is affected, is always egoistical, often irreligious, and indelicate: but on elevated and important subjects writes with great sense, vigor, eloquence, and honesty.

We shall return home the beginning of November, stay till the end of the year, and then go to Bristol; that is, if the Church of England lasts so long; but there is a strong impression that there will be a rising of Curates. Should anything of this kind occurr, they will be committed to hard preaching on the tread-pulpit (a new machine), and rendered incapable of ever hereafter collecting great or small tythes.

God bless you dear Lady Holland. I remain always your affectionate and obliged friend.

Sydney Smith

564. J. A. MURRAY

Weston House, Oct. 24th, 1830

My dear Murray,

There will be no changes in the Government before Christmas; and by that time the Duke will probably have gained some recruits. He does not want numbers, but defenders. Whoever goes into his cabinet, goes there as an inferior, to register the Duke's resolutions, - not as an equal, to assist in their formation; and this is a situation into which men of spirit and character do not choose to descend. The death of Huskisson has strengthened him very materially; his firmness, powers of labour, sagacity, and good-nature, and his vast military reputation, will secure his power. Averse from liberal measures, he will be as liberal as the times require; and will listen to instructed men on subjects where he has no opinions, or wrong ones.

During the first moments of the French Revolution, La Fayette had almost resolved upon a republic, but was turned the other way by the remonstrances and representation of the American Minister.*

The new Beer Bill* has begun its operations. Everybody is drunk. Those who are not singing are sprawling. The sovereign people are in a beastly state.

You are rich and rambling; pray come and see us next year. Your very sincere and affectionate friend,

Sydney Smith

567. LADY GREY

Combe Florey, Taunton, Nov. 21st, 1830

My dear Lady Grey

I never felt more sincere pleasure than from Lord Grey's appointment* – After such long toil, such Labor, privation, and misrepresentation, that a man should be placed where providence intended him to be, that honesty and Virtue should at last meet with its reward is a pleasure which rarely occurs in human Life, and one which I confess I had not promised myself –

I am particularly glad Brougham (if my poor* friend Lord Lyndhurst must go out) is Chancellor for *many* reasons. I should have preferred Goodrich for Home, Melborne for Colonial; The Duke of Richmond is well imagined.* I am very glad Lord Durham is in the Cabinet, because I like him, and for better reasons. Sr J. Graham* surprises me; the appointment is excellent but I should have expected there must have been so many great people who would have been claimants. I hope Captain Elliot* is Lord Minto's Cousin. Pray give John Russel an Office,* and Mcauley is well worth your attention;* make him Solicitor General. Adieu my dear Lady Grey – give my sincere and affectionate regards to Lord Grey. Thank God he has at last disappeared from that North Wall, against which so many sunless years of his Life had been past –

Your sincere and affectionate friend
Sydney Smith

I think the Selection upon the whole is *remarkably* good –

568. HON. CAROLINE FOX

⟨After Dec. 8th, 1830⟩*

My dear Miss Fox,

Merely to say that these and 20 other such handbills were not, as you suppose, written by me, but by a neighbouring curate. They have had an excellent effect. There is one from Miss Swing threatening to destroy crimping-irons for caps and washing machines, and patent tea-kettles; vowing vengeance also on the new bodkin which makes 2 holes instead of one.

Justices' wives are agitated and female constables have been sworn in. Ever yours

S S

571. MRS. MEYNELL

Bristol, Jan. 3rd, 1831

My dear Mrs. Meynell,

Brougham has kindly offered me an exchange of livings, which I declined with many thanks. I think the Administration will last some time, because I think the country decided upon Reform; and if the Tories will not permit Lord Grey to carry it into effect, they must turn it over to Hunt and Cobbett.*

I think the French Government far from stable, – like Meynell's horses at the end of a long day's chase. The Government of the country is in the hands of armed shopkeepers; and when the man with the bayonet deliberates, his reasons are more powerful than civilians can cope with. I am tired of liberty and revolution! Where is it to end? Are all political agglutinations to be unglued? Are we prepared for a second Heptarchy, and to see the King of Sussex fighting with the Emperor of Essex, or marrying the Dowager Queen of Hampshire?

It would be amusing enough if the chances of preferment were, after all, to make me your neighbour. Many is the quarrel and making up we should have together. Thank you, my dear friend, for saying that proximity to me would make your life happier! The rose that spreads its fragrance over the garden might as well thank the earth beneath for bearing it.

You see Jeffrey has been nearly killed at his election.* How funny to see all the Edinburgh Reviewers in office! God bless you, my dear friend!

Sydney Smith

572. J. A. MURRAY

8, Glocester-place, Clifton, Bristol,
Jan. 24th, 1831

My dear Murray,

pray tell me how you are all going on in Scotland. Is Jeffrey much damaged? They say he fought like a Lyon, and would have been killed had he been more visible, but that several people struck at him who could see nothing and so battered infinite space instead of the Advocate.

How did you find Brougham? He despatches Causes quickly but whether he satisfies the profession I do not know. ⟨I⟩ have some thoughts of going to Town the middle of February; is there any chance of seeing you there?

I think Lord Grey will give me some preferment if he stays in long enough; but the Upper Parsons live vindictively, and evince their aversion to a Whigg Ministry by an improved health. The Bishop of Ely* has the rancor to recover after three paralytic strokes, and the Dean of Lichfield* to be vigorous at 82 – and yet these are the men who are called Christians.

Things seem to be improving. I am afraid of Lord Anglesey's indiscretion, and still more of the indiscretion of his adviser Plunket.*

We are all well, are here upon duty and remain here until the middle of February. I think we shall all be in Town, but that must depend upon the state of my exchequer.

[The rest of the letter has been cut off.]

579. LADY GREY

Sidmouth, April 25th, 1831

My dear Lady Grey

Bold King. Bold Ministers. The immediate effect of this measure* is that I had no sleep all last Night – a meeting of free-holders at the Inn at Sidmouth, much Speaking and frequent Sound of Lord Grey's name thro' the wall; I had a great mind (being a Devonshire freeholder) to have appeared suddenly in

Night Cap and dressing Gown and to have made a Speech.

I have left off writing myself but I have persuaded a friend of mine a Mr. Dyson* to publish his Speech to the freeholders, which I believe will be in your hands by Wednesday or Thursday from Ridgeway. You may suppose it to be mine, but it is not, and I ask it as a *particular favor* from Lord Grey and you that you will not mention you have received it from me, or that I have had any influence in producing it –

It is a mite to the public Stock of Liberal principles, and not worth caution or trouble, but my plan has always been to contribute my *mite*, and in my own particular Way. I am making the tour of the Devonshire Watering places with my family, shall be at home on Saty, and at Holland House Friday 6th, and in London at the Hibberts Saty 14.

My sincere hope is that all this political agitation may not worry you nor injure the health of Lord Grey

I remain my dear Lady respectfully and affectionately yrs

Sydney Smith

Sidmouth – which place I pronounce to be an imposture

590. MRS. MEYNELL

Saville-row, Sept. 1831

My dear G.,

I am just stepping into the carriage to be installed by the Bishop,* but cannot lose a post in thanking you. It is, I believe, a very good thing, and puts me at my ease for life. I asked for nothing – never did anything shabby to procure preferment. These are pleasing recollections. My pleasure is greatly increased by the congratulations of good and excellent friends like yourself. God bless you!

Sydney Smith

591. LADY MORLEY

Bristol, ⟨Oct.⟩* 1831

Dear Lady Morley,

I have taken possession of my preferment. The house is in Amen-corner, - an awkward name on a card, and an awkward annunciation to the coachman on leaving any fashionable mansion. I find too (sweet discovery!) that I give a dinner every Sunday, for three months in the year, to six clergymen and six singing-men, at one o'clock. Do me the favour to drop in as Mrs. Morley. I did the duty at St. Paul's; the organ and music were excellent.

Seeing several carpenters at work at Lord Dudley's, I called; and after he had expatiated at some length on the danger of the times, I learnt that he was boarding up his windows in imitation of the Duke of Wellington, who has been fortified in a similar manner ever since the Coronation. I am afraid the Lords will fling out the Bill, and that I shall pocket the sovereign of Mr. Bulteel; in that case, I believe and trust Lord Grey will have recourse to Peer-making.

I went to Court, and, horrible to relate! with strings to my shoes instead of buckles, - not from Jacobinism, but ignorance. I saw two or three Tory lords looking at me with dismay, was informed by the Clerk of the Closet of my sin, and gathering my sacerdotal petticoats about me (like a lady conscious of thick ankles), I escaped further observation. My residence is in February, March, and July.

Lady Holland is to have an express from the Lords every ten minutes, and is encamped for that purpose in Burlington-street. Adieu, dear Lady Morley! Excuse my nonsense. A thousand thanks for your hospitality and good-nature.

Sydney Smith

595. LORD GREY

November, 1831

I take it for granted you are quite resolved to make Peers to an extent which may enable you to carry the Measure; the Measure is now one of such indispensable necessity that you will be completely justified by public opinion, and as completely overwhelmed by public opinion if you shrink from such a Step – so I have done with this. Cultivate Whishaw, he is one of the most sensible men in England, and his opinions valuable if he will give them –

The honest Clergymen that I know are few. It would give great Satisfaction if a Prebend were in course of time given to Malthus. Lord Carlisle's Brother Howard* is a good Scholar, a Gentleman of a mind not unecclesiastical, timid in manner, insignificant in appearance, thoroughly honest and to be depended upon. Caldwell* is fit for any Ecclesiastical situation – for his prudence, Sense, character and honesty; a great friend of Whishaw's. Wrangham* Wood will tell you about; you may trust him as long as you have any thing to give him. –

Wait till after Xmas for the meeting of parliament I am sure this is right. I give you great Credit for Lambs Conduit fields.* – Pray keep well, and do your best with a gay and careless heart. What is it all but the Scratching of Pismires on an heap of Earth – Rogues are careless and gay, why may not honest men? Think of the bill in the Morning, and take your Claret in the Evening totally forgetting the bill. You have done admirably up to this point, I warrant you will get thro' the rapids: and that we shall laugh over it all in the Hall of Howick.

I presume you have Ferguson of Rahte* in your list of peers if wanted; no Children, large fortune, – Good Whigg. Fling Bristol into the Circuit,* this will be worth a Riot.

599. LADY GREY

20, Saville-row, Tues. Dec. 6th, 1831

My dear Lady Grey

I went to the debate. Lords Littleton* and Scamperdown* were horrible. I wish apologies were abolished by act of parliament.

They are all Children to Lord Grey. He made an excellent Speech as prudent as it was spirited. I submit the following little Criticism; Lord Grey should stand further from the Bench and more in the body of the house, should stand more upright, and raise his arm - (which no Englishman does, and all foreigners do) from the Shoulder, and not from the Elbow. But he speaks beautifully, and is a Torch among tapers. Next to Lord Grey I liked Lord Harrowby.* Lord Aberdeen* speaks like a School boy.

The whole debate was rather conciliatory. You will be glad to hear that the Physicians pronounced Mrs Hibbert to be going on today as well as possible. Lady Holland ate a good dinner yesterday; pray mention this to Lady G. who is tenderly anxious on the Subject.

ever yours dear Lady Grey
Sydney Smith

606. LADY GREY

March, 1832

My dear Lady Grey

I did not like to say much to you about public affairs today, because I thought you were not very well, but I must take the Weight off my Soul. I am alarmed for Lord Grey, so are many others.

Is there a strong probability (amounting almost to a certainty) that the bill will be carried without a creation of peers?* No. Then make them. But the King will not. Then resign.

But if the King *will* create, we shall lose more than we gain: I doubt it. Many threaten who will not vote against the bill; at all

Events you will have done all you can to carry it. If you do *not* create and it fails, you are beaten with disgrace; – if you *do* create and it fails, – you are beaten with Honor; and the Country will distinguish between its Enemies and its friends.

The same reasoning applies to dissensions in the Cabinet of which (though perhaps unfounded) I have heard many rumors: –

Turn out the Anti-Reformers You will then be either victorious, or defeated with Honor.

You are just in that predicament in which the greatest boldness is the greatest prudence.

You must either carry the bill or make it as clear as the day that you have done all in your power to do so.

There is not a moment to lose.

The Character of Lord Grey is a very valuable public possession; it would be a very serious injury if it were destroyed, it will be looked for hereafter in vain, and there will be no public man in whom the people will place the smallest confidence.

Lord Grey must say to his Colleagues tomorrow – 'Brothers, the time draws near, you must chuse this day between good and Evil; either you or I* must perish this night before the Sun falls. I am sure the bill will not pass *without* Creation, it may pass *with* Creation, it is the only expedient for doing what from the bottom of my heart I believe the Country requires. I will create and create immediately or resign.'

Mcintosh, Whishaw, Robert Smith, Rogers, Luttrell, Jeffrey, Sharp, Orde,* Mcauley, Fazackerley, Ld Ebrington, where will you find a better Jury, one more able, and more willing to consider every point connected with the honor, character, and fame of Lord Grey? There would not be among them a dissentient Voice. If you want to be happy three months hence, create Peers. If you wish to avoid an old Age of Sorrow and Reproach, create Peers. If you wish to retain my friendship, it is of no sort of consequence whether you make Peers or not – I shall always retain for you the most sincere gratitude and affection without the slightest reference to your political Wisdom or your political Errors – and may God bless and support you in one of the most difficult Moments that ever occurred to any public man.

Sydney Smith

615. CHARLES COCKERELL*

No. 24, Hanover-square, Wednesday Eveng,
[endorsed June 1832]

Dear Sir

I have been attacked today with my old enemy Lumbago so as to prevent my intended inspection with you tomorrow at St. Paul's. I had a long conversation with the Dean. We are agreed to husband our feeble resources as much as possible, and to divide the expense of painting the Chapterhouse. We shall do no more therefore this year than to paint the outside. I trust no more will be done with the Dog-spikes in the stonework till I have seen you and conversed with you on the subject. I make the same observation with regard to the Iron staircase of the West Tower. I enclose a paper agreed upon between the Dean and myself to which I cannot anticipate the slightest objection, and to which I will beg the favour of you to adhere. I will also in future sign my name to all the Bills that I audit.

I could not find from enquiry that the deputy Surveyor kept any written documents of the work done or materials employed in the Cathedral; I am to see Hodson and the tradesmen tomorrow and you shall immediately hear from me again about the bills.

Very truly yours
Sydney Smith

623. LADY GREY

Combe Florey, Taunton, Aug. 27th, 1832

My dear Lady Grey

Are you gone to Howick? You must have great pleasure the greatest pleasure in going there triumphant and all powerful; it must be I fear an hasty pleasure and that you cannot be long spared. One of your great difficulties is the Church. You must positively in the course of the first Session make a provision for the Catholic Clergy of Ireland, and make it out of the Revenues of the Irish Protestant Church. I have in vain racked my brains to think how this can be avoided, but it cannot. It will divide the Cabinet, and agitate the Country, but you must face the danger, and conquer or be conquered by it. It cannot be delayed, there is no alternative between this and a bloody War and reconquest of Ireland.

I hope you will make the Bishops if possible bring in their own reform Bill; they will throw it on the Government if they can. I foresee the probability of a protestant tempest, but you must keep the Sea, and not run into Harbor. – Such indeed is not your practice. The Tories are daunted and intimidated here, and I think the Members returned will be Reformers.

Pray put down the Unions* as soon as the New parliament meet.

We are all well. Cholera has made one successful Effort at Taunton and not repeated it though a month has elapsed. Lord John Russel comes here Saty, and the Fazakerlys* Friday, So we shall be a strong reform Party for a few days. My Butler said in the Kitchen he should let the Country people peep through the Shutters at Lord John for a penny a piece – a very reasonable price. I wonder what he will charge for Lord Grey if he should come here. The Cholera will have killed by the end of the year about one person in every thousand. Therefore it is a Thousand to one (supposing the Cholera to travel at the same rate) that any person does not die of the Cholera in any one year. This calculation is for the Mass, but if you are prudent, temperate and rich your chance is at least five times as good that you do not die of cholera; in other words 5000 to 1. and if it is 5000 to 1 that you do not die of Cholera in a year, it is not far from two Million to one that you do not die any one day of Cholera. –

It is only 730,000 to one that your house is not burnt down any one day; therefore it is nearly three times as likely that your home should be burnt down any one day as that you should die of Cholera, or it is as probable that your home should be burnt down 3 times in any one year as that you should die of Cholera.

Pray tell Lord Grey that the most reforming Reformer we have in these parts is Sr Thomas Lethbridge, so that his hopes are not yet Extinguished.* An Enormous harvest here – and every appearance of peace and plenty. God bless you dear Lady Grey – my very kind regards to Lord Grey, and Georgiana. Ever your sincere friend

Sydney Smith

My Love to Miss Craster

630. MRS. MEYNELL

Combe Florey, Dec. 16th, 1832

Dear Mrs. Meynell,

I often think of you, though I do not write to you. I am delighted to find the elections have gone so well. The blackguards and democrats have been defeated almost universally, and I hope Meynell is less alarmed, though I am afraid he will never forgive me Mrs. Partington; in return I have taken no part in the county election, and am behaving quite like a dignitary of the Church; that is, I am confining myself to digestion.

Read Memoirs of Constant,* Buonaparte's valet-de-chambre, and Mrs. Trollope's 'Refugees in America.'* The story is foolish, but the picture of American manners excellent; and why should not the Americans be ridiculed, if they are ridiculous?

I see no prospect of a change of Ministry, but think the Whigs much stronger than they were when we were in town. I have come to the end of my career, and have nothing now to do but to grow old merrily and to die without pain. Yours,

Sydney Smith

643. —— GUILLEMARD*

November 22nd, 1833

Dear Guillemard,

To go to St. Paul's is certain death. The thermometer is several degrees below zero. My sentences are frozen as they come out of my mouth, and are thawed in the course of the Summer, making strange noises and unexpected assertions in various parts of the church; but if you are tired of a world which is not tired of you, and are determined to go to St. Paul's, it becomes my duty to facilitate the desperate scheme. Present the enclosed card to any of the vergers, and you will be well placed.

Ever truly yours
Sydney Smith

658. THE BISHOP OF LONDON*

May 1st, 1834

My dear Lord

I observe in bishops a great readiness to break in pieces the larger livings of their diocese, but none in those who have the better sees to dedicate any portion of their own superior emoluments to the improvement of smaller Bishoprics, but on the contrary a perfect readiness to mount up into the still higher and more wealthy offices of the Church. Do not be angry with me for this observation. I do not mean it as a sarcasm but state it fairly as an argument which materially influences my decision on the present occasion; – for if the Laity are to be conciliated by putting an end to the inequalities of the Church property it is a striking injustice not to begin where that inequality is the greatest and the most visible, and especially so where the Reformer of abuses on one side of the hedge is the same person who Enjoys them to a much greater extent on the other.

There is not (as you well know) enough of property in the Church to pay to each man a decent competence; they must therefore be paid by a lottery of Preferment, some more, some less. I do not want to lessen the value of your See and to give it to others. I shall be glad on the contrary (because I think you the most sensible man on the Bench) to see you hereafter Archbishop of Canterbury with all its honours and emoluments, but then the argument that is good for you is good for those who are below you. If there is an undissolved Bishop of London there may surely be an integral Vicar of Edmonton. I cannot preserve your colossal stature and refuse to Mr. Warren* the more modest portion of space which he has hitherto been allowed to occupy.

I see no reason why the Parish may not go on quite as well with a Curate* under the Rector as with a small autocratical clergyman in the midst of it, and if a Bishop can exercise a pastoral care over 300 Parishes, a vicar may easily do so over one chapel of ease close to his own residence. The rent of the pews wd to a man fit for the office produce £180 pr. an. and this with £100 pr. an. (which I am sure Mr. Warren wd give) appears to me sufficient for any young man who might officiate there.

No complaint has reached us thro' yr Lordship or by any other means of any neglect of duty at Winchmore Hill, and seeing no evil I do not know why we should employ any remedy.

I have been out of town for some days, or wd have answered your letter before. I write now in my way to my Parish, – remaining always my dear Lord with respect and good wishes, yours

Sydney Smith

661. THE LORD CHANCELLOR

Combeflorey, Taunton, May 23rd,* 1834

My dear Lord

Pray consider for a moment some of the provisions of yr bill respecting the Parochial clergy and the effect they will have upon us. Our present leave of absence is surely not unreasonable. Clergymen with families are placed often in the most remote and solitary situations, and to get into towns for 3 months is an object of the greatest importance for the education of children who are to live perhaps by those accomplishments which can only be learnt in towns. The Parishes are properly taken care of in their absence, and I never heard of any scandal or complaint of these permitted absences where a man resided Bonâ-fide the rest of the time; but if you reduce us to two months which I think hard it is surely a very great vexation not to let us take these two months consecutively; so that a poor Devil who comes from Northumberland or Cornwall to spend a few weeks in London with his friends is forced to go and return in the middle of his visit to avoid the penalties of the Law. You have no idea of the consternation and complaint this occasions among the country clergy. The Bishops will not oppose it because they are utterly careless of the restrictions and inconveniences to which their clergy are exposed if their own power is not abridged; so that it must depend on your own good nature.

Your Bill for Residence and against pluralities was I think inevitable and therefore the consequences are no argument, but those effects will be to make the clergy contemptible in a rich country for their poverty, and vexatious from their fanaticism.

Ever sincerely yrs
Sydney Smith

663. Mrs. Baring

Weymouth-street, Portland-place, ⟨July,⟩ 1834

Dear Mrs. Baring*

I have a favour to ask: could you lend our side such a thing as a Chancellor of the Exchequer?* Some of our people are too little – some too much in love – some too ill. We will take great care of him, and return him so improved you will hardly know him.

You will be glad to hear my eyes are better – nearly well. Ever sincerely yours

Sydney Smith

P.S. What is real piety? What is true attachment to the Church? How are these fine feelings best evinced? The answer is plain: by sending strawberries to a clergyman. Many thanks.

S. S.

664. Mrs. Meynell

Combe Florey, July, 1834

My dear Mrs. Meynell,

The thought was sudden, so was the execution: I saw I was making no progress in London, and I resolved to run the risk of the journey. I performed it with pain, and found on my arrival at my own door my new carriage completely disabled. I called on no one, but went away without beat of drum. I know nothing of public affairs – I have no pleasure in thinking of them, and turn my face the other way, deeply regretting the abrupt and unpleasant termination of Lord Grey's political life.

I am making a slow recovery; hardly yet able to walk across the room, nor to put on a christian shoe. On Monday I shall have been ill for a month. Perhaps it is a perquisite of my time of life, to have the gout or some formidable illness. We enter and quit the world in pain! but let us be just however; I find my eyesight much improved by gout, and I am not low-spirited.

Pray let me hear from you from time to time, as you shall from me. Remember me to the handsome widow with handsome daughters; and believe me, my dear G., yours affectionately,

Sydney Smith

668. LADY GREY

Combe Florey, Taunton, Oct. 12th, 1834

My dear Lady Grey

I should be glad to hear a word about the dinner; you must have been in the 7th. heaven: I am heartily rejoiced at the great, and just honors Lord Grey has received, which I am sure will give him great pleasure in retirement.

I have spent a Summer of Sickness, never having been 10 days without some return of Gout or Opthalmia. At present I am very well, and laying up the aliments, and Elements of future Illnesses. I shall be in London the 11th of November with Mrs. Smith in Weymouth Street where you paid me those charitable Visits for which God's blessing be upon you. I went to Bowood for a week, and paid for it by a Sharp fit of opthalmia. It was agreeable. Luttrell was there, very unwell. I think Brougham has damaged the Administration from 10 to 20 p Ctm, and I wish our friend John George* would not speak so much. I really cannot agree with him about Reform. I am for no more movements, they are not relished by Canons of St Paul's. You will be glad to hear that St Paul behaved extremely well to me last year, and well it was he did so for I have had some thumping Bills from Cambridge, however I have paid them, and great alterations are promised, and I believe sincerely intended.* When I say no more movement I except the case of the Universities which I think ought to be immediately invaded with Enquiries and Commissioners. They are a crying Evil.

I have had a great Number of persons coming to C. Florey, and they all profess themselves converts to the beauty of this Country. The Hibberts leave us next week and Mrs. Sydney and I shall be left Tete a Tete, all the young Birds flown.

Terrible work with the new Poor Law* – nobody knows what to do – or what Way to go. how did Lord Grey stand all his fatigues? has Rogers been with you? who should pay me a visit here but Poodle Byng?* his very look turns Country into Piccadilly.

ever dear Lady Grey your sincere friend
Sydney Smith

670. LADY GREY

3, Weymouth-street, Portland-place,
Nov. 19th, 1834

My dear Lady Grey

Nothing can equal the fury of the Whiggs. They mean not only to change everything upon Earth, but to alter the Tides, to suspend the principles of Gravitation, and Vegetation and to tear down the Solar System.

I saw Brougham in a fine Waistcoat at Mrs. Petre's intensly rabid and a good contrast to Petre.* I am truely sorry for Holland House.

The Duke's success (as it appears to me) will entirely depend upon his imitation of the Whiggs. I am heartily glad that Lord Grey is in port. I am (thanks to him) in Port also, and have no intention of resigning St. Paul's. *I* (as the Chancellor says) have not resigned. Still the King has used them ill; if he always intended to turn them out as soon as Lord Spencer died he should have told Lord Melbourne so and not made him as ridiculous as he has made him – at least as far as circumstances (over which he has no control) can make an honest, able and high minded man ridiculous.

I am better in health avoiding all fermented Liquors, and drinking nothing but London Water with a million of insects in every drop; he who drinks a tumbler of London Water has literally in his stomach more animated beings than there are men, Women and Children on the face of the Globe.

London is very empty but by no means disagreable. I find plenty of friends and feel an affection for Cousins, which somehow or another disappears in the more brilliant Seasons of the year. When do you come to London? Pray be there early in January. I shall practice as I preach and be there from January to Easter.

Lady Jersey* they say wants to be Lord Lieutenant of Ireland. It is supposed that the Messenger who is gone to fetch Bob Peel to come and ruin his Country, will not catch him before Bob is at Paestum. In the meantime the Duke of Wellington holds all offices civil, military and Ecclesiastical, and is to be Bishop of Ely (if Ely dies) till Peel arrives.

Only think of a Prebendary of Norwich, and a very large

Pluralist killing himself* – amiable, gay and agreeable into the bargain.

Pray give my kindest regards to Georgiana, and to the Earl, and believe me always your affectionate friend

Sydney Smith

672. LORD HOLLAND

November, 1834

My dear Lord Holland,

If any chance had remained of my being made a Bishop I should probably (that I might not be suspected of interested motives) have said nothing about the matter, – but I cared much more for the *slight* than the *sacrifice*. I think your observation (unexplained) might in all fairness have led to the inference I drew from it without supposing in me any extraordinary degree of irritability; and if I *did* draw the inference you must in fairness admit it would be to any man a very painful one. I was the more easily led into the mistake because it so happens that I am utterly ignorant on what the claims of Dr. Butler* consist. I never heard that Butler had written anything which proved him to be a great Scholar, or a great Theologian, nor did I ever hear that in the worst times of Protestantism he had ever put himself *forward* as the friend of Catholic Emancipation, and sacrificed himself for his party. I do not *deny* that he may have done all this, but I can safely say that living with all sorts of people I *never heard* it, had I therefore imagined that he was one of those men of prudent and suppressed Liberality who were selected not *for what he had done for friends*, but that he might *not alarm enemies*. A Ministry may think it their duty to do this; it *may* be their duty. I think otherwise, and don't call it mean or base, but *wrong* and *unjust*. I care very little what 3/4ths of the late Cabinet think about me, but I care a good deal what *you* think about me. You have often said to me '*I would get drunk on the day you were made a Bishop*'. You then say that Butler ought to have been the man. I ask kindly and civilly for an explanation, and you say 'I am only one of many. If it had depended on me alone, from joint considerations of regard, and fitness I would have chosen *you*, from fitness alone, *Butler*.

This is perfectly fair and I am obliged to you for taking the trouble to explain yourself to me, – but I wonder you should wonder at my feeling. And now there being an end of the Mitre for ever, I must say that Lord Grey, and the Cabinet, have chosen a man who instead of staunchly defending those bold Church measures for the destruction of the Irish Protestant Church and the payment of the Catholic Clergy which will become more necessary every day will (if I am rightly informed) be as great a Bigot and as foolish and blind a Churchman as any Bishop on the Bench. It is an appointment in which I am sure the Ministry are 'wholly wrong'.

Ever yrs.
Sydney Smith

673. Lady Holland

November 25th, 1834

[Private and Confidential]

My dear Lady Holland

Lord Holland (who before coming into Office had expressed so strongly and frequently his wish to see me a Bishop) tells me that he thinks another person ought to have been the man; it was very natural for me to say to myself, What Have I done? – why am I laid aside? why is Lord Holland's opinion changed? and feeling all this I am sure it was much wiser to express than to suppress it. The Contest was not about a Bishopric but about something of much greater Consequence, a slight and a degradation. Lord Holland has been so kind as to explain to me his views and opinions; I am much obliged to him for having done so, I am satisfied, and silent.

I never asked Lord Holland why he had not made me a Bishop, but why he thought I ought not to be one. I selected Lord Holland because he is the only person in the Cabinet with whom I am intimate and the only person who (as far as I know) had ever expressed any wish to make me a Bishop, and the only person who told me that if Allen had not been the man it ought not to have been me. I now know that many others thought so but I did not know it before Lord Holland told me. To such members of the Cabinet I would say that they are a set of political Cowards not worth serving, who desert a bold and honest man who has always turned out in danger and difficulty for a prudent and plausible man who has done nothing for his party; but thank God I never acted from the hope of preferment but from the Love of Justice and truth which was bursting within me. When I began to express my opinions on Church politics what hope could any but a mad man have of gaining preferment by such a Line of Conduct?

You can see* when such tremendous Questions are coming on who are the men the Whiggs have placed upon the Bench as the advocates of those liberal measures on which the Safety of the State depends 1, a dishonest Bankrupt* who always votes against them; 2, the greatest fool in Europe,* who always votes against them; 3. A learned and honest man* so weak and injudicious that the greatest favour he can do his party is to hold his tongue and pen; 4, an insignificant man* who has suckled Lord Althorpe, and who will in all trying Questions – desert them.

In what I have said of the Cabinet I cannot of course in the most distant manner mean to include Lord Holland for he has distinctly said that if the appointment had rested solely in him I should have been the man. All you say of my first preferment is strictly true, I am deeply grateful for it – why should you for a moment suppose that my loyalty and affection to you and Lord Holland is lessened one atom – because I felt hurt at what Lord Holland said. You would have had much more reason to think so, if the supposed loss of his good opinion had been a matter of indifference to me.

I beg you to consider this Letter as private and confidential.

There is nothing in my Life of which I am more proud than the favor and patronage of Holland House. I am quite sure I should have got up in the World somehow or another, but I am not the less indebted to those who have treated me with such exemplary kindness.

God bless you dr Lady Hd. your affectionate friend

Sydney Smith

I was coming this day to H H, but cannot have the Carriage, of course I shall come to see you as often as you will let me.

675. LADY GREY

18, Stratford-place, Oxford-road, Jan. 14th, 1835

Knowing (as you do my dear Lady Grey) Lady Holland so well, and having known her so long, you will I am sure be sorry to hear the misfortune which has befallen her. You know how long she has been alarmed by diseases of the heart; terrified to an agony by some recent death from that cause, she was determined that Brodie* should examine the chest thoroughly with a stethoscope. He spent a long time there, bestowed the greatest attention upon the case, and ended with saying that in the course of his practice he had never witnessed a more decided case of healthy circulation, and that she had not a single complaint belonging to her. I have seen her since, and never saw anyone so crestfallen and desponding. She did all she could to get me to help her to some fresh complaint, but I was stubborn.

I believe the new ministry are purporting some great Coup de Teatre, and that when the curtain draws up, there will be seen, ready prepared, Abolition of Pluralities, Commutation of Tithes, Provision for the Catholic Clergy, etc., etc. Somebody asked Peel the other day how the Elections were going on. Peel said 'I know very little about them and in truth I care little. We have such plans as I think will silence all opposition, or at least such as will conciliate all reasonable men.' Do not doubt that he said this. – Brougham is already entirely forgotten; was there ever such a fall?* You must have a great appetite for revenge if you are not satiated. Lady Holland wants to bring in Lord Grey again.

I had last week the gout upon crutches, and it came into my Eye, but by means of Colchicum I can now see and walk. Of course I had the best advice. I am glad to hear from Hammick,* and the Hollands such good accounts of Howick House and that you are to be in Town so soon.

I write to you not to make you write to me, for what can you tell me where you are but that Craster of Craster is well or ill? but because I am in London and you are not. You may say that you are happy out of office, but I have great disbelief on this subject.

We are here till the end of April in the same house where we were last year. My kind regards to the Earl and Lady G. Your cheese will arrive in London as soon as you do. God bless you dear Lady Grey. Your sincere friend

Sydney Smith

676. Sir Wilmot-Horton, Bart.*

January 15th, 1835

Dear Horton,

It is impossible to say what the result of all these changes will be. I do not think there is any chance of the Tories being suffocated at the first moment by a denial of confidence; if the more heated Whigs were to attempt it, the more moderate ones would resist it. If I were forced to give an opinion, I should say Peel's government would last through a session; and a session is, in the present state of politics, an eternity. But the remaining reforms, rule who may, must go on. The Trojans must put on the armour of the Greeks whom they have defeated.

Never was astonishment equal to that produced by the dismissal of the Whigs. I thought it better at first to ascertain whether the common laws of nature were suspended; and to put this to the test, I sowed a little mustard and cress seed, and waited in breathless anxiety the event. It came up. By little and little I perceived that, as far as the outward world was concerned, the dismissal of Lord Melbourne has not produced much effect.

I met T—— yesterday at Lady Williams's,* a sensible and very good-natured man, and so stout that I think there are few wild elephants who would care to meet him in the wood. I am turned a gouty old gentleman, and am afraid I shall not pass a green old-age, but, on the contrary, a blue one; or rather, that I shall be spared the trouble of passing any old-age at all. Poor Malthus!* everybody regrets him; – in science and in conduct equally a philosopher, one of the most practically wise men I ever met, shamefully mistaken and unjustly calumniated, and receiving no mark of favour from a Liberal Government, who ought to have interested themselves in the fortunes of such a virtuous martyr to truth.

I hope you will disorient yourself soon. The departure of the wise men from the East seems to have been on a more extensive scale than is generally supposed, for no one of that description seems to have been left behind. Come back to Europe, where only life is worth having, where that excellent man and governor, Lord Clare,* is returning, and where so many friends are waiting to receive you *à bras ouverts*, – among the rest the Berries, whom I may call fully ripe at present, and who may, if your stay is protracted, pass that point of vegetable perfection, and exhibit some faint tendency to decomposition.

The idea lately was, that Lord ——* would go to India, but they are afraid his religious scruples would interfere with the prejudices of the Hindoos. This may be so; but surely the moral purity of his life must have excited their admiration. I beg my kind and (an old parson may say) my affectionate regards to Lady Horton.

Yours, my dear Horton, very sincerely,
Sydney Smith

679. LADY GREY

Saty., Feb. 7th, 1835

Thank you for the Speech, very good and very honest. I agree with you entirely dear Lady Grey as to the difficulty of finding any body in the relics of the Whiggs fit to govern the Country. Abercrusty is only fit to set in an Ivy Bush, and to shake his head, and move his Eye Brows. Johnny Russel is more calculated for Love than civil Strife;* and of all the obstinate shallow conceited men in the World Duncannon* is the person in whom these defects are the most glaringly combined. Light farces and Melodramas are so little conducive to the well being of nations that Mulgrave* will be of little Use.

The bear* is ill, and licking his Paws. Holland and Lansdowne (with every other qualification for governing) want that Legion of Devils in the interior without whose aid Mankind cannot be ruled. The Legion has been too kind and too prodigal of aid to Brougham.

An Englishman settled at Marseilles dined the other day at a Table D'Hôte, and was very civilly accosted by a fellow Countryman who talked of many of their common acquaintance and was very gracious. All Nations upon Earth were at Table. The Unknown Briton descanted upon the politics of Europe, was acquainted with the Secrets, and movements of every Cabinet and astonished every body (waiters included) by his fluency, and political information. At last the Anglo Marsalian* by diverse twitches of the Nose began to suspect who it was, and resolved to bring a friend the next day to such an amusing Exhibition; but the next day they found he had gone to another Table D'Hôte, in another Quarter of Marseilles, where they ascertained he had excited the same astonishment by the same display. It is absolutely impossible he can ever be Chancellor again unless in times where Whittle Harvey* is Chancellor of the Exchequer – No Government can be so insane as to take him, insane as he is.

I have no doubt whatever but that Bob or as they call him Bobbin Peel is quite sincere in his Church Reform;* Bishops nearly equalized – Pluralities, Canons, and Prebendaries abolished, Tithes commuted, and Residence enforced – a much more severe bill than the Whiggs could have ventured upon. Pray excuse my writing to you so often but I am learning to write clear and straight, and it is necessary I should write a Letter every day. – I hear you are to be here by the end of the Month; If you put it off for a Week or two you will perhaps not be here till the end of the Monachy –

Your affectionate Chaplain
Sydney Smith

683. LORD HOLLAND

18, Stratford-place, April 18th, 1835

My dear Lord Holland,

I wrote to you some time since when you were out of office about being a Bishop. My own opinion of myself is that I should make a very good Bishop, that I should be a firm defender of Liberal opinions, and I hope I am too much a man of honor to take an office without fashioning my manners and conversation so as not to bring it into discredit.

You have said and written that you wish to see me a Bishop, and I have no doubt would try to carry your wishes into effect. If proper vacancies had occurred in the beginning of Lord Grey's administration I believe this would have been done. Other politicians have succeeded who entertain no such notion and Lord Melbourne always thinks *that* man best qualified for any office whom he had seen and known the least. Liberals of the eleventh hour abound, and there are some of the first hour of whose work in the toil and heat of the day I have no recollection. These are the obstacles to my promotion; but there is a greater obstacle and that is that I have entirely lost all wish to be a Bishop; the thought is erased from my mind, and in the very improbable event of a Bishopric offered to me I would steadily refuse it; in this I am *perfectly honest and sincere* and I make this communication to you to prevent your friendly exertion in my favor, and perhaps to spare you the regret of making that exertion in vain. My letter requires no answer. I remain always your sincere and affectionate friend

Sydney Smith

I congratulate you sincerely on recovering the Duchy of Lancaster.

687. Dr. Henry Holland

Combe Florey, Taunton, June 8th, 1835

My dear Holland,

We shall have the greatest pleasure in receiving you and yours – and if you were twice as numerous it would be so much the better. The Hibberts are arrived well and safe – they had a prosperous journey. Illness must be peculiarly disagreeable to the Duchess of Sutherland, as I take it all Duchesses descend when they die, and there are some peculiar circumstances in the life of that Lady that will certainly not occasion any exemption in her favor. The defunct Duke must by this time be well informed of her infidelities and their first meeting in Tartarus will not therefore be of the most agreeable description.*

What do you think of this last piece of Legislation for Boroughs?* It was necessary to do a good deal: the question is one of degree. I shall be in town on Tuesday 23rd, and be at Hibbert's house in Weymouth Street – I hope under better auspices than last year. I have followed your directions and therefore deserve a better fortune than fell to my lot on that occasion. Sr Henry Halford* is the Mahomet of rhubarb and magnesia – the greatest medical impostor I know. – if once ill he will soon go.

I am suffering from my old complaint, the Hay-fever (as it is calld). My fear is of perishing by deliquescence. – I melt away in Nasal and Lachrymal profluvia. My remedies are warm Pediluvium, Cathartics, topical application of a watery solution of Opium to eyes ears, and the interior of the nostrils. The membrane is so irritable, that light, dust, contradiction, an absurd remark, the sight of a dissenter, – anything, sets me a sneezing and if I begin sneezing at 12, I don't leave off till two o'clock – and am heard distinctly in Taunton when the wind sets that way at a distance of 6 miles. Turn your mind to this little curse. If Consumption is too powerful for Physicians at least they should not suffer themselves to be outwitted by such little upstart disorders as the Hay-fever.

I am very glad you married my daughter, for I am sure you are both very happy, and I assure you I am proud of my son-in-law.

I have ordered a Brass Knocker against you come and we have a case of Chronic Bronchitis next door – some advanced cases of Dyspepsia not far off – and a considerable promise of acute Rheumatism at no great distance – a neighboring Squire has water forming on the chest so that I hope ⟨things*⟩ will be comfortable and your visit not unpleasant.

I did not think that Copplestone with all his nonsense could have got down to Tar-water. I have as much belief in it as I have in Holy water. – it is the water has done the business, not the tar. They could not induce the sensual prelate* to drink water but by mixing it up with nonsense and disguising the simplicity of the receipt. You must have a pitch battle with him about his tar-water, and teach him what he has never learnt – the rudiments of common sense. Kindest love to dear Saba. Ever your affectionate father ·
                                               Sydney Smith

693. MRS. AUSTIN*

Combe Florey, July, 1835

Many thanks, dear Mrs. Austin, for your kindness in thinking of me and my journey after the door was shut: but you have a good heart, and I hope it will be rewarded with that aliment in which the heart delights, – the respectful affection of the wise and just.

I will write to you before I come to Boulogne, and am obliged to you for the commission. I have been travelling one hundred and fifty miles in my carriage, with a green parrot and the 'Life of Mackintosh.' I shall be much surprised if this book does not become extremely popular. It is full of profound and eloquent remarks on men, books, and events. What more, dear lady, can you wish for in a book?

I found here seven grandchildren, all in a dreadful state of perspiration and screaming. You are in the agonies of change; always *some* pain in leaving! I could say a great deal on that subject, only I am afraid you would quiz me. And, pray, what am I to do for my evening parties in November, if you are not in London? Surely you must have overlooked this when you resolved to stay at Boulogne.

Mr. Whishaw is coming down here on the 8th of August, to stay some days. He is truly happy in the country. What a pleasure it would be if you were here to meet him! But to get human beings together who ought to be together, is a dream.

Keep a little corner in that fine heart of yours for me, however small it may be; a clergyman in your heart will keep all your other notions in good order. God bless you!

Sydney Smith

695. MRS. AUSTIN

Combe Florey, Sept. 7th, 1835

Health to Mrs. Austin, and happiness, and agreeable society, carelessness for the future, and enjoyment of the present!

Who can think of your offer now, and before, but with kindness and gratitude? My brother, who loves paradoxes, says, if he saw a man walking into a pit, he would not advise him to turn the other way. My plan is on the contrary, to advise, to interfere, to remonstrate, at all hazards. I hate cold-blooded people, a tribe to which you have no relation; and the brother who talks this nonsense would not only stop the wanderer, but jump halfway down the pit to save him. We will go by the Lower Road. The consequence of all this beautiful weather will be, our liquefaction in our French expedition.

I send you a list of all the papers written by me in the Edinburgh Review. Catch me, if you can, in any one illiberal sentiment, or in any opinion which I have need to recant; and that, after twenty years' scribbling upon all subjects.

Lord John Russell comes here next week with Lady John. He has behaved prudently, but the thing is not yet over.* I am heartily glad of the prospect of agreement. Who, but the idiots of the earth, would fling a country like this into confusion, because a Bill (in its mutilated state a great improvement) is not carried as far, and does not embrace as much, as the best men could wish? Is political happiness so cheap, and political improvement so easy, that the one can be sported with, and the other demanded, in this style? God bless you, dear Mrs. Austin! From your friend

Sydney Smith

708. J. A. MURRAY

January 6th, 1836

My dear Murray,

It seems a long while since we have heard anything about you and yours, in which matters we always take a very affectionate concern. I saw a good deal of the Ministers in the month of

November, which I passed (as I always do pass it) in London. I see no reason why they should go out, and I do not in the least believe they are going. I think they have done more for the country than all the Administrations since the Revolution. The Poor-law Bill alone would immortalize them. It is working extremely well.

I see you are destroying the Scotch Church. I think we are a little more popular in England than we were. Before I form any opinion on Establishments, I should like to know the effect they produce on vegetables. Many of our clergy suppose that if there was no Church of England, cucumbers and celery would not grow; that mustard and cress could not be raised. If Establishments are connected so much with the great laws of nature, this makes all the difference; but I cannot believe it.

God bless you, dear Murray!

Sydney Smith

710. LADY GREY

Combe Florey, Taunton, Feb. 1st, 1836

I write a line my dear Lady Grey to say that my tributary Cheese is only waiting in Somersetshire because you are waiting in Northumberland, and it will come to Town to be eaten as soon as it is aware that you are there to eat it.

I hope that Lord Grey and you are well – no easy thing seeing that there are about 1500 diseases to which Man is subjected.

Without having thought much about them (and as I have no part to play I am not bound to think about them) I like all the Whiggs have done: I only wish them to bear in mind that the consequences of giving so much power to the people have not yet been tried at a period of bad harvests, and checked Manufactures; the prosperity of the Country during all these changes has been without Example.

Mrs. Sydney and I have been leading a Derby* and Joan Life for these 2 months, without Children. This kind of Life might have done very well for Adam and Eve in Paradise, where the weather was fine, and the Beasts as numerous as in the Zoological Gardens, and the plants equal to anything in the Gardens about London; but I like a greater Variety. It is a great proof of Wisdom and corage in the government that they have not re-united themselves to Brougham. It is the fashion now to pity him. I lament over the loss of so much talent but remain steadily convinced of the necessity of excluding him from any share in the administration.

I am become a nearer neighbour to you in London, having purchased the Lease of a Small House in Charles St Berkley Square, looking up John St, No. 33. I shall be in Town by the 15th and I hope in my house by the end of the Month.

Mcintosh kept all Letters; he had a bundle of mine which his Son returned to me. I found a letter written 35 years ago or thereabouts giving to him Mcintosh an account of my first introduction to Lord and Lady Holland. I sent it to Lady Holland who was much amused by it. I call her a *magnificent structure of flesh and blood** By the bye I never saw anybody so improved* as Howick; he is affable, good humored pleasant and very agreeable. Sensible, and well informed he always was.

Remember me very kindly to Lord Grey and Georgiana – I remain always dear Lady Grey your grateful and affectionate friend

Sydney Smith

I had no idea that in offering my humble caseous tribute every year I should minister in so great a degree to my own Glory. I bought the other day some Cheshire Cheese at Cullums in Bond St, desiring him to send it to Mr. Sydney Smith. – He smiled and said Sr your name is very familiar to me. No I replied Mr Cullum, I am not Sr Sydney Smith but Mr Sydney Smith – "I am perfectly aware of that he said I know whom I am addressing, I have often heard of the Cheeses you send to Lord Grey". So you see there is no escaping from Fame. –

712. Sir George Philips

February 28th, 1836

My dear Philips,

You say I have many comic ideas rising in my mind; this may be true; but the champagne bottle is no better for holding the champagne. Don't you remember the old story of Carlin,* the French harlequin? It settles these questions. I don't mean to say I am prone to melancholy; but I acknowledge my weakness enough to confess that I want the aid of society, and dislike a solitary life.

Thomas Brown* was an intimate friend of mine, and used to dine with me regularly every Sunday in Edinburgh. He was a Lake poet, a profound metaphysician, and one of the most virtuous men that ever lived. As a metaphysician, Dugald Stewart was a humbug to him. Brown had real talents for the thing. You must recognize, in reading Brown, many of those arguments with which I have so often reduced you to silence in metaphysical discussions. Your discovery of Brown is amusing. Go on! You will detect Dryden if you persevere; bring to light John Milton, and drag William Shakespeare from his ill-deserved obscurity!

The Whigs seem to me stronger than ever; I agree in all their measures. I have no doubt about Irish Municipalities.

Sydney Smith

713. Lady Holland

33, Charles-street, Berkley-square, ⟨1836⟩*

My dear Lady Hd

On Saty I dine with Sr Stratford* or as they call him Sr Straightforward Canning, and can only dine at H H on Sunday as I am on religious guard at St. Pauls where I pray incessantly that John Allen may be reconciled to the Church, but I am afraid Canterbury (his friend) would not hear of it without fresh Baptism. This I call pious pedantry; at the same time to see John in his riper years at the font, to witness the first entrance of Creed into his mind, and the 39 Articles comfortably settling themselves in his understanding, it really would be a spectacle not devoid of interest, nor one which Mrs. Brown* could behold without pleasure.

health and respect.
S S.

714. LORD MELBOURNE

33, Charles-street, Berkley-square,
March 25th, 1836

Dear Lord Melbourne,

I have a son who strange to say has an aversion to going into holy orders, and I want to put him in some public office. I shall take it as an act of kindness if you will do this for me. I care not how small the salary is. I merely want the Occupation.

I except from my request the Treasury where there is an Examination – not that the young man is incompetent but nervous, and might fail from agitation rather than from deficiency.

Wyndham my son is between 21 and 22,* has just taken his degree at Cambridge, has some natural shrewdness with only a moderate attachment to Greek and Roman Learning, but he will be diligent and quiet.

I have mentioned the Treasury as an exception, but I believe many other suchlike appointments are at your disposal such as the Audit office, etc., etc. If you will do something of this kind for me I shall be seriously obliged to you.

A sad affair this inaugural Lecture of Hampden;* instead of being like the worldly Hampden, martial and truculent, it is elegiac, precatory, and hypocritical. I would have fetched blood at every sentence, perpetually enquiring placetne vobis Domini Doctores? placetne vobis Domini Magistri?

Ever yours
Sydney Smith

719. MRS. AUSTIN

July, 1836

Dear Mrs. Austin,

I shall have great pleasure in calling for you to go to Mrs.
Charles Buller* Wednesday, but we are going to the Duchess of
Sutherland's concert, and as Mrs. Sydney cannot go alone I must
leave Mrs. Buller's at 1/2 past 9. I can put you down then if it is
not too early for you. Mrs. Sydney's arm is rather better, many
thanks for the inquiry.

Very high and very low temperatures extinguish all human
sympathy and relations. It is impossible to feel any affection
beyond 78 and below 20 Fahrenheit; human nature is too solid or
too liquid beyond these limits. Man only lives to shiver or to per-
spire. God send that the glass may fall, and restore me to my regard for you which in the temperate zone is invariable.

ever yrs
Sydney Smith

729. LADY DACRE*

33, Charles-street, ⟨Jan. ?⟩ 1837

Many thanks, dear Lady Dacre, for your beautiful translations
in your beautiful book –

I read forthwith several beautiful sonnets upon Love, which
paint with great fidelity some of the worst symptoms of that
terrible disorder, than which none destroys more completely the
happiness of common existence, and substitutes for the activity
which Life demands a long and sickly dream with moments of
pleasure and days of intolerable pain. The Poets are full of false
views: they make mankind believe that happiness consists in falling in love, and living in the country – I say: live in London; like
many people, fall in love with nobody. To these rules of life I
add: read Lady Dacre's Translations, and attend her Monday
evening parties.

Ever yours,
Sydney Smith

734. LORD JOHN RUSSELL

33, Charles-street, Berkley-square,
April 3rd, 1837

My dear John,

At 11 o'clock in the morning, some years since, the AB of Canterbury called upon the AB of York (my informant) and said, 'I am going to the King (George the 3d) to meet Perceval who wants to make Mansell* Bishop of Bristol. I have advised the King not to assent to it and he is thoroughly determined *it shall not be*. I will call in an hour or two and tell you what has past.' Canterbury did not return before 11 o'clock at night. 'Quite in vain' he said 'Perceval has beaten us all; he tendered his immediate resignation. If he were not considered to be a fit person for recommending the dignitaries of the Church he was not a fit person to be at the head of the Treasury. After a conflict carried on all day, we were forced to yield.'

Such a conflict carried on once and ending with victory never need be repeated. Pretended Heterodoxy is the plea with which those rascally Bishops endeavour to keep off from the Bench every man of spirit and independence, and to terrify you into the appointment of feeble men who will be sure to desert you (as all your Bishops have lately and shamefully done) in a moment of peril. When was a greater clamour excited than by the appointment of Maltby? or when were there stronger charges of Heterodoxy? Lord Grey disregarded all this and they are forgotten.

I know not, by alluding to the chess-board, whether you mean the charges which Canterbury might make against *me*, or against liberal men in general. I defy Canterbury to quote a single passage of my writing contrary to the doctrines of the Church; for I have always avoided speculative, and preached practical, religion. I defy him to mention a single action in my life which he can call immoral. The only thing he could charge me with, would be high spirits and much innocent nonsense. I am distinguished as a preacher and sedulous as a parochial clergyman. His real charge is, that I am an high-spirited honest uncompromising man, whom he and all the Bench of Bishops could not turn, and who would set them all at defiance upon vital questions. This is the reason why (as far as depends upon others) I am not a Bishop; *but I am thoroughly sincere in saying I would not take any Bishopric whatever, and to this I pledge my honor and character as a gentleman.* But, had I been a Bishop you wd have seen me, on a late occasion, charging Canterbury and London with a gallantry which would have warmed your heart's blood, and made Melbourne rub the skin off his hands.

The only good the Ministry can do me is to give my son some place of some emolument in some public office. He is at present a clerk in the Audit Office at £90 pr. ann. This is all I wish and want in this world, and this would be a receipt in full for that Mitre to which long life of depression for liberal principles bravely avowed had doomed me to the age of 63. – Pray shew this letter to Lord Melbourne and believe me dear John always sincerely yours

Sydney Smith

Make Ed Stanley and Caldwell,* a friend of Ld Lansdowne's and mine; both unexceptional men.

745. ARTHUR KINGLAKE*

Combe Florey, Sept. 30th, 1837

Dear Sir,

I am much obliged by the present of your brother's book.* I am convinced digestion is the great secret of life; and that character, talents, virtues, and qualities are powerfully affected by beef, mutton, pie-crust, and rich soups. I have often thought I could feed or starve men into many virtues and vices, and affect them more powerfully with my instruments of cookery than Timotheus could do formerly with his lyre. Ever yours, very truly,

Sydney Smith

747. MRS. PENNINGTON*

November 9th, 1837

Ah, dear Lady! is it you? Do I see again your handwriting? and when shall I see yourself? (as the Irish say). You may depend upon it, all lives out of London are mistakes, more or less grievous; – but mistakes.

I am alone in London, without Mrs. Smith, upon duty at St· Paul's. London, however, is full, from one of these eternal dissolutions and reassemblage of Parliaments, with which these latter days have abounded. I wish you were back again: nobody is so agreeable, so frank, so loyal, so good-hearted. I do not think I have made any new female friends since I saw you, but have been faithful to you. But I love excellence of all kinds, and seek and cherish it.

The Whigs remain in; they are in no present danger. Did you read my pamphlet against the Bishops, and how did you like it?

I have not seen your friend Jeffrey for these two years. He did not come to town last year. I hear with the greatest pleasure of his fame as a judge.

I am going back to Combe Florey the end of the month, to remain till the beginning of March; and then in London for some months, where I sincerely hope to see you. To see you again will be like the resurrection of flowers in the spring: the bitterness of solitude, I shall say, is past.

God bless you, dear Mrs. Pennington,
Sydney Smith

756. R. MONCKTON MILNES*

33, Charles-street, Berkeley-square,
June 20th, 1838

My dear Sir,

I began years ago to breakfast with Rogers, and I must go on unless he leaves off asking me, but I must not make any fresh alliance of this sort, for it deranges me for the whole day, and I

am a very old gentleman, and must take care of myself, a duty I
owe to my parish, or rather I should say two parishes. But you
have, luckily for you, no such plea, and therefore you must come
and breakfast with me on Saturday morning next, at ten o'clock
precisely. Say that you will do this.

Yours truely
Sydney Smith

758. Miss G. Harcourt

Charles-street, ⟨July,⟩ 1838

My dear Georgiana,

You see how desirous I am to do what you bid me. In general,
nothing is so foolish as to recommend a medicine. If I am doing a
foolish thing, you are not the first young lady who has driven an
old gentleman to this line of action.

That loose and disorderly young man, E—— H——,* has
mistaken my wishes for my powers, and has told you that I proposed to do, what I only said I should be most happy to do. I
have overstayed my time so much here, that I *must* hasten home,
and feed my starving flock. I should have left London before, but
how could I do so, in the pains and perils of the Church, which I
have been defending at all moral hazards? Young tells me that
nothing will induce the Archbishop to read my pamphlets, or to
allow you to read them.

The summer and the country, dear Georgiana, have no charms
for me. I look forward anxiously to the return of bad weather,
coal fires, and good society in a crowded city. I have no relish for
the country; it is a kind of healthy grave. I am afraid you are not
exempt from the delusions of flowers, green turf, and birds; they
all afford slight gratification, but not worth an hour of rational
conversation: and rational conversation in sufficient quantities is
only to be had from the congregation of a million of people in one
spot. God bless you!

Sydney Smith

759. LADY HOLLAND

September 6th, 1838

If all the friends, dear Lady Holland, who have shared in your kindness and hospitality, were to give a little puff, you would be blown over to Calais with a gentle and prosperous gale. I admire your courage; and earnestly hope, as I sincerely believe, that you will derive great amusement and satisfaction, and therefore improved health, from your expedition.

I am out of temper with Lord Melbourne, and upon the subject of the Church; but in case of an election, I should vote as I always have done, with the Whigs. As for little John, I love him, though I chastise him. I have never lifted up my voice against the Duke of Lancaster; I should be the most ungrateful of men if I did.

We have had a run of blue-stocking ladies to Combe Florey this summer, a race you despise. To me they are agreeable, and less insipid than the general run of women; for *you know*, *my Lady*, *the female mind does not reason*.

Kindest regards to the Duke of Lancaster.

S. S.

760. LORD LANSDOWNE

Taunton, Sept. 14th, 1838

Dear Lord Lansdowne,

Do what you like with the Church, it will never make the slightest alteration in my respect and regard for you. All that I require is full permission in shilling pamphlets to protest that we are the most injured, persecuted, and ill-treated persons on the face of the Earth. Against Lord Holland and you personally I could not, and would not, write a single syllable, and of course you must both laugh at such nonsense I put forth from time to time.

After all the Residence and Plurality Bill was (as it came out of the Commission) a very bad Bill. I could point out eleven or twelve very material points, bearing strongly upon the happiness of the parochial clergy, which have been omitted or completely changed in the passage of the Bill through Parliament; to all of these I objected, and though I do not of course imagine that I had weight and authority to produce these changes, yet it shows that my hostility was not frivolous and vexatious.

The Bill is now a very good Bill. The original Bill was bad, because John Russell, legislating on what it is not likely he could understand, took his information from bishops, who were sure to mislead him because they consulted their own power. In the same way I am sure that his Dean and Chapter Bill may be very materially improved, and that the errors it contains proceed from the same source.

Many thanks for the venison, which arrived here safely today, and apparently in very good condition. We have had a great run of blue-stocking ladies here this summer, and are expecting more. I have had a fit of the gout, which I chased away speedily with Colchicum. Are you going to make your promised tour to Lynton? If so, pray come and see us, you and yours.

I am very much obliged by your good-natured and sensible letter, which gave me great pleasure and satisfaction; for I should have been heartily sorry that my defence of my profession should have been construed into the most distant intention of ill-will and hostility to *you*; and to show you how little I consider the venison as deprecatory, I will put into my next pamphlet any abuse of yourself which you choose to dictate, but decline entirely to insert any of my own –

Ever sincerely yours
Sydney Smith

765. LADY GREY

33, Charles-street, Berkley-square,
Nov. 14th, 1838

My dear Lady Grey,

I have been here since the beginning of the month but have no news to tell you.

I think Lord Durham has made a great mistake,* but he is a man of great Ability and we shall see what sort of a case he makes. In the mean time old Satan Brougham is in raptures and tells the

Duke of Wellington if he will turn these people out that he Brougham will leave the Country for 2 Years. The Duke of Wellington says he is quite mad. I have dined twice with the Hollands; I never saw them or the Atheist* better. – Their Expedition answered perfectly, they are delighted with Louis Philippe, Versailles, and everything, and very much flattered with the order they obtained from the government that the Post Horses were to go only 3 miles an hour with Lady Holland.

They are beginning to open Batteries against Lord Melburne and the Queen; the Spectator of last week represented Roebuck and Brougham rushing in, pulling Lord Melburne from under the table and stabbing him.* Lord Glenelg* will not go out. They talk of Minto* going to Canada – and that Hobhouse* is to be a Peer. All this you probably know better than I do but I give it you as I have it.

Mrs. Sydney would not leave her garden; her health is very much improved. I return to C Florey the end of this month where all the Hibberts join me immediately to pass the Winter and I shall be in Town the end of February. I hear that the Carlisles are prospering in Italy.

We have never been a single day at C Florey without a succession of Company principally learned blue Stocking Ladies, whose Society Lord Grey so particularly loves.

They are going to bring in Mcauley into Cutler Ferguson's situation* Ferguson cannot recover. Mcaulay had resolved to lead a Literary Life but cannot withstand the temptation – like Ladies who resolve upon celibacy if they have no offers – I find London very agreeable and as full as I wish it. I have dined out almost every day since I have been in London. The Bishop of Glocester has attacked me in his charge almost by name; I will repay him with 5 p. Cent Compound Interest. – *Oh Simon Simon I have somewhat to say unto thee.** The Bishop of London has also defended the Commission; with the blessing of God I will overturn them both, and smite them sorely. Pray tell me something about yourself and the Greys, about your health and my Lord, and Georgiana, and believe me dear Lady Grey affectionately and sincerely your old and true friend

                                                    Sydney Smith

766. C. COCKERELL*

33, Charles-street, Berkley-square,
Nov. 22nd, 1838

Sr

knowing the time and trouble I have given up to the Cathedral
I think it is but fair that the paid architect of the Cathedral
should render me some assistance when I request his advice. If I
am not successful in obtaining this I must but shall do it with the
greatest reluctance obtain other professional assistance and
firmly state to the Trustees my reasons for doing so; I sincerely
hope however you will not drive me to this Expedient. I have
done so now out of my own pocket, but cannot again subject
myself to this Expence. I cannot but observe that while you tell
me that ill health prevents you from attending me in the Cathedral you have come there at an hour when you knew I was not
there. Your letter to me is dated from the Bank and you leave
Town for 10 days on business – I will not trouble you to call
upon me when you return – I have obtained elsewhere the
knowledge and information I thought I had a right to ask from
you. I am

Sr yr obt st
Sydney Smith

767. C. COCKERELL

33, Charles-street, Berkley-square,
Nov. 26th, 1838

Sr

Repayment to me for any little Expence I may have incurred
is of course wholly and entirely out of the Question.

I request of you to meet me at St Pauls upon important
business and mention the hours at which I am there giving you
in addition your chance of any other hour; a Week after you
come to St. Pauls without seeing me and a Week after that write
me word from the Bank, stating that your health is so bad that
you have not been able to call and that you are going out of Town

on business. All this is intelligible enough if you mean to say – '*I will not be put to inconvenience by your exertions, but will enjoy my Salary for doing nothing*' – but I ask you if there is common prudence in such conduct if you mean to be civil to me and attentive to your trust? I wish to go on with you quietly, civilly, and good naturedly as I do with Hodgson* and Sellon and other Officers of the Establishment. I honor your Genius and your tallents but then I must require in my turn, civility, and common attention.

I beg you will not give yourself the trouble of calling when you come to Town. I have made up my mind upon certain points and have really nothing now to communicate. When we meet in March we will talk over the State of the Cathedral. From me you will always experience that respect which your Situation as a Gentleman and your great Eminence in your profession have a right to command – When your health will permit I hope and believe I shall receive in return from you that professional attention which my Zeal for the Cathedral really deserves. What is past is of course forgotten

truely yrs
Sydney Smith

I am so far from standing on any etiquette that I will at any time call upon you, when you inform me that you are not well enough to come out.

777. Lady Hardy*

33, Charles-street, March 26th, 1839

My dear Lady Hardy,

I would rather have the approbation of Sir Thomas Hardy than that of several bishops. If Bishops approved, the sermons must be pompous, intolerant and full of useless Theology. If Sir Thomas likes them, they are true, honest and useful; and if you add your sanction, then at least I think I am not dull and that I am helping to pay off the debt we all owe you for looking so well and talking so agreeably.

Ever yours
Sydney Smith

778.* LADY HOLLAND

Oil 4 Tables
Vinegar 2
Salt 3 Tea Spoons
Essence of Anchovy 1
Mustard 1
the Yellow of two Eggs boild hard
2 or 3 potatoes boild and straind through a Sieve
1/2 a Tea Spoon of onion chopped very fine
Mix the Salad thoroughly just before it is used.

Turn over

too cold for Mrs. Sydney – many thinks.

782. MRS. MEYNELL

Charles-street, April, 1839

My dear Mrs. Meynell,

The Government is always crazy, but I see no immediate
signs of dissolution. The success of my pamphlet* has been very
great. I always told you I was a clever man, and you never would
believe me.

You must study Macaulay when you come to town. He is
incomparably the first lion in the Metropolis; that is, he writes,
talks, and speaks better than any man in England.

Kind regards to your husband.

Sydney Smith

783. CHARLES DICKENS

Charles-street, Berkeley-square,
June 11th, 1839

My dear Sir,

Nobody more, and more justly, talked of than yourself.

The Miss Berrys, now at Richmond, live only to become
acquainted with you, and have commissioned me to request you

to dine with them Friday, the 29th, or Monday, July 1st, to meet a Canon of St. Paul's, the Rector of Combe Florey, and the Vicar of Halberton, – all equally well known to you; to say nothing of other and better people. The Miss Berrys and Lady Charlotte Lindsay have not the smallest objection to be put into a Number, but, on the contrary, would be proud of the distinction; and Lady Charlotte, in particular, you may marry to Newman Noggs.* Pray come, it is as much as my place is worth to send them a refusal.

Sydney Smith

784. MRS. GROTE*

33, Charles-street, June 24th, 1839

I will dine with you, dear Mrs. Grote, on the 11th, with great pleasure.

The 'Great Western'* turns out very well, – grand, simple, cold, slow, wise, and good. I have been introduced to Miss ——; she abuses the privilege of literary women to be plain; and, in addition, has the true Kentucky twang through the nose, converting that promontory into an organ of speech. How generous the conduct of Mrs. ——,* who, as a literary woman, might be ugly if she chose, but is as decidedly handsome as if she were profoundly ignorant! I call such conduct honourable.

You shall have a real philosophical breakfast here; all mind-and-matter men. I am truly glad, my dear Mrs. Grote, to add you to the number of my friends (*i.e.* if you will be added). I saw in the moiety of a moment that you were made of fine materials, and put together by a master workman; and I ticketed you accordingly. But do not let me deceive you; if you honour me with your notice, you will find me a theologian and a bigot, even to martyrdom.

Heaven forbid I should deny the right of Miss ——, or of any other lady to ask me to dinner! the only condition I annex is, that you dine there also. As for any dislikes of mine, I would not give one penny to avoid the society of any man in England.

I do not preach at St. Paul's before the first Sunday in July; send me word (if you please) if you intend to come, and I (as the Americans say) will locate you. But do not flatter yourself with the delusive hope of a slumber; I preach violently, and there is a strong smell of sulphur in my sermons. I could not get Lady —— to believe you did not know her; she evidently considered it affectation. Why do you not consult Dr. Turnbull* upon tic-douloureux? I told you a long story about it, of which, I thought at the time, you did not hear a single word.

Adieu, dear Mrs. Grote! Always, with best compliments to Mr. Grote, very sincerely yours,

Sydney Smith

792. LADY GREY

⟨Charles-street, Oct. 1839⟩

My dear Lady Grey

I am in the great City, and the rumors I gather are I presume not very different from the opinions which prevail at Howick.

The appointment of Thomson* to Canada nothing but Success will justify. Mcauley is too professional a Speaker, he is brought in for the express purpose of Speechification, and an air of ridicule is thrown over the appointment. Mantalini* is all weakness, Lord Clarendon* is an useful acquisition. The most formidable event for the Whiggs will be the Queen's Marriage. Her attachment to Melbourne will be lessened, and she will become more a Tory. They have had a great loss in Howick and Wood, and they lose 3 Votes by the death of the two Dukes.

Lady Holland was in considerable danger last week from an obstruction; Dr. Holland says she behaved with great Corage. When the fire broke out at Lord Lilford's* Lady Holland woke up Allen, who hearing the Crackling of the flames, and smelling the Smoke and seeing Lady Hd conceived he had slipt off in the Night to a very serious place at an high Temperature; he attempted to recollect a prayer, but entirely failed, and was fairly pulled out of bed by Lady Hd and the maids –

I am quite delighted with my new house in Green St I have

one leg in it and the other here; it is everything I want or Wish.

I suppose the State of politics will make no difference in your movements, that you will come late in the Spring as usual; pray tell me how this is, and if Lord Grey and you are tolerably well. Had you the great Western Mr. Webster? and how did he answer? Lord Grey I know hates Lions. pray write to me to 56 Green Street Grosvenor Square.

Brougham by way of Joke made Shafto write the account of his (Brougham's) death; can anything be more silly?* He sinks lower every Week.

The Court Doctor* has done himself no good by his Statement. I cannot understand Melbourne's behaviour. - Ld Hastings asks him in a meaning manner who first mentioned the Subject to him, and Melbourne immediately guesses the name of Lady Tavistock.* I would have seen Ld Hastings at the bottom of the Caspian Sea before I would have told him.

The Whiggs are quite delighted with the article in the Edinburgh Review against Lord Lyndhurst; it is by Lytton Bulwer.* Pray remember me very kindly to the Earl, and all my Howick friends and believe me dear Lady Grey your old and affectionate friend

Sydney Smith

795. LADY HOLLAND

December 28th, 1839

I will dine with you on Saturday, my dear Lady Holland, with the greatest pleasure.

I have written against ——* one of the cleverest pamphlets I ever read, which I think would cover —— and him with ridicule. At least it made me laugh very much in reading it; and there I stood, with the printer's devil, and the real devil close to me; and then I said, 'After all, this is very funny, and very well written, but it will give great pain to people who have been very kind and good to me through life; and what can I do to show my sense of that kindness, if it is not by flinging this pamphlet into the fire?'

So I flung it in, and there was an end! My sense of ill-usage remains of course the same. The dialogue between —— —— and —— is, or I should rather say, was, most admirable.

Sydney Smith

798. MRS. CROWE*

January 6th, 1840

I am very glad to find, dear Mrs. Crowe, that you are so comfortably arranged at Edinburgh. I am particularly glad that you are intimate with Jeffrey. He is one of the *best*, as well as the *ablest*, men in the country: and his friendship is to you, honour, safety, and amusement.

I hate young men, and I hate soldiers; but I will be gracious to ——, if he will call upon me.

Among the many evils of getting old, one is, that every little illness may probably be the last. You feel like a delinquent who knows that the constable is looking out after him. I am not going to live at Barnes, or to quit Combe Florey; if ever I do quit Combe Florey, it will probably be to give up my country livings, and to confine myself to London only.

My 'Works' are now become too expensive to allow of the dispersion and presentation of many copies, but I shall with pleasure order one for you: the bookseller will send it. I printed my reviews to show, if I could, that I had not passed my life merely in making jokes; but that I had made use of what little powers of pleasantry I might be endowed with, to discountenance bad, and to encourage liberal and wise, principles. The publication has been successful. The Liberal journals praise me to the skies; the Tories are silent, grateful for my attack upon the Ballot.

Yours truly,
Sydney Smith

808. LADY HOLLAND

52, Marine-parade, Brighton, June, 1840

My dear Lady Holland,

You will (because you are very good-natured) be glad to hear that Brighton is rapidly restoring Mrs. Sydney to health. She gets better every three hours; and if she goes on so, I shall begin to be glad that Dr. —— is not here.

I am giving a rout this evening to the only three persons I have yet discovered at Brighton. I have had handbills printed to find other London people, but I believe there are none. I shall stay till the 28th. You *must* allow the Chain Pier to be a great luxury; and I think all rich and rational people living in London should take small doses of Brighton from time to time. There cannot be a better place than this to refresh metropolitan gentlemen and ladies, wearied with bad air, falsehood, and lemonade.

I am very deep in Lord Stowell's 'Reports,'* and if it were wartime I should officiate as Judge of the Admiralty Court. It was a fine occupation to make a public law for all nations, or to confirm one; and it is rather singular that so sly a rogue should have done it so honestly. Yours ever,

Sydney Smith

812. LADY GREY

⟨August, 1840⟩*

I was sure my dear Lady Grey that you would all feel Lord Durham's death severely, for in spite of his defects which were apparent there was a great deal of real excellence in him – poor Lady Durham!!!

Mrs. Sydney is better than she has been for some years. Gout and Asthma increase upon me.

I am glad the Marriage* is over; it was protracted too long; you have acquired a charming Daughter in Law. I send a little Note I have written to the Bp of London.

The Weather is glorious and the Crops good and well got in. There is staying with us that very singular and clever woman Mrs. Grote the queen of the radicals – the natives think her insane; I like her very much. It gave me sincere pleasure dear Lady Grey to see your handwriting. I have a great affection for you and Lord Grey and the little bit of Life which remains to us all does not make me love you less ——

Lady Holland in consequence of Marsh's death* has given up all thoughts of her Western Excursion and the Ducks and fowls and Turkies about Combe Florey have had a reprieve – She is collecting her Autumnal friends about her and giving loose to affections which are in abeyance when London is full and are never developed till the fall of the Leaf – The fallen Prebendaries like the Devils in the first book of Milton, are shaking themselves, and threatening War against the Bp of London. I am endeavoring to imitate Satan.*

I am sorry you did not see Castle Howard, though with all your aversion for Sights I think you will hardly be able to avoid it. Poor Lady Carlisle is very little calculated to bear up against the Storms of Life – She has lived all her days in the Greenhouse of prosperity – and shrinks from the open air. Remember me most kindly to Ld Grey, and Georgiana and believe me your affectionate friend

S. S.

814. BISHOP BLOMFIELD

The Times, 5 Sept., 1840

A few words more, my dear Lord, before we part, after a controversy of four years:—

In reading your speech, I was a good deal amused by your characteristic indignation at the idea of any man, or any body of men, being competent to offer you advice; at the same time I have a sort of indistinct recollection of your name, as defendant in courts of justice, where it appeared, not only to the judges who decided against you, but to your best friends also, that you would have made rather a better figure if you had begged a few contributions of wisdom and temper from those who had any to share: till these cases are erased from our legal reports, it would perhaps be expedient to admit for yourself a small degree of fallibility, and to leave the claim of absolute wisdom to Alderman Wood.*

You say that you always consult your archdeacon and rural dean; this I believe to be quite true – but then you generally consult them after the error, and not before. Immediately after this aspernation of all human counsel, I came to the following sentence, – such a sentence as I believe mortal and mitred man never spoke before, and the author of which, as it seems to me, should be loaded with four atmospheres of advice instead of one, and controlled regularly by that number of cathedral councils. In speaking of the 3,000 clergymen who have petitioned against the destruction of the church, you say –

'I could easily get as many to petition upon any subject connected with the church. The mode by which in the present case a great proportion of these signatures have been obtained is as follows: – the Archdeacon, who has always great influence with the parochial clergy, and justly so, as visiting them every year, and as being in habits of more familiar intercourse with them than their Bishop, and who is moreover considered by them as acting, in some degree, with the sanction of the Bishop, circulates printed forms of petition against the bill amongst the Rural Deans; the Rural Dean goes with them to the parochial clergy; and he must be a bold or a very well-informed man who refuses to sign a petition so recommended by his immediate ecclesiastical superiors.' – Pp. 6 and 7.

Now I am afraid you will be very angry with me, but for the life of me I cannot discover in this part of your speech any of those marks of unerring and unassistable wisdom – that perfect uselessness of counsellors to the Bishop of London of which you seem to be so intimately convinced; and this, remember, is not a lapse to be forgiven in the fervour of speaking, but a cold printed insult; or what is the plain English of the passage? 'Archdeacons and rural deans are a set of base and time-serving instruments, whom their superiors can set on for any purpose to abuse their power and influence over the lower clergy, and the lower clergy themselves are either in such a state of intellectual destitution that they cannot comprehend what they sign, or they are so miserably enthralled by their ecclesiastical superiors that they dare not dissent. I could put this depraved machinery in action for any church purpose I wished to carry.' If Lord Melbourne, in the exercise of his caprice, had offered me a bishopric, and I had been fool enough to have accepted it, this insult upon the whole body of the parochial clergy should not have been passed over with the silent impunity with which it was received in the House of Lords. You call me in the speech your facetious friend, and I hasten with gratitude in this letter to denominate you my solemn friend; but you and I must not run into commonplace errors; you must not think me necessarily foolish because I am facetious, nor will I consider you necessarily wise because you are grave; but whether foolish or facetious or what not, I admire and respect you too much not to deplore this passage in your speech; and, in spite of all your horror of being counselled by one of your own canons, I advise you manfully to publish another edition of your speech, and to expunge with the most ample apology this indecent aggression upon the venerable instructors of mankind.

In our future attacks upon the Catholics let us wisely omit our customary sarcasms on their regard for oaths. The only persons who appear to me to understand the doctrine of oaths are the two honest sheriffs whom Lord John put into prison for respecting them.

In the eighth page of your speech you say – 'I am continually brought into contact, in the discharge of my official duties, with vast masses of my fellow-creatures living without God in the world. I traverse the streets of this crowded city with deep and solemn thoughts of the spiritual condition of its inhabitants. I pass the magnificent church which crowns the metropolis, and is consecrated to the noblest of objects, the glory of God, and I ask of myself, in what degree it answers that object. I see there a dean and three residentiaries, with incomes amounting in the aggregate to between 10,000 l. and 12,000 l. a year. I see, too, connected with the cathedral 29 clergymen, whose offices are all but sinecures, with an annual income of about 12,000 l. at the present moment, and likely to be very much larger after the lapse of a few years. I proceed a mile or two to the E. and N.E., and find myself in the midst of an immense population in the most wretched state of destitution and neglect, artisans, mechanics, labourers, beggars, thieves, to the number of at least 300,000.'

This stroll in the metropolis is extremely well contrived for your Lordship's speech; but suppose, my dear Lord, that instead of going E. and N.E., you had turned about, crossed London-bridge, and, resolving to make your walk as impartial as possible, had proceeded in a S.W. direction, you would soon in that case have perceived a vast palace, containing, not a dean, three residentiaries, and 29 clergymen, but one attenuated prelate with an income enjoyed by himself alone, amounting to 30,000 l. per annum, twice as great as that of all these confiscated clergymen put together; not one penny of it given up by act of Parliament during his life to that spiritual destitution which he so deeply deplores, and 15,000 l. per annum secured to his successor: though all the duties of the office might be most effectually performed for one third of the salary.

Having refreshed yourself, my dear Lord, by the contemplation of this beautiful and consistent scene, and recovered a little from those dreadful pictures of spiritual destitution which have been obtruded upon you by the sight of St. Paul's, you must continue our religious promenade to the banks of the Thames; but, as the way is long, let us rest ourselves for a few minutes in your palace in St. James's-square, no scene certainly of carnal and secular destitution. Having halted for a few minutes in this mansion of humility, we shall now be able to reach your second palace of Fulham, where I think your animal spirits will be restored, and the painful theme of spiritual destitution be for the moment put to sleep. 20,000 l. per annum to the present possessor increasing in value every hour, not a shilling legally given up during life to 'the masses who are living without God', and 10,000 l. per annum secured to the successor. I know that you are both of you generous and munificent men, but 2,000 l. or 3,000 l. subscribed, though much more observed, is much more economical also, than a fixed and legal diminution of an income, now out of all character and proportion, for those who feel the spiritual destitution so deeply. But these feelings upon spiritual destitution, my Lord, are of the most singular description; they seem to be under the most perfect control when bishops are to be provided for, and of irresistible plenitude and power when prebends are to be destroyed; such charity is the charity of my poor dear friend, old Lady C——, who was so powerfully affected (she said) by my sermon, that she borrowed a sovereign of some gentleman in the pew and put it in the plate.

My Lord, you are a very able, honest, and good man, but I pray you, as one of your council, be a little more discreet. You have taught the enemies of the church a fearful lesson, and they are very good scholars. In the midst of your ecclesiastical elegies upon spiritual destitution, take care they do not turn upon you and say, 'We can place the bench of Bishops in a position by which their usefulness will be materially increased, and 60,000 l per annum be saved for the spiritual destitution of the church.'

'But, my Lords, the learned counsel and those whom he represents, are grievously mistaken if they imagine that the calm, or rather lull, which now prevails, will be of long continuance, if no effective measures are taken to remove or lessen the anomalies which our Bishops now present, and to make them really conducive to the spiritual instruction of the people. The winds are chained for a season in their cavern; but ere long they will burst forth with redoubled violence, and shipwreck perhaps the vessel of the established church. Bishops may repose a few years longer in their stalls, unshorn of a single item of dignity or revenue; but by and by reform will come upon them as a strong man armed, and will take from them their armour wherein they trusted, and divide the spoils.' – p. 15.

Your foolish printer has injured the passage by printing it 'Deans and Chapters' instead of Bishops.

It is very easy, my Lord, to swing about in the House of Lords, and to be brave five years after the time, and to point out to their Lordships the clear difference between moral and physical fear, and to be nodded to by the Duke of Wellington, but I am not to be paid by such coin. I believe that the old-fashioned, orthodox, hand-shaking, bowel-disturbing passion of fear had a good deal to do with the whole reform. You choose to forget it, but I remember the period when the Bishops never remained unpelted;

they were pelted going, coming, riding, walking, consecrating, and carousing; the Archbishop of Canterbury, in the town of Canterbury, at the period of his visitation, was only saved from the mob by the dexterity of his coachman. If you were not frightened by all this, I was, and would have given half my preferment to save the rest; but then I was not a Commissioner, and had no great interests committed to my charge. If such had been my lot, I would have looked severely into my own soul.

You have laid yourself open to some cruel replies and retorts in various parts of your pamphlet speech; but the law is past, and the subject is at an end.

You are fast hastening on, with the acclamations and gratitude of the Whigs, to Lambeth, and I am hastening, after a life of 70 years, with gout and asthma, to the grave. I am most sincere, therefore, when I say, that in the management of this business you have (in my opinion) made a very serious and fatal mistake: you have shaken the laws of property, and prepared the ruin of the church by lowering the character of its members, and encouraging the aggressions of its enemies. That your error has been the error of an upright, zealous, and honest man, I have not the most remote doubt. I have fought you lustily for four years, but I admire your talents, and respect your character as sincerely as I lament the mistakes into which you have been hurried by the honest and headlong impetuosity of your nature.

I remain, my Lord, your obedient humble servant,

Sydney Smith

815. LADY CARLISLE

⟨Combe Florey⟩, Sept. 5th, 1840

I should be very glad to hear how all is going on at Castle Howard, dear Lady Carlisle, and whether my Lord and you keep up health and spirits with tolerable success; – a difficult task in the fifth act of life, when the curtain must ere long drop, and the comedy or tragedy be brought to an end.

Mrs. Sydney is still living on the stock of health she laid up at

Brighton; I am pretty well, except gout, asthma, and pains in all the bones, and all the flesh, of my body. What a very singular disease gout is! It seems as if the stomach fell down into the feet. The smallest deviation from right diet is immediately punished by limping and lameness, and the innocent ankle and blameless instep are tortured for the vices of the nobler organs. The stomach having found this easy way of getting rid of inconveniences, becomes cruelly despotic, and punishes for the least offences. A plum, a glass of champagne, excess in joy, excess in grief, - any crime, however small, is sufficient for redness, swelling, spasms, and large shoes.

I have found it necessary to give ——* a valedictory flagellation. I know you and my excellent friend, Earl Carlisle, disapprove of these things; but you must excuse all the immense differences of temper, training, situation, habits, which make Sydney Smith one sort of person, and the Lord of the Castle another, - and both right in their way. Lord Carlisle does not like the vehicle of a newspaper; but if a man wants to publish what is too short for a pamphlet, what other vehicle is there? Lord Lansdowne, and Philpotts, and the Bishop of London make short communications in newspapers. The statement of duels is made in newspapers by the first men in the country. To write anonymously in a newspaper is an act of another description; but if I put my name to what I write, the mere vehicle is surely immaterial; and I am to be tried, not by *where* I write, but *what* I write. I send the newspaper.

Ah, dear Lady Carlisle! do not imagine, because I did not knock every day at your door, and molest you with perpetual inquiries, that I have been inattentive to all that has passed, and careless of what you and Lord Carlisle have suffered. I have a sincere respect and affection for you both, and never forget your great kindness to me. God bless and preserve you!

Sydney Smith

818. Mrs. ——*

56, Green-street, Nov. 18th, 1840

An earthquake may prevent me. dear Mrs. ——, a civil commotion attended with bloodshed, or fatal disease, – but it must
be some cause as powerful as these. Pray return the enclosed
when you have read it, as I have borrowed it. Yours affectionately,
S. S.

I have heard from Mrs. Grote, who is very well, and amusing
herself with Horticulture and Democracy, – the most approved
methods of growing cabbages and destroying kings.*

822. Mrs. Meynell

Combe Florey, Dec. 1840

My dear Georgina,
It is indeed a great loss to me; but I have learnt to live as a
soldier does in war, expecting that, on any one moment, the best
and the dearest may be killed before his eyes.

Promise me, in the midst of these afflicting deaths, that you
will remain alive; and if Death does tap at the door, say, 'I can't
come; I have promised a parson to see him out.'

These verses were found in Lord Holland's room in his handwriting: –

> 'Nephew of Fox, and friend of Grey, –
> Enough my meed of fame,
> If those who deign'd to observe me say
> I tarnish'd neither name.'

I have gout asthma and seven other maladies, but am otherwise
very well. God bless you, Gem of Needwood Forest!

Sydney Smith

1027. ARCHDEACON HALE*

Combe Florey, Taunton, Dec. 20th, 1840

My dear Sr

You are a romantic Canon to talk about warming St. Pauls. the only real way of doing it is to warm the County of Middlesex, to which our revenues are hardly adequate – but of this, and the immence field of Caloric in which your imagination is floating of the gigantic Tubes, and Brobdinag Thermometers you are constructing we will consult in the middle of February.

Lingard is the deputy Surveyor I generally give the orders through him. If it was any part where the beauty of stability or important repairs of the Cathedral were concerned I consulted Cockerell, if not, I gave the orders myself through Lingard. I mean where the work was to be done at the expense of the fabric. I see no sort of occasion for, nor objection to a conference with Cockerell.

Our excellent and good hearted Bishop* makes such dreadful work when he undertakes anything of this kind that I have strongly recommended him (but of course without alledging this reason) to wait till we are all assembed in London before he meddles with the Chorister School; but if he will not fall in with this advice, I agree to what is settled in my absence; but Hawes* has strong Statutable rights and is very litigious. I am afraid of a Law suit, the late action by a singing man was entirely brought about by his mismanagement – pray stop him if you can – and so with the appointment of a Vicar Choral – why make an illegal appointment ? Why not wait for the alteration in the bill ?* What hurry is there ? Hodgson divides the Fines* as they arise. We balance with Sellon once a year at the Audit in March, you may always see his books. The Cupola money* is never noticed by the Chapter nor ought to be so, for many reasons I will hereafter give you. You will find the Gas Lights alteration a very expensive measure and if any considerable change is meditated it ought I think to be agitated in Chapter. I need not say to a person of your sense and prudence that it will be better to wait a little and become acquainted with the Cathedral thoroughly before you plan any great alteration.

> I remain my dear Sr
> Yours very truely
> Sydney Smith

I hope in the time of fine weather to have an opportunity of shewing you my very pretty Parsonage.

To the Very Revd
  Archdeacon Hale
    Charter House
      London

823. LADY HOLLAND

> Combe Florey, Jan. 3rd, 1841

My dear Lady Holland,

I hope you are better than when I left town, and that you have found a house. I have had two months' holiday from gout. Do not imagine I have forgotten my annual tribute of a cheese, but my carriage is in the hands of the doctor, and I have not been able to get to Taunton; for I cannot fall into that absurd English fashion of going in open carriages in the months of December and January, – seasons when I should prefer to go in a bottle, well corked and sealed.

The Hibberts are here, and the house full, light, and warm. Time goes on well. I do all I can to love the country, and endeavour to believe those poetical lies which I read in Rogers and others, on the subject; which said deviations from truth were, by Rogers, all written in St. James's-place.

I have long since got rid of all ambition and wish for distinctions, and am much happier for it. The journey is nearly over, and I am careless and good-humoured; at least good-humoured for me, as it is not an attribute which has been largely conceded to me by Providence.

Accept my affectionate and sincere good wishes.

> Sydney Smith

827. Mrs. Crowe

Combe Florey, Jan. 31st, 1841

Dear Mrs. Crowe.

I quite agree with you as to the horrors of correspondence.
Correspondences are like small-clothes before the invention of
suspenders; it is impossible to keep them up.

That episode of Julia is much too long.* Your incidents are
remarkable for their improbability. A boy goes on board a frigate
in the middle of the night, and penetrates to the captain's cabin
without being seen or challenged. Susan climbs into a two-pair-
of-stairs window to rescue two grenadiers. A gentleman about to
be murdered, is saved by rescuing a woman about to be drowned,
and so on. The language is easy, the dialogue natural. There is a
great deal of humour; the plot is too complicated. The best part
of the book is Mr. and Mrs. Ayton; but the highest and most
important praise of the novel is that you are carried on eagerly,
and that it excites and sustains a great interest in the event, and
therefore I think it a very good novel, and will recommend it.

It is in vain that I study the subject of the Scotch Church. I
have heard it ten times over from Murray, and twenty times from
Jeffrey, and I have not the smallest conception what it is about.
I know it has something to do with oatmeal, but beyond that I am
in utter darkness. Everybody here is turning Puseyite. Having
worn out my black gown, I preach in my surplice; this is all the
change I have made, or mean to make.

There seems to be in your letter a deep-rooted love of the
amusements of the world. Instead of the ever gay Murray and
the never silent Jeffrey, why do you not cultivate the Scotch
clergy and the elders and professors? I would then have some
hopes of you.

Sydney Smith

1029. ARCHDEACON HALE

Combe Florey, Taunton, Feb. 9th, 1841

My dear Sr

My eyes are bad and I hope to be in Town next week, these are reasons why I must answer your Letter concisely. With respect to what people say you will agree with me that we must do what is right, and let people say what they will. Every Cathedral is surrounded with an Atmosphere of nonsense and impertinence – we must pass through it and never mind it.

I have investigated with great pains many Complaints and have often found them to proceed from the unreasonable partialities and expectations of parents. There is one father with an handsome Roman countenance who I daresay has sent me two Quires of Writing and is always in the Wrong. I forget his name.

All that I think it necessary for a Chorister to learn are, besides Music, Reading, Writing, the Knowledge of his religion and Arithmetic, and these things they have hitherto learnt very fairly.

The whole Institution of Singing boys is a gross absurdity and instead of doubling them I should be glad to reduce them to one half.

I think their distance from the Cathedral a great advantage instead of an evil. It would in my opinion be quite improper to put them in the Chapter House for many reasons I will give you, but as that if even desireable could not be done immediately the discussion may be postponed.

The most preferable method of educating Choristers is to pay them for their singing as is done in Westminster and to pay to each parent a sum for the educating his own Child. This I am sure might easily be done at the decease or resignation of Hawes, as easily as it is done at Westminster.

As to Hawes we must proceed with him cautiously according to the facts; he understands his rights is litigious and would be supported.

Do not I beseech you raise up Minor Canon Insurrections. If in the depth of Winter there are enough on week days to carry on the Service, leave well alone, they will plague your heart out and we shall have eternal battles in the papers. We are in a state of transition to the new condition of the Minor Canonry let us descend quietly as we can.

Having given up the care of the Cathedral to you, I have no disposition to meddle with your arrangements about the future all that I require is that the *Dean and Chapter Money* is not expended without either an order of Chapter or without my consent. The fabric money I advise you to spend and not to suffer it to accumulate. You will do more good by spending it.

I make no apology to a Gentleman of your excellent Sense for writing plainly upon matters of business and I remain my dear Sr yours always very truely

Sydney Smith

854. LADY DAVY

Combe Florey, Taunton,
Aug. 31st, 1841

My dear Lady Davy,

I thank you for your very kind Letter which gave to Mrs. Sydney and me much pleasure and carried us back agreeably into past times. We are both tolerably well bulging out like old Houses but with no *immediate* intention of tumbling down.

The Country is in a state of political transition and the Shabby are preparing their consciences and opinions for a Tack. The Queen likes it least of anybody, and declares loudly that the coming Prince of Wales she is sure will resemble Peel in countenance and manner. A short prayer against this tucked into the Litany might possibly do some Good.

I think all our common friends are doing well, some are fatter some more spare, none handsomer, but such as they are I think you will see them all again – but pray do you mean to see any of us again or do you mean to end your days at Rome? a Town I am told you have entirely enslaved, and where in spite of your protestantism you are omnipotent – Your *Protestantism* but I confess that reflection makes me sometimes melancholy; your attachment to the Clergy generally, the activity of your mind, the Roman Catholic spirit of proselytism, all alarm me. I am afraid they will get hold of you and we shall lose you from the Church of England. Only promise me that you will not give up till you have subjected their arguments to my examination and given me a chance of reply. Tell them that there is *un Canonico dottissimo* to whom you have pledged your theological faith. Excuse my zeal, it is an additional proof of my affection, which wants however no additional proof. God bless you my dear Lady Davy. Your affectionate friend

Sydney Smith

855. *From* ROBERT SMITH*

Cheam, Sept. 5th, 1841

My dear Sydney,

I go on as most old fellows do, *nec recte nec suaviter*! I should like to be with you at Combe Florey, but I have not energy enough to go. The number of hours matters little; it is the preparation and the displacement. . . . I am not sorry the Whigs are out. The country was tired of them, I think, and always will be after a short time. There is too much botheration in their politics for our people, who, though they have reformed more than all the nations of Europe put together, do not like scheming and planning reforms when the work is not in hand, and called for by some pressing occasion; they have something else to do, and talking about reform disturbs them. I do myself think the state of things best suited to our condition is a Tory Government, checked by a strong opposition, and under the awe of a tolerably Liberal public opinion. That is pretty near what we shall have if Peel can keep his army in order. But who will answer for that? I am glad to hear so good an account of you all. God bless you, dear Sydney! Love to your wife.

Your affectionate brother
Robert Smith

859. MRS. AUSTIN

Green-street, Oct. 29th, 1841

My dear Mrs. Austin,

It grieves me to think you will not be in England this winter. The privations of winter are numerous enough without this. The absence of leaves and flowers I could endure, and am accustomed to; but the absence of amiable and enlightened women I have not hitherto connected with the approach of winter, and I do not at all approve of it.

Great forgeries of Exchequer Bills* in England and all the world up in arms; the evil to the amount of £200,000 or £300,000. Sanguine people imagine Lord Monteagle will be hanged.* I am a holder of Exchequer Bills to some little amount, and am quaking for fear. Poor Jeffrey is at Empson's,* very ill, and writing in a melancholy mood of himself. He seems very reluctant to resign his seat on the Bench, and no wonder, where he gains every day great reputation, and is of great use; – still he may gain a few years of life if he will be quiet, and fall into a private station.

Mrs. Grote is, I presume, abroad, collecting at Rome, for Roebuck and others, anecdotes of Catiline and the Gracchi. She came to Combe Florey again this year, which was very kind and flattering. I have a high opinion of, and a real affection for her; she has an excellent head, and an honest and kind heart.

The Tories are going on quite quietly, and are in for a dozen years. I am living in London this winter quite alone; – pity me, and keep for me a little portion of remembrance and regard. Your affectionate friend,

Sydney Smith

861. THOMAS MOORE

November 12th, 1841

Dear Moore, –

I have a breakfast of philosophers tomorrow at ten *punctually*. Muffins and metaphysics; crumpets and contradiction. Will you come?

862.* MISS COURTENAY

56, Green-street, Nov. 13th, 1841

My dear Miss Courtenay,

I never preach well – but I shall preach worse for not numbering you among my Congregation.

There never was such a confusion of Tongues since the Poly-
glossary of the Tower of Babel.

There are those who think these questions of little consequence
– I look back with remorse and regret at the time I have wasted,
and the late period of Life at which my attention has been
awakened to esculent investigations – I will talk the matter over
with you not write it – in the mean⟨time⟩ let me beg of you to
put down on paper any dicta upon the Table which fall from
your father however loosely or carelessly spoken – when his
Works are published in two Courses how inestimable will your
collection be – how Boswell will fall into the shade.

Yours dear Lady very sincerely
Sydney Smith

I see a book advertised, *Hasty thoughts on Pickles*. Am I right
in my conjecture as to the Author?

863. LADY GREY

56, Green-street, Grosvenor-square,
Nov. 15th, 1841

My dear Lady Grey

being in London I think it is but a Christian proceeding to
write to my Country friends.

London is still full for the time of Year. The Exchequer Bills
and the queen's Accouchment* have kept multitudes away from
the Country.

I was very much frightened about Exchequer Bills having
£1200 in that sort of paper, but they all proved to be good. Couts
the Banker is [is] got into a Scrape which is not considered as
very creditable to him; he suffers in false Bills to the amount of
£40,000; the same bargain had been offered to Glyn, and

Masterman and had been rejected by them. Lady Holland is as well as I have seen her for many years, and has laid aside the character though not the dress of a Widow. I meet Lord Melbourne there very often who giggles, and rubs his hands and sweats as when in Office. I hope Lord Grey has read and likes Mcauley's* review of Warren Hastings, it is very much admired. I believe Mcauley is unaffectedly glad to have given up Office. Literature is his Vocation. Nothing would do him more good than a course of the Waters of Lethe; if he could forget half of what he reads he would be less suffocating than he is; he breakfasted with me this morning in company with three other very clever men much disposed to talk, but it was not Mcauley's disposition that they should say a word, I might as well have had three Mutes from a funeral.

Rogers has gone to Paris with the Dowager Lady Essex and her niece;* it is not yet known which of the two he has married. no great Mischief is done at the Tower.*

The Tories seem to be going on very quietly – I shall stay in Town till the end of the first week in December, and then go to the Country till the Middle of February. God bless you dear Lady Grey, I beg my kind regards to all

Yours affecly.
Sydney Smith

879*b*.* SAMUEL ROGERS

56 Green St., Apr. 12th, 1842

My dear Rogers, –

I have always intended to send you these volumes,* but have been always unwilling to place such ordinary matter upon a library table around which the great and the wise are so often gathered. I remember, however, that you are not only an author of the highest distinction, but a politician of unblemished honesty, and that if you thought little of my powers you would still value my principles – nor was my vanity forgotten, for I trusted your guests would say, 'If Sydney Smith was not a Liberal and an upright man we should not find his books on the table of Samuel Rogers.'

Sydney Smith

880. R. MONCKTON MILNES

56, Green-street, April 22nd, 1842

Dear Milnes,

Never lose your good temper, which is one of your best qualities, and which has carried you hitherto safely through your *startling eccentricities*. If you turn cross and touchy, you are a lost man. No man can combine the defects of opposite characters. The names of *the Cool of the evening, London Assurance, Inigo Jones*, are, *I give you my word*, not mine. They are of no sort of importance, they are safety valves, and if you could by paying sixpence get rid of them, you had better keep your money.

You do me justice in acknowledging that I have spoken much good of you. I have laughed at you for those follies which I have told you of to your face; but nobody has more loudly and more constantly asserted that you were a very agreeable, clever man, with a very good heart, unimpeachable in all the relations of life, and that you *amply deserved* to be *retained* in the place to which you have too hastily elevated yourself by manners unknown to our cold and phlegmatic people.

I thank you for what you say of my good-humour. Lord Dudley, when I took leave of him, said to me, 'You have been laughing at me for the last seven years, and you never said anything that I wished unsaid.' This pleased me.

Ever yours
S S

882. CHARLES DICKENS

May 14th, 1842

My dear Dickens,

I accept your obliging invitation conditionally. If I am invited by any man of greater genius than yourself, or one by whose works I have been more completely interested, I will repudiate you, and dine with the more splendid phenomenon of the two.

Ever yours sincerely,
Sydney Smith

889. J. A. Murray

Combe Florey, Sept. 12th, 1842

My dear Murray,

How did the Queen receive you?* What was the general effect of her visit? Was it well managed? Does she show any turn for metaphysics? Have you had much company in the Highlands?

Mrs. Sydney and I are both in fair health, – such health as is conceded to moribundity and caducity.

Horner applied to me, and I sent him a long letter upon the subject of his brother, which he likes, and means to publish in his Memoirs. He seeks the same contribution from Jeffrey. Pray say to Jeffrey that he ought to send it. It is a great pity that the subject has been so long deferred. The mischief has all proceeded from the delays of poor Whishaw, who cared too much about reputation, to do anything in a period compatible with the shortness of human life. If you have seen Jeffrey, tell me how he is, and if you think he will stand his work.*

We have the railroad now within five miles. Bath in two hours, London in six, – in short, everywhere in no time! Every fresh accident on the railroads is an advantage, and leads to an improvement. What we want is, an overturn which would kill a bishop, or, at least, a dean. This mode of conveyance would then become perfect. We have had but little company here this summer. Luttrell comes next week. I have given notice to the fishmongers, and poulterers, and fruit-women! Ever, dear Murray, your sincere friend,

Sydney Smith

891. Lady Holland

Combe Florey, Sept. 13th, 1842

My dear Lady Holland,

I am sorry to hear Allen is not well; but the reduction of his legs is a pure and unmixed good; they are enormous, – they are clerical! He has the creed of a philosopher and the legs of a clergyman; I never saw such legs, – at least, belonging to a layman.

Read 'A Life in the Forest', skipping nimbly; but there is much of good in it.*

It is a bore, I admit, to be past seventy, for you are left for execution, and are daily expecting the death-warrant; but, as you say, it is not anything very capital we quit. We are, at the close of life, only hurried away from stomach-aches, pains in the joints, from sleepless nights and unamusing days, from weakness, ugliness, and nervous tremors; but we shall all meet again in another planet, cured of all our defects. Rogers* will be less irritable; Macaulay more silent; Hallam will assent; Jeffrey will speak slower; Bobus will be just as he is; I shall be more respectful to the upper clergy; but I shall have as lively a sense as I now have of all your kindness and affection for me.

Sydney Smith

894. LADY DAVY

September 21st, 1842

My dear Lady Davy,

There is a demand for you in England, and a general inquiry whether you have given us up altogether. I always defend you, and say, if you have so done, that it is from no want of love for us, but from a rooted dislike of rheumatism, catarrh, and bodily *mal-être*, such as all true Britons undergo for eleven months and three weeks in the year.

What have I to tell you of our old friends? Lady Holland is tolerably well, with two courses and a French cook. She has fitted up her lower rooms in a very pretty style, and there receives the shattered remains of the symposiasts of the house. Lady —— has captivated Mr. ——, though they have not proceeded to the extremities of marriage. Mr. Luttrell is going gently down-hill, trusting that the cookery in another planet may be at least as good as in this; but not without apprehensions that for misconduct here he may be sentenced to a thousand years of tough mutton, or condemned to a little eternity of family dinners.

I have not yet discovered of what I am to die, but I rather believe I shall be burnt alive by the Puseyites. Nothing so remarkable in England as the progress of these foolish people. I have no conception what they mean, if it be not to revive every absurd ceremony, and every antiquated folly, which the common sense of mankind has set to sleep. You will find at your return a fanatical Church of England, but pray do not let it prevent your return. We can always gather together, in Park-street and Green-street, a chosen few who have never bowed the knee to Rimmon.

Did you meet at Rome my friend Mrs. ——*? Give me, if you please, some notion of the impression she produced upon you. She is very clever, very good-natured, and good-hearted, but the Lilliputians are afraid of her. We shall be truly glad to see you again, but I think you will never return. Why should you give up your serene heavens and short winters, to re-enter this garret of the earth? Yet there are those in the garret who know how to appreciate you, and no one better than your old and sincere friend,

Sydney Smith

895. Mrs. Meynell

Combe Florey, Sept. 23rd, 1842

Dearest Gee,

Nothing could exceed the beauty of the grapes, except the beauty of the pine-apple. How well you understand the clergy!

I am living, lively and young as I am, in the most profound solitude. I saw a crow yesterday, and had a distant view of a rabbit today. I have ceased to trouble myself about company. If anybody thinks it worth while to turn aside to the Valley of Flowers, I am most happy to see them; but I have ceased to lay plots, and to toil for visitors. I save myself by this much disappointment.

Sydney Smith

898. MRS. AUSTIN

Combe Florey, Oct. 13th, 1842

My dear Mrs. Austin,*

You lie heavy upon my conscience, unaccustomed to bear any weight at all. What can a country parson say to a travelled and travelling lady, who neither knows nor cares anything for wheat, oats, and barley? It is this reflection which keeps me silent. Still she has a fine heart, and likes to be cared for, even by me.

Mrs. Sydney and I are in tolerable health, – both better than we were when you lived in England; but there is much more of us, so that you will find you were only half acquainted with us! I wish I could add that the intellectual faculties had expanded in proportion to the augmentation of flesh and blood.

Have you any chance of coming home? or rather, I should say, have we any chance of seeing you at home? I have been living for three months quite alone here. I am nearly seventy-two, and I confess myself afraid of the very disagreeable methods by which we leave this world; the long death of palsy, or the degraded spectacle of aged idiotism. As for the *pleasures* of the world, – it is a very ordinary, middling sort of place. Pray be my tombstone, and say a good word for me when I am dead! I shall think of my beautiful monument when I am going; but I wish I could see it before I die. God bless you!

Sydney Smith

899. LADY HOLLAND

November 6th, 1842

My dear Lady Holland,

I have not the heart, when an amiable lady says, 'Come to "Semiramis"* in my box,' to decline; but I get bolder at a distance. 'Semiramis' would be to me pure misery. I love music very little, – I hate acting; I have the worst opinion of Semiramis herself, and the whole thing (I cannot help it) seems so childish and so foolish that I cannot abide it. Moreover, it would be rather out of etiquette for a Canon of St. Paul's to go to an opera; and where etiquette prevents me from doing things disagreeable to myself, I am a perfect martinet.

All these things considered, I am sure you will not be a Semiramis to me, but let me off.

Sydney Smith

900. LADY GREY

56, Green-street, Grosvenor-square.
Nov. 18th, 1842

There are plenty of people in London dear Lady Grey as there always are and I am leading a life almost as riotous as in the middle of June. The Widow Holland is remarkably well, has changed her lacrymal habits and gives herself up to dining.

You have seen the love of the Sex for Rogers – Orpheus another poet a contemporary of Rogers was torn to pieces by the Bacchanals.* What perilous loveliness that a man cannot walk the Streets unmolested and without being forced to defend himself with an Umbrella which is now commonly called a *Para-femme*. By the bye this is not only the* peril our dear Samuel has been subjected to; in dressing he set fire to his Shirt and was nearly burnt alive. Lady Holland tells the story to large Table-fulls of people, and with Tears in her Eyes.

I saw the other day John Lord Ponsonby* who looks old I think but well, he seems in very good Spirits and determined to amuse himself for the rest of his Life, a resolution which I have long since adopted, and which I recommend to you. Quinine is not a greater Specific for ague than Lady Morley* is for Lord Grey. She is a very charming remedy and is enough to make any disease popular for which she is prescribed.

Have you read Mcaulay's Lays?* they are very much liked. I have read some, but I abhor all Grecian and Roman Subjects.

I am just recovered from a fit of the Gout but am quite well, enjoying Life, and ready for death. Mrs. Sydney is remarkably well having lessened her size by taking Iodine. Would not this be useful for the national debt? There are no Whiggs to be seen; there are descriptions of them in books, but they are a lost variety of the Species like the Dodo* or the Sea Cow. Kind regards to

my Lord and Georgiana the honest and the true and much
affection to you from your old friend

Sydney Smith

902. LADY ASHBURTON

Dogmersfield Park,* 〈Nov. 1842〉

You have very naturally, my dear Lady Ashburton, referred
to me for some information respecting St. Anthony. The principal anecdotes related of him are, that he was rather careless of his
diet; and that, instead of confining himself to boiled mutton and
a little wine and water, he ate of side-dishes, and drank two
glasses of sherry, and refused to lead a life of great care and
circumspection, such as his constitution required. The consequence was, that his friends were often alarmed at his health;
and the medical men of Jerusalem and Jericho were in constant
requisition, taking exorbitant fees, and doing him little good.

You ought to be very thankful to me (Lord Ashburton and
yourself) for resisting as firmly and honourably as I do, my
desire to offer myself at the Grange; but my health is so indifferent, and my spirits so low, and I am so old and half-dead, that
I am mere lumber; so that I can only inflict myself upon the
Mildmays, who are accustomed to Mr. ——; and I dare not
appear before one who crosses the seas to arrange the destinies
of nations, and to chain up in bonds of peace the angry passions
of the people of the earth.

Still I can preach a little; and I wish you had witnessed, the
other day, at St. Paul's, my incredible boldness in attacking the
Puseyites. I told them that they made the Christian religion a
religion of postures and ceremonies, of circumflexions and genu-
flexions, of garments and vestures, of ostentation and parade;
that they took up tithe of mint and cummin, and neglected the
weightier matters of the law, – justice, mercy, and the duties of
life; and so forth.

Pray give my kind regards to the ambassador of ambassadors;
and believe me, my dear Lady Ashburton, with benedictions to
the whole house, ever sincerely yours,

Sydney Smith

903. MISS MARTINEAU*

Combe Florey, Dec. 11th, 1842

Dear Miss Martineau,

I am seventy-two years of age, at which period there comes over one a shameful love of ease and repose, common to dogs, horses, clergymen, and even to *Edinburgh Reviewers*. Then an idea comes across me sometimes that I am entitled to five or six years of quiet before I die. I fought with beasts at Ephesus for twenty years. Have not I contributed my fair share for the establishment of important truths, and for the discomfiture of quacks and fools? Is not the spirit gone out of me? Can I now mix ridicule with reason, so as to hit at once every variety of opposition? Is not there a story about Gil Blas and the Arch-bishop of Granada?*

I am just come from London, where I have been doing duty at St. Paul's, and preaching against the Puseyites – I. Because they lessen the aversion to the Catholic faith, and the admiration of Protestantism, which I think one of the greatest improvements the world ever made. II. They inculcate the preposterous sur-render of the understanding to bishops. III. They make religion an affair of trifles, of postures, and of garments.

Nothing is talked of in London but China. I wrote to Lord Fitzgerald,* who is at the head of the Board of Control, to beg, now that the army was so near, that he would conquer Japan. I utterly deny the right of those exclusive Orientals to shut up the earth in the way they are doing, and I think it one of the most legitimate causes of war. But this argument we will have out when we meet.

I believe Peel to be a philosopher disguised in a Tory fool's-cap, who will do everything by slow degrees which the Whigs proposed to do at once. Whether the delay be wise or mischiev-ous is a separate question, but such I believe to be the man in whom the fools of the earth put their trust.

I am living here, with my wife and one son, in one of the prettiest parsonages in England. I am at my ease in point of income, tolerably well for an old man, giving broth and physic to the poor, but no metaphysical dissertations on the Thirty-nine

Articles. I have many friends, and always pronounce violent panegyrics on you whenever your name is mentioned.

Sydney Smith

911. LADY GREY

56, Green-street, Grosvenor-square,
Feb. 28th, 1843

My dear Lady Grey

Many and sincere thanks for your kind Enquiry. My younger Brother died suddenly at the beginning of this month.* For the last 18 years he has avoided his family and has lived almost entirely estranged from them. I cannot pretend to feel grief for his loss. He has left behind him 2 Testamentary papers unsigned and unwitnessed and I believe quite invalid. If they are set aside as I believe they will and I have little doubt of it, I shall benefit to the amount of about £30,000 or more, which will come just in time to gild the nails of my Coffin. Bulteel* has stated his case to to me, and I have given him my advice upon it. Has a Bishop a right to make as a condition of Ordination *that*, which the Law does not make a condition—that no man shall be ordained who has not taken an English degree? Suppose he were to say that no man should be ordained who travels on the Continent, who has studied the Italian Language or who is not 6 feet high? Where does this power end? How does he prove that the Tutor knew this rule? – What right has he to say that a man (even knowing it) may not go to be ordained where he chuses? – and 50 other questions to which the Case gives birth. I have advised Bulteel to take it at once to the Commons* and lay it before Dr Adams or the Queen's Advocate. If the Bishop will not alter his resolution it must not go to sleep –

Lady Holland is suffering from a bad Eye; she has broken a small blood vessel in the eye by coughing. I have no news to tell you – I heard from the best authority today that trade is really reviving at Manchester; all the Machine Makers are employed and at full and increased Wages.

Mrs. Sydney and I are both in fair preservation.

When I say my Brother died Suddenly, I should state that he died most probably from Apoplexy. He fell down in the street and was dead in ten minutes. God bless you dear Lady Grey please give my kindest regards to Lord Grey and Georgiana and believe me your affectionate friend

Sydney Smith

912. RODERICK MURCHISON

Green-street, March 10th, 1843

Dear Murchison,

Many thanks for your address,* which I will diligently read. May there not be some one among the infinite worlds where men and women are all made of stone? Perhaps of Parian marble? How infinitely superior to flesh and blood! What a Paradise for you, to pass eternity with a greywacke woman!

Ever yours,
Sydney Smith

P.S. – Very good indeed! The model of an address from a scientific man to practical men! Great zeal, and an earnest desire to make others zealous.

The style and language just what they ought to be. No lapses, no indiscretions. The only expression I quarrel with is, mono-graph; either it has some conventional meaning among geologists, or it only means a pamphlet, – a book.

914. LADY GREY

March 31st, 1843

My dear Lady Grey

I am here till the 12th. of July, and shall be most happy to see you and yours again. I am gradually stepping into my fortune and find it not unpleasant – Nothing new here; the only conversation is Brougham. What is Brougham doing? where is he going? will he wear a red Coat at Belvoir?* and such other matters. By the by – his name for Lady Palmerston is admirable, he calls her *Pamela or Virtue rewarded.** Dr Holland has been down to Lord Carlisle at Trentham* and pronounces him not in danger but that he is very weak and that his confinement will probably be tedious. I remain always dr Lady Grey yours affectionately

Sydney Smith

You must read Horner's book*

915. DR. WHEWELL*

April 8th, 1843

My dear Sir,

My lectures are gone to the dogs, and are utterly forgotten. I knew nothing of moral philosophy, but I was thoroughly aware that I wanted £200 to furnish my house. The success, however, was prodigious; all Albemarle-street blocked up with carriages, and such an uproar as I never remember to have been excited by any other literary imposture. Every week I had a new theory about conception and perception; and supported by a natural manner, a torrent of words, and an impudence scarcely credible in this prudent age. Still, in justice to myself, I must say there were some good things in them. But good and bad are all gone. By 'moral philosophy' you mean, as they mean at Edinburgh, mental philosophy; *i.e.* the faculties of the mind, and the effects which our reasoning powers and our passions produce upon the actions of our lives.

I think the University uses you and us very ill, in keeping you so strictly at Cambridge. If Jupiter could desert Olympus for twelve days to feast with the harmless Ethiopians, why may not the Vice-Chancellor commit the graduating, matriculating world for a little time to the inferior deities, and thunder and lighten at the tables of the Metropolis?

I hope you like Horner's 'Life'. It succeeds extremely well here. It is full of all the exorbitant and impracticable views so natural to very young men at Edinburgh; but there is great order, great love of knowledge, high principle and feelings, which ought to grow and thrive in superior minds.

Our kind regards to Mrs. Whewell. Ever, my dear Sir, sincerely yours,

Sydney Smith

918. J. A. MURRAY

Green-street, June 4th, 1843

My dear Murray,

I should be glad to hear something of your life and adventures, and the more particularly so, as I learn you have no intention of leaving Edinburgh for London this season.

Mrs. Sydney and I have been remarkably well, and are so at present; why, I cannot tell. I am getting very old in years, but do not feel that I am become so in constitution. My locomotive powers at seventy-three are abridged, but my animal spirits do not desert me. I am become rich. My youngest brother died suddenly, leaving behind him £100,000 and no will. A third of this therefore fell to my share, and puts me at my ease for my few remaining years. After buying into the Consols and the Reduced, I read Seneca 'On the Contempt of Wealth!'* What intolerable nonsense! I heard your *éloge* from Lord Lansdowne when I dined with him, and I need not say how heartily I concurred in it. Next to me sat Lord Worsley,* whose enclosed letter affected me, and very much pleased me. I answered it with sincere warmth. Pray return me the paper. Did you read my American Petition, and did you approve it?

.   .   .   .

Why don't they talk over the virtues and excellencies of Lansdowne? There is no man who performs the duties of life better, or fills a high station in a more becoming manner. He is full of knowledge, and eager for its acquisition. His remarkable politeness is the result of good-nature, regulated by good sense. He looks for talents and qualities among all ranks of men, and adds them to his stock of society, as a botanist does his plants; and while other aristocrats are yawning among Stars and Garters, Lansdowne is refreshing his soul with the fancy and genius which he has found in odd places, and gathered to the marbles and pictures of his palace. Then he is an honest politician, a wise statesman, and has a philosophic mind; he is very agreeable in conversation, and is a man of an unblemished life. I shall take care of him in my Memoirs!

Remember me very kindly to the *maximus minimus*,* and to the Scotch Church. I have urged my friend the Bishop of Durham* to prepare kettles of soup for the seceders, who will probably be wandering in troops over our northern counties.

Ever your sincere friend,
Sydney Smith

929. LADY DUFFERIN*

Combe Florey ⟨Early Aug. 1843⟩

I am just beginning to get well from that fit of gout, at the beginning of which you were charitable enough to pay me a visit, and I said – the same Providence which inflicts gout creates Dufferins! We must take the good and the evils of life.

I am charmed, I confess, with the beauty of this country. I hope some day you will be charmed with it too. It banished, however, every Arcadian notion to see ——* walk in at the gate today. I seemed to be transported instantly to Piccadilly, and the innocence went out of me.

I hope the process of furnishing goes on well. Attend, I pray you, to the proper selection of an easy chair, where you may cast yourself down in the weariness and distresses of life, with the absolute certainty that every joint of the human frame will receive all the comfort which can be derived from easy position and soft materials; then the glass, on which your eyes are so often fixed, knowing that you have the great duty imposed on the Sheridans, of looking well. You may depend upon it, happiness depends mainly on these little things.

I hope you remain in perfect favour with Rogers, and that you are not admitted in any of the dress breakfast parties. Remember me to the Norton: tell her I am glad to be sheltered from her beauty by the insensibility of age; that I shall not live to see its decay, but die with that unfaded image before my eyes: but don't make a mistake, and deliver the message to ——,* instead of your sister.

I remain, dear Lady Dufferin, very sincerely yours,

Sydney Smith

934. Miss G. Harcourt

Combe Florey, Sept. 1843

My dear Georgiana,

I am retiring from business as a diner-out, but I recommend to attention as a rising wit, Mr. Milnes,* whose misfortune I believe it is not to be known to you. . . .

Little Tommy Moore sent me some verses after leaving Combe Florey, which I send to you even though they are laudatory of me, trusting in your constant goodness and kindness to the subject of his panegyric. Moore has one or two notes, and looks when he is singing like a Superannuated cherub.

You and I are both inn-keepers, and are occupied from one end of the week to the other in looking after company. I think we ought to have soldiers billeted upon us. My sign is 'The Rector's Head', yours 'The Mitre'. My Devonshire curate and his wife are just come, and are drinking in the tap. Mrs. Sydney and I are tolerably well; I have quite got rid of my gouty knee, but the hot weather makes me very languid.

I suppose you will soon be at Bishopsthorpe, surrounded by the sons of the prophets. What a charming existence to live in the midst of holy people, to know that nothing profane can approach you, to be certain that a dissenter can no more be found in the Palace than a snake can exist in Ireland, or ripe fruit in Scotland. To have your society strong and undiluted by the laity, to bid adieu to human learning, to feast on the Canons, and revel in the Thirty-Nine Articles. Happy Georgiana!

My curate's name is Tin Lin. I must go and do the honours. God bless you, dear Georgiana. Look at the map where those dwell who have a regard and affection for you, and make a strong mark in the neighbourhood of Taunton.

Sydney Smith

935. LADY GREY

Combe Florey, Taunton, Sept. 9th, 1843

Another Line if you please my dear Lady Grey to say how the remaining part of the Journey was performed. As far as Lambton Castle all seems to have gone on beautifully; I am very desirous to learn that the end was as good as the beginning.

I have been a good deal annoyed and am considerably annoyed now, by my footman having poisoned himself, not intentionally, but Seeing some Arsenical paste made for poisoning Rats he ate as much as contained 40 Grains of Arsenic. I was called up in the middle of the Night, worked with White Vitriol Stomach pump and Lime Water; he now lies with pulse at 120 and quite incapable of bearing anything on his stomach, and in great danger.

This foolish Man will die of eating unknown paste but how can I blame him when the first Physician in Taunton died this morning of a whole filbert which he swallowed Shell and all a year ago, and which produced mortification of the intestines. how absurd is human existence. Mrs. Sydney and I are in decent health – surrounded by Hollands of all ages and Sexes.

The Harvest here very great in produce is got in admirably. Manufactures are clearly reviving: where is the ruin which we Whiggs have so often predicted? The Queens Voyage seems to be planned in good Sense, and may conciliate, but I never read a Word of her banquets and her proceedings, nor of the Prince of Wales' airings. Don't attempt to teach Sr Stephen Hammick the Northumberland method of farming; he cares for nothing but Piccadilly and the Hospitals and Lady Holland, and is miserable out of London, as miserable as Dr. Holland in the Country. In coming home last week from a dinner party our Carriage was stopped and as I was preparing my Watch and Money a man put his head in the Window and said We want Dr Holland. They took him out and we have heard nothing of him since; we think of advertising

ever affly Yrs
Sydney Smith

kind regards to Lord G and Lady Georg:

936. LORD LANSDOWNE

Combe Florey, Sept. 16th, 1843

Dear Lord Lansdowne,

I received the haunch of venison, but as there was no intimation on the package from whence it came, I could not thank my benefactor as I now do. It struck me at the time that to send venison to the clergy without saying from whence it came was an act of profound and high-principled piety.

Ever sincerely yours
Sydney Smith

938. J. A. MURRAY

Combe Florey, Sept. 29th, 1843

My dear Murray,

Jeffrey has written to me to say he means to dedicate his Essays to me. This I think a very great honour, and it pleases me very much. I am sure he ought to resign. He has very feeble health; a mild climate would suit the state of his throat. Mrs. Jeffrey thinks he could not employ himself. Wives know a great deal about husbands; but, if she is right, I should be surprised. I have thought he had a canine appetite for books, though this sometimes declines in the decline of life. I am beautifying my house in Green-street; a comfortable house is a great source of happiness. It ranks immediately after health and a good conscience. I see your religious war is begun in Scotland. I suppose Jeffrey will be at the head of the Free Church troops. Do you think he has any military talents?

You are, I hear, attending more to diet than heretofore. If you wish for anything like happiness in the fifth act of life, eat and drink about one-half what you *could* eat and drink. Did I ever tell you my calculation about eating and drinking? Having ascertained the weight of what I could live upon, so as to preserve health and strength, and what I did live upon, I found that, between ten and seventy years of age, I had eaten and drunk forty four-horse waggon-loads of meat and drink more than would have preserved me in life and health! The value of this mass of nourishment I considered to be worth seven thousand pounds sterling. It occurred to me that I must, by my voracity, have starved to death fully a hundred persons. This is a frightful calculation, but irresistibly true; and I think, dear Murray, your waggons would require an additional horse each!

Lord and Lady Lansdowne, who are rambling about this fine country, are to spend a day here next week. You must really come to see the West of England. From Combe Florey we will go together to Linton and Lynmouth, than which there is nothing finer in this island. Two of our acquaintance dead this week, – Stewart Mackenzie* and Bell!* We must close our ranks. God bless you, my dear Murray!

Sydney Smith

945. Mrs. Sydney Smith

Green-street, Oct. 23rd, 1843

Dearest Kate,

I meant to have gone to Munden today, but am not quite stout, so have postponed my journey there till next Saturday the 28th. I went over yesterday to the Tates* at Edmonton. The family consists of three delicate daughters, an aunt, the old lady, and her son, then curate of Edmonton; the old lady was in bed. I found there a physician, an old friend of Tate's, attending them from friendship, who had come from London for that purpose. They were in daily expectation of being turned out from house and Curacy. . . . I began by inquiring the character of their servant; then turned the conversation upon their affairs, and expressed a hope the Chapter might ultimately do something for them. I then said, 'It is my duty to state to you (they were all assembled) that I have given away the living of Edmonton; and have written to our Chapter clerk this morning, to mention the person to whom I have given it; and I must also tell you that I am sure he will appoint his curate. (A general silence and dejection.) It is a very odd coincidence', I added, 'that the gentleman I have selected is a namesake of this family; his name is Tate. Have you any relations of that name?' 'No, we have not.' 'And, by a more singular coincidence, his name is Thomas Tate; in short,' I added, 'there is no use in mincing the matter, you are vicar of Edmonton.' They all burst into tears. It flung me also into a great agitation of tears, and I wept and groaned for a long time. Then I rose, and said I thought it was very likely to end in their keeping a buggy, at which we all laughed as violently

The poor old lady, who was sleeping in a garret because she could not bear to enter into the room lately inhabited by her husband, sent for me and kissed me, sobbing with a thousand emotions. The charitable physician wept too. . . . I never passed so remarkable a morning, nor was more deeply impressed with the sufferings of human life, and never felt more thoroughly the happiness of doing good.

God bless you!
Sydney Smith

949. R. Monckton Milnes

Green-street, Nov. 8th, 1843

My dear Sir,

I am glad the business is in such good hands; it is the important measure of the day.* As to any share I may take in it, it must depend upon my foot, ankle, and knee. If the Americans will not book up, they must take the consequences.*

I am just going to pray for you at St. Paul's, but with no very lively hope of success.

Sydney Smith

950. Lady Grey

56, Green-street, Grosvenor-square,
Nov. 8th, 1843

My dear Lady Grey

I cross examine every body who has any intelligence from Howick and I study your Letters – The result is that Lord Grey's general health appears to be improved, – though I am afraid the Eyes* are not so. My elder Brother is just in the same way; he dined with me yesterday and I was forced to lead him in, and out of the room, and to assist him at table. I hear a rumor that Lord Grey is coming to Town and it appears to me to be a very wise measure. Surely his main dependance now must be upon Society and where except in London is Society to be attained of the quality, and quantity required –

I hope you have read my Letter to the Americans, it is generally found fault with as being too favorable and to this I plead guilty, but I find I get more mild as I get older and more unwilling to be severe; but if they do not (as men of business phrase it) book up by Christmas, I shall set at them in good earnest.

Lady Holland represents London at present – I believe no other dinners are heard of but hers, and I doubt if there is any other house in London at this Season where more than 2 or 3 are gathered together – She is just migrating into Gt Stanhope St and has insisted upon dining with me on Saty. on me* without Servants Spoons Forks – Wife or Cook.

I am so convinced the Americans will not pay that I mean to sell out this Week at the price of 60 –

God bless you dear Lady Grey
S S

kindest regards to my Lord

955. LADY GREY

Combe Florey, Taunton, Dec. 10th, 1843

My dear Lady Grey

I have heard from different persons painful accounts of Lord Grey's health, and I only write a line to you to say that I am not unmindful of this Subject but that on the contrary I take a deep interest in it. I do not write to you to induce you to write to me, I beg you will not think of so doing. I am returned here to spend the Winter months with my old Woman, not the most cheerful part of life when all the young ones are fled from the nest and nothing remaining but the old old Birds, and those old Birds sick Birds also. I hope you were amused with my attack upon the

Americans, they really deserved it. It is a monstrous and increasing Villainy; fancy a meeting in Philadelphia convened by public advertisement where they came to resolutions that the debt was too great for the people to pay, that the people could not pay it, ought not to pay it, and would not pay it. I have not a conception that the Creditors will ever have a single Shilling.

I left Lady Holland dining, and complaining in parties of 18 people that every body had deserted her. Tell Lord Grey that I recommend to his attention in the 4thcoming* Edinburgh Review an article upon Ireland by Senior* the Master in Chancery which I think admirable. – it contains in my humble Estimation an enumeration of the Medicines and a statement of the treatment necessary for your distracted Country in defence of which I always state it has at least produced Lady Grey.

I keep my health tolerably well; occasionally fits of gout, but my Eyes in good preservation, and while I can read and write I have no care about age. I should add though another Condition that I must have no pain.

Remember me very kindly and affectionately to my friend and Patron Ld Grey – and believe me as affectionately yrs

Sydney Smith

do not think of answering this

956. MRS. HOLLAND

Combe Florey, Dec. 15th, ⟨1843⟩

My dearest Daughter

Many pardons for not having written to you according to my promise but the Calf and the Kitchen maid both kept their beds, George Strong had a Diarrhea and the Shafts were broken. I had a very agreeable journey down, going in the public Carriages – an infinitely more agreeable method than in a private vehicle. I felt as little fatigue as in my own arm Chair in this Library and could have gone on to the West Indies without being tired. I find your mother very well and much less, not bigger than two Haycocks. She has stopped the Iodine for fear of not only becoming less but vanishing altogether. The whole Country is divided between Coles Clerk of the Peace and Captain Mars who has challenged him. Mars the God of War challenging the Clerk of the Peace; I am studying the question deeply, as is Cecil.*

Not a breath of Wind, a solemn Stillness, all nature fast asleep, Storm and Tempest bound over to keep the peace; there never was such a period.

I have had a letter from Harriet Martineau praising me up to the Skies and exhorting me to a Tilt and Tournament against the Corn Laws. I say all that is kind to the poor dying Woman* whom I believe to be the most honest person in Great Britain. I don't mean an honest Woman in the common Sense but a thoroughly highminded person in all the relations of Life. –

Love to Holland and the Children

> your affectionate father
> Sydney Smith

959. MRS. GROTE

December 18th, 1843

My dear Mrs. Grote,

I hope the Irish fossils have reached you by this time, and that they are approved of.

．　．　．　．　．　．　．

My bomb has fallen very successfully in America, and the list of killed and wounded is extensive. I have several quires of paper sent me every day, calling me monster, thief, atheist, deist, etc. Duff Green sent me three pounds of cheese, and a Captain Monigan a large barrel of American apples. The last news from America will, I think, lower the Pennsylvanian funds.

I wonder how you are occupied. I am reading Montaigne. He thinks aloud, that is his great merit, but does not think remarkably well; mankind have improved in thinking and writing since that period. Have you read Senior's article for the forthcoming Edinburgh Review? It is excellent, and does him great credit.

I went, while in town, one night to the Sartoris', where Mrs. Sartoris was singing divinely.* Your sincere friend,

> Sydney Smith

960. LADY GREY

Combe Florey, Taunton, Dec. 21st, 1843

My dear Lady Grey

What is the most unpleasant news to me is the great pain Lord Grey appears to suffer. I trust you keep up a constant communication with Hammick, and learn from him all the palliatives and managements that the highest state of the medical art can suggest – Children and relations are a great blessing but were I in great pain I should like Lord Grey be very loath to see any one. Talking of Children I have thought it expedient that my Son* and I should have separate Establishments. I allow him £500 per Annum, and he lives at Southampton. Our habits were incompatible; he was tired to death of the Solitude of this place and the arrangement was as agreeable to him as to me. He is to visit us here from time to time and we have parted good friends.

So Mrs Sydney and I after a life of bustle and parturition are left alone. – We mean to have a large Turkey on Xmas day just the same as when there were people to eat it and we mean to have a twelfth Cake and draw King and Queen, a remarkable instance of the power of habit.

The weather here is absolutely sultry, we are forced to sit with open doors and sleep with open Windows, but I suppose they are preparing their Snow and Hail. I am reading the Letters to George Selwyn* by which I am amused. Many of them are written with Wit and Spirit, they bring before me people of whom I knew a little and the notes are so copious that the book makes an history of those Times, certainly an history of the Manners and mode of Life of the upper orders of Society. I hope you were all pleased with my giving the Living of Edmonton to Taite's Son; it has raised them all up from the dust. I never saw a more affecting Scene than when I went over to announce it to them; 3 Sick daughters, a Sick aunt, a mother in bed with a fever and broken heart, a miserable Curate, all expecting every day to be turned out on the Wide World with the interest of £3000 for the whole of their Support. – I never was more powerfully affected. Pray give my kindest regards and warmest Wishes to your invalid and believe me your affectionate friend

Sydney Smith

963. SIR GEORGE PHILIPS

Combe Florey, Dec. 28th, 1843

My dear Philips,

I am going to Bowood for five or six days next week. I shall find Bobus there, who will come on from thence here. He is very blind, but bears up against the evils of age heroically. The great question of the next Session will be the support of the Catholic clergy. Will Peel dare to bring it on? Will he be able to carry it in and out of the House, if he does? Longman has printed my American Letters in the shape of a small pamphlet, and it has a very great circulation. I receive presents of cheese and apples from Americans who are advocates for paying debts, and very abusive letters in print and in manuscript from those who are not. I continue to think the Pennsylvanians will not pay; and so thinks, as I hear, Jones Loyd.*

Your old and affectionate friend
Sydney Smith

966. LADY GREY

⟨Undated: Jan. 3rd, 1844⟩

My dear Lady Grey

God bless you and support you in great tryals such as the illness is of so good and so great a man, and one who has played so distinguished a part in the Events of these times; convey to him my most ardent Wishes for his Safety, and exemption from pain. I am a believer in his Constitution and feel sure that we shall yet have many Conversations about the Wonderful things of this World.

I receive every day from America letters and pamphlets without end; and I send you a very honest and sensible Sermon, so little like another Sermon that I think our dear Earl might read it or have it read to him, but let that honest Howick read it who loves everything that is bold and true and honest and send it back to me when it is done with.

Only think of that fool young Taite,* no sooner does he find himself extricated from poverty and misery than the first thing he does is to turn out a poor Curate the son of the late Rector before his father; his conduct has been quite abominable.

I go on Tuesday for 2 or 3 days to Bowood where a large party is assembled among the rest Lady Holland unless she has sent an excuse which as it gives most trouble is the plan she will probably adopt.

We are all dying here of heat. I sleep with my Windows open every night, the Birds are all taken in, and are building, the foolish flowers are blowing, human creatures alone are in the Secret – and know what is to happen in a week or two.

I met Melburne* in Town not having seen him before since his illness. I have never joined in the general admiration ⟨of⟩ this person; I think his manners rude and insolent, his Conversation is an eternal persiflage and is therefore wearisome, it seems as if he did not think it worth while to talk Sense or seriousness before his Company and that he had a right to abandon himself to any nonsense which happened to come uppermost, which nonsense many of his Company remembered to have come uppermost often before.

I verily believe the United States are cracking – a nation cannot exist in such a state of Morals. Read Miss Martineau upon the management of a sick room,* they say it is full of good things.

Give my kindest and most affectionate regards to Lord Grey and believe me ever dr Lady Grey Your sincere friend

Sydney Smith

971. Mrs. Grote

Combe Florey, Jan. 31st, 1844

My dear Mrs. Grote,

Your fall entirely proceeded from your despising the pommel of the saddle, – a species of pride to which many ladies may attribute fractures and death. When I rode (which, I believe, was in the middle of the last century) I had a holding-strap fixed somewhere near the pommel, and escaped many falls by it.

Nothing ever does happen at Combe Florey, and nothing has happened.

· · · · · ·

Old-age is not so much a scene of illness as of *malaise*. I think every day how near I am to death. I am very weak, and very breathless. Everett,* the American Minister, has been here at the same time with my eldest brother. We all liked him, and were confirmed in our good opinion of him. A sensible, unassuming man, always wise and reasonable.

.   .   .   .   .   .

'If I take this dose of calomel, shall I be well immediately?' 'Certainly not,' replies the physician. 'You have been in bed these six weeks; how can you expect such a sudden cure? But I can tell you you will never be well without it, and that it will tend materially to the establishment of your health.' So, the pay to the Catholic Clergy. They will not be immediately satisfied by the measure but, they will never be satisfied without it, and it will have a considerable tendency to produce that effect. It will not supersede other medicines, but it is an indispensable preliminary to them.

If you dine with Lady ——, it is a sure proof that you are a virtuous woman; she collects the virtuous. I have totally forgotten all about the American debt, but I continue to receive letters and papers from the most remote corners of the United States, with every vituperative epithet which human rage has invented.

> Your affectionate friend,
> Sydney Smith

974. Lady Grey

⟨Postmark Feb. 27th, 1844⟩

My dear Lady Grey

I am quite delighted to learn from so many sources that Lord Grey is so much better and I trust we shall see him in Town after Easter.

What news have I to tell you? Nothing but what the papers will tell you better. – Howick's Speech* is universally praised for its honesty, and ability. I think O'Connel will have 2 years imprisonment and the Government and the Irish Courts have come off much better than it was supposed they would have done.

We have bad accounts from Castle Howard though your intelligence is as good as ours from this quarter. – There is a rumour that Lord Ashburton is employed in Italy in flirting with the pope; the common idea that a premunire is incurred by these flirtations or that there is any Law enacting penalties for communications with his Holiness is erroneous. Lady Holland is remarkably well and less Saucey than usual.

Rogers has rallied and is much as he has been for years. I can neither walk nor breathe but in other particulars am well. Four Volumes of Burke's Letters to Ld Fitzwilliam I mean the Marquis of Rockingham* are about to be published –

I am not sorry to come to London. I have been living on commonplaces and trueisms for 3 months; I always fatten and stupefy on this diet; I want to lose flesh and gain understanding. I saw at Bowood Lady Shelburne* and did not like her, she is too much like her mother not to make one suspect similarity of temper; she is cold, distant and apparently cross, a painful contrast with Lady Kerry* who has a manner to make the Shrubs blossom as she passes.

Shelburne is what the Coachmen call a *queer Chap* but I rather like him:

The new Lady Abbinger* dined with Lady Holland on Sunday. I thought she would have fainted. The page always has sal Volatile on hand for first introductions.

God bless you Lady Grey

Affly yrs
S S

kindest regards to Ld Grey

981. LADY GREY

⟨Between April 13th and 22nd, 1844⟩

My dear Lady Grey

I never believe one single Word she says so that it matters very little what her assertions are; nor is it I believe of much more importance to the World at large than to me; still I do not wonder at your being provoked.

Your account seems good of Lord Grey, I envy him the taste of fresh air after such long confinement, to say nothing of the fine feeling which cessation of pain produces; not that therefore I would be ill, but that I consider these feelings as some little abatement of the evil – I have read Miss Martineau on Sick rooms, but I cannot understand it, it is too sublime for me. I have accustomed myself (perhaps a bad habit) to examine into the meaning of Words before I part with my admiration. The Government are to have this Year I understand a very splendid Budget, but obtained of course by the pernicious auxiliary of the Income Tax.

What a singular event these divisions upon the Working hours of the Common People. I am a decided Duodecimalist. Ashley* is losing his head and becoming absurd; then if he brings forward his Suckling act he will be considered as quite mad. No Woman to be allowed to suckle her own Children without medical Certificates – 3 Classes *free sucklers – half sucklers –* and *Spoon meal Mothers* – Mothers whose supply is uncertain to *suckle upon Affidavit*. How is it possible that an act of parliament can supply the place of nature and natural affections; have you any nonsense equal to this act in Northumberland.

God bless you

S S

Kindest regards to Ld Grey

984. Sir Robert Peel

May 5th, 1844

Sir,

I am informed there will be a vacancy in July of a clerkship in the Record Office, in that department of it over which Mr. Hardy, I believe, presides. There is a family of the name of Kingston, residing in ——, who have formerly been in affluence, but have fallen with the fall of the West Indies. The mother and daughter are teaching music. The son is an excellent lad, understanding and speaking French and German, and is a humble candidate for this situation of Clerk of the Records, worth about eighty pounds per annum. Mr. Hardy, a very old friend of the family, is very desirous of getting the young man into his office. A better family does not exist, or one fighting up more bravely against adversity. The mother has been repeatedly to me, to beg I would state these things to you. I stated to her that I had so little the honour of your acquaintance, that, though I had met you, I should hardly presume to bow to you in the street. But the poor lady said I had evidence to give, if I had not influence to use; and at last I consented to do what I am doing. I beg therefore to observe, I am not asking anything of you (no man has less right to do so); I am merely stating facts to you respecting an office of which you have the disposal. I have no other acquaintance with the family than through their misfortunes, borne with such unshaken constancy.

I beg you will not give yourself the trouble to answer this letter. If my evidence induces you to make any inquiries about the young lad, that will be the best answer. If not, I shall attribute it to some of the innumerable obstacles which prevent a person in your situation from giving way to the impulses of compassion and good-nature.

I have the honour to be, etc –
Sydney Smith

1037. ARCHDEACON HALE

56 Green-street, June 11th, 1844

My dear Sr

I really must object to Dr Phillimore* he is an excellent man but not intended by nature for a giver of opinions, but I hardly see at present where the points for Consultation are. It is I presume thoroughly understood between us that nothing is to be done except by our agreement out of Chapter or by our Votes in it. I wish particularly that everything should be delayed till after Friday, when I shall be much better informed on the Subject. As the Vote has past the Chapter you have a *perfect right* that the plan shall be persevered in till revoked or changed. I have no doubt of the goodness of your motives but your zeal will wear off a little by time and experience. You will find that the way to go through the World is with one Eye open and the other shut unless you mean to lead a Life of endless contention and litigation and I am very sure you are too good natured a person to have any such meaning.

Yrs ever
Sydney Smith

990. EUGÈNE ROBIN*

London, June 29th, 1844

Sir,

Your application to me does me honour, and requires, on your part, no sort of apology.

It is scarcely possible to speak much of self, and I have little or nothing to tell which has not been told before in my preface.

I am seventy-four years of age; and being Canon of St. Paul's in London, and a rector of a parish in the country, my time is divided equally between town and country. I am living amongst the best society in the Metropolis, and at ease in my circumstances; in tolerable health, a mild Whig, a tolerating Churchman, and much given to talking, laughing, and noise. I dine with the rich in London, and physic the poor in the country; passing from the sauces of Dives to the sores of Lazarus. I am, upon the whole, a happy man; have found the world an entertaining world, and am thankful to Providence for the part allotted to me in it. If you wish to become more informed respecting the actor himself, I must refer you to my friend Van de Weyer, who knows me well, and is able (if he will condescend to do so) to point out the good and the evil within me. If you come to London, I hope you will call on me, and enable me to make your acquaintance; and in the meantime I beg you to accept every assurance of my consideration and respect.

Sydney Smith

995. MISS G. HARCOURT

Combe Florey, soon after July 22nd, 1844

My dear Georgiana,

Nothing can exceed the beauty of the country; I am forced to admit that. Mrs. Sydney also revives, I see the Westmorelands are come to England. Lady Westmoreland produced a great impression upon me. Pray recall me to her recollection, mentioning my leading attributes of mind and body. Slender, grave, silent, and modest, but don't overdo me in this last quality. I thought her a very interesting woman.*

I have treated that poor musical family, the Kingstons, with three weeks of fresh air, as they were all sick and fading away. They came here on Monday, so that you will find me, when we meet, much improved in my singing – not in singing your praises, for in that exercise I have long been perfect.

Believe me always your affectionate friend

Sydney Smith

998. LADY GREY

July 30th, 1844

My dear Lady Grey

I like the news of today very much and think it better than any I have received for a long time; pray send me as good next week.

We have staing here with us the Musical family and the remarkable little Musical boy whom Georgiana and Lady Caroline* heard at my house when they were in London – Their singing is certainly very remarkable and the little Boy at the age of seven composes Hymns, I mean sets them to music.

You are very kind to enquire after Mrs. Sydney. She is much better than when in London but I have great doubts if this relaxing climate of the West of England agrees either with her or with me – I suppose there is the difference of a thick great coat between Howick, and Combe Florey, and at this Season of the year, the difference is in your favor.

I think I have already mentioned to you the Life of Ld Eldon by Horace Twiss.* It is not badly done, and I think it would very much amuse Ld Grey as it is the history almost of his times. He seems (Lord Eldon) to have been a cunning canting old Rogue whose object was to make all the money he ⟨could⟩ by office at any expence of the public happiness. In addition he was the bigotted Enemy of every sort of improvement and retarded by his influence for more than 25 years those changes which the State of the Country absolutely required. I know where he is now in that particular part of certain regions which are set apart for Canting and Hypocrisy – God bless you, dear Lady Grey; kindest regards to the Earl; all here swear by him and in the midst of their Swearing earnestly pray for his recovery

Yrs affly

S S

1000. LADY GREY

Combe Florey, Taunton, Aug. 6th, 1844

My dear Lady Grey

I have no belief in a french War so long as Louis Philippe lives, and live he will for they cannot hit him, and seem to have left off Shooting at him in despair.

The account of Lord Grey seems to be very good. Wilson* must be a clever man – by the bye I was sorry to see Hammick had laid down his Carriage in his old age, not only because comforts should not be abridged in old age but because it is Evidence that he is losing his business.

The Wet Weather has succeeded to the Drought and threatens the Safety of the Harvest. There is also a great famine of Hay and as I have all to buy I am almost ruined by the Expence of my Stables.

Howick said he would come here this year on his way to Lady Elizabeth Bulteel; I suppose he is not yet liberated from his politics. I have taken a considerable liking to Howick and Lady Howick.

I continue extremely well and am spending the little Life which remains to me very agreeably. I hear from all quarters that Lady Holland is coming here.

I am prepared and hope in *this*, (as I endeavour to do in all situations) I shall behave with proper resolution and corage.

Remember me always most kindly and affectionately to my excellent Lord Grey.

God bless you dear Lady Grey

Yours affly
Sydney Smith

1013. LADY GREY

C. Florey, Taunton, Oct. 11th, 1844

Take care always to give my kind and affectionate regards to Lord Grey.

My dear Lady Grey

I rather think that last week they wanted to kill me, but I was too sharp for them. I am now tolerably well but am weak and taking all proper care of myself, which care consists in eating nothing that I like and doing nothing that I wish.

I sent you yesterday the triumph of a fellow sufferer with Lord Grey; tell me fairly the effect such a narrative produces upon him; the greatest consolation to me is to find that others are suffering as much as I do. I would not inflict sufferings upon them, I would contribute actively to prevent it, but if they do come after this I must confess – that I am always affly yours

Sydney Smith

I shall be in London between the 22nd. and 25th. see what rural Life is on the other Side

Combe Florey Gazette

Mr. Smith's large red Cow is expected to calve this week.

Mr Gibbs has bought Mr Smith's Lame Mare –

it rained yesterday, and a correspondent observes that it is not unlikely to rain today.

Mr Smith is better

Mrs Smith is indisposed

a nest of black Magpies was found near this Village yesterday

1017. LADY CARLISLE

56, Green-street, Oct. 1844

My dear Lady Carlisle,

From your ancient goodness to me, I am sure you will be glad to receive a bulletin from myself, informing you that I am making a good progress; in fact, I am in a regular train of promotion from gruel, vermicelli, and sago, I was promoted to panada, from thence to minced meat, and (such is the effect of good conduct) I was elevated to a mutton-chop. My breathlessness and giddiness are gone – chased away by the gout. If you hear of sixteen or eighteen pounds of human flesh, they belong to me. I look as if a curate had been taken out of me. I am delighted to hear such improved accounts of my fellow-sufferer at Castle Howard. Lady Holland is severe in her medical questions; but I detail the most horrible symptoms, at which she takes flight.

Accept, my dear Lady Carlisle, my best wishes for Lord Carlisle and all the family –

Sydney Smith

2. *my churches:* at Netheravon and Fittleton.

– *Bath:* Sydney's parents were at this time living at Bath.

3. *My Brother:* Robert Percy Smith (1770–1845) known as 'Bobus', was born one year before Sydney and died a fortnight after him, thus fulfilling Sydney's prayer in letter 233. He was an intimate friend at Eton of Canning, John Hookham Frere, and Lord Holland. At King's, Cambridge, he distinguished himself especially as a Latin versifier.

4. *Aristocrat or ... Democrat:* William Petty (1737–1805), 1st Marquess of Lansdowne (1784), but best known as Earl of Shelburne (1761–84), one of the ablest of the Whig leaders, but very unpopular in political circles. He was a patron of the arts and his house Bowood 'was the centre of the most cultivated and liberal society of the day' (*D.N.B.*). Bentham, in particular, lived much at Bowood and owed an incalculable debt to Shelburne for his friendship. For an interesting comment on his personality cf. Lady Holland's *Journal*, i. 175–6.

– *Mithoffer:* the name of the valet who is several times mentioned: and S. sometimes changes it to 'Metaphore' for fun.

6. Lord Webb Seymour (1777–1819), son of the Duke of Somerset, became while an undergraduate at Christ Church a devoted student of science and philosophy. For these pursuits he settled in Edinburgh in 1798, where he became intimate with the same circle as Sydney Smith. Ill health prevented his producing any memorable work, but he was much respected and loved by his friends, There is a biographical notice of him by Henry Hallam in *Memoirs of Francis Horner*, vol. i, pp. 473–86.

– Dugald Stewart (1753–1828), Professor of Moral Philosophy at Edinburgh for many years and held in great repute, especially among the Whigs. He and his wife became great friends of the Sydney Smiths. He greatly admired Sydney's preaching (cf. *M.*, ch. iv).

– Andrew Dalzel (1742–1806), Professor of Greek 1779–1805.

– Baron Norton of the Scottish Exchequer: see Letter 21.

(   ) *my dear Sr:* the word, obliterated by the wafer, was probably 'Adieu'.

9. *I am in hopes ... my village:* he did carry these ideas into execution afterwards at Foston.

10. A new Swiss governess.

– Abomelique = Bluebeard. In the burlesque played at the Gaiety Theatre, London, in 1883, Bluebeard is Baron Abomelique de Barbe Bleue, played by Nellie Farren.

11. *Kemble:* probably John Philip Kemble (1757–1823), the most celebrated of the brothers of Mrs. Siddons. His brother Stephen (1758–1822) was managing the Edinburgh Theatre 1797–1800.

13. Sir Robert Williames Vaughan, 2nd Bt. (1768–1843), of Nannau House near Dolgelley, was M.P. for Merioneth 1792–1836.

14. *Madame de Monteny*: (if that is the name: it is strictly illegible) was the Swiss governess mentioned on p. 10.

– *Practical Education.*

– Henry Kett (1761–1825), Fellow of Trinity College, Oxford, was Bampton Lecturer in 1790 when S. was an undergraduate at New College.

– So the MS. Apparently S. omitted 'time ago' by inadvertence.

– See p. 16.

16. Miss Browne was related to Lady Hicks, Mr. Hicks Beach's mother. She married William Gore Langton, of Newton St. Loe, M.P. for Somerset 1795–1806.

17. *Macintosh:* so S. habitually wrote the name of one of his intimate friends, Sir James Mackintosh (1765–1832), a brilliant member of the Holland House circle, who attained early celebrity by his *Vindiciae Gallicae* (1791) in reply to Burke's *Reflections on the French Revolution*, and wrote various historical and philosophical books, articles in *E.R.*. &c.

– as they would reason upon x: so the MS. The pious prudence of the original editor led her into mistaking this algebraical symbol for the X as the abbreviation of 'Christ', and then into perpetrating one of her pious frauds and printing 'as they would upon a divinity', to the complete mystification of any attentive reader!

18. Dr. Samuel Parr (1747–1825), 'the Whig Johnson', celebrated for his wig, his pipe, and his prolixity. He was a friend of Bentham, Mackintosh, and many distinguished men. He preached 'a Spital Sermon' before the Lord Mayor at Christ Church, Bishopsgate, on Easter Tuesday, 15 Apr. 1800, and published it with an immense mass of notes in 1801. In the sermon he attacked his friend Godwin's *Political Justice*; and S. reviewed both Parr's sermon and Godwin's reply in the first number of *E.R.*, articles II and III – excellent examples of S.'s jovial wit and sound judgement.

Hon. Caroline Fox (1767–1845), the sister of Lord Holland, deservedly one of the best loved persons of her time. On the death of her widowed mother in 1778 she lived first with her step-aunt Henrietta, Countess of Warwick, then (1781) partly with her great-aunt Gertrude, Duchess of Bedford, partly and from 1789 to 1804 entirely at Bowood with her uncle, the 1st Marquess of Lansdowne. Here Bentham, twenty years her senior, is said to have proposed marriage (*The Home of the Hollands*, p. 108). He kept up a correspondence with her to the end of his long life. From 1804 she and her youngest step-aunt Elizabeth Vernon lived together at the farm in the grounds of Holland House. She was one of the most intimate friends of the Sydney Smiths, and god-mother to Saba's first child, Caroline.

19. Mr. Allen: see Letter 100. He took with him the following letter of introduction from S. (reprinted by kind permission from *The Home of the Hollands*, p. 177): 'The bearer of this note is Mr. Allen, of whom I have said so much already that it is superfluous to say any more. That he is a very sensible man you cannot long be ignorant, tho' I sincerely hope you may that he is a very skilful physician. You will speedily perceive that my friend Mr. Allen (who has passed his life in this monastery of infidels) has not acquired that species of politeness which consists in attitudes and flexibilities, but he is civil, unaffected and good-natured. What to compare his French to, I know not: I never heard a sound so dreadful.'

– In this sentence 'create' might be read as 'evoke', 'commotion' as 'animation' or 'conversation'. 'Routes' is a spelling of 'routs' (= evening parties) quoted in *O.E.D.* from *The Rambler* (1751).

– Robert Nares (1753–1829), author of the well-known Nares's *Glossary* (1822) and other works in philology and in divinity. He established *The British Critic* in 1793 and edited it till 1813: it is to this that S. refers in the 'hangman for these ten years . . .'. He was chaplain to the Duke of York and held many ecclesiastical benefices in plurality. The review here in question (*E.R.* i, Art. XX) was of a sermon, 'A Thanksgiving for Plenty, and warning against avarice' (London, 1801). It is one of the nine articles which S. contributed to the first number of the *E.R.* (as well as collaborating with Brougham in another).

20. Archdeacon: of Stafford – one of Nares's numerous ecclesiastical offices.

22. *Archibald Constable:* from Lord Cockburn's *Life of Jeffrey*, i. 134.

23. *Tuxford:* in Nottinghamshire.

25. The only child of Jeffrey's first marriage was born in Sept. 1802 and died on 25 Oct. of the same year. His wife died on 8 Aug. 1805.

– the light, etc.: from Gray's *The Bard*, 40, 41:

> Dear as the light that visits these sad eyes,
> Dear as the ruddy drops that warm my heart:

lines themselves reminiscent of Shakespeare and other poets.

26. *Knight of the Shaggy Eyebrows:* Francis Horner, Jeffrey's letters to whom contain frequent appeals and objurgations to contribute

more to *E.R.* and to complete reviews he has undertaken. Francis Horner (1778–1817), son of an Edinburgh merchant, was one of the founders of *E.R.* and one of S.'s dearest friends. During his short career he was one of the most respected politicians of his day with special authority in the House of Commons on financial and economic questions. His letters, edited by his brother in 1843 (*Memoirs and Correspondence*, 2 vols.) are long, but have charm and interest.

27. Rev. Archibald Alison (1767–1839), from 1800 Minister of the Episcopal Chapel in the Cowgate, Edinburgh. His essay on *Taste* (1790) was much admired by Jeffrey. He and S. were original members of the Friday Club started by Walter Scott, J. A. Murray, and Jeffrey in 1803. He was father of Sir Archibald Alison, the historian.

– *Bishop of London:* Beilby Porteus. I have no clue to the 'business' here mentioned.

28. Thomas Brown (1778–1820), one of the first Edinburgh Reviewers, who withdrew after 'editorial interference' with an article of his in *E.R.* iii. Cf. Cockburn's *Life of Jeffrey*, i. 137. This probably explains S.'s remark that he was 'an impracticable, excellent creature'. He was a precocious pupil of Dugald Stewart, and after studying law and qualifying in medicine, settled down to philosophy, was elected colleague to Stewart, 1810, and was a very popular lecturer. He published a considerable quantity of amiable but uninspired verse. Cf. Letter 712.

– James Scarlett (1769–1844) was the most successful advocate during his career of more than forty years at the bar, and as M.P. and Attorney-General was active in measures of reform, though he strongly opposed the Reform Bill. He was created Baron Abinger on becoming Lord Chief Baron of the Exchequer in 1834. Samuel Foart Simmons (1750–1813), physician, to St. Luke's Hospital 1781–1811, attended George III when insane in 1803 and 1811.

– Dr. Langford. I have not found this name among the numerous doctors named in reference to George III's attacks of insanity.

30. *little poet:* Thomas Campbell (1777–1844), already famous for his *Pleasures of Hope* and ballads, and a literary friend of Lord Holland and other Whig leaders.

– Sir Francis Baring, Bt., M.P., founder of the banking house (1740–1810), was the first Chairman of the London Institution founded in May 1805 to do for the City what the Royal Institution was doing for Westminster.

31. Anne Bannerman: author of a small volume of *Poems* published at Edinburgh in 1800, 12mo. A second edition in quarto, with

the poems rearranged and some omissions and additions, was published, also at Edinburgh, in 1807. From this passage in S. and the fact that the book was dedicated to Lady Charlotte Rawdon, it is a fair inference that it was published by subscription. John Allen (1771–1843) was a learned and impecunious M.D. of Edinburgh and friend of Jeffrey and S. when he became travelling companion to Lord Holland and his wife on a tour in Spain. From that time he was an inmate of Holland House, putting his stores of learning and powers of argument at the service of Lord Holland and the Whig leaders, carving at Lady Holland's dinner-parties and being treated by her, according to Macaulay, no better than a negro slave. They were, however, a devoted family party. Allen contributed to *E.R.* and published a standard work on the Royal Prerogative (1830). He had a great reputation to which testimony is borne by Byron, Brougham, Macaulay, and Greville, as well as S. Cf. the excellent account of him in *The Home of the Hollands*, pp. 176–81.

- *Darcy:* Dugald Stewart's second wife, sister of Scott's friend George Cranstoun, later Lord Corehouse, a Scottish judge. The allusion is to the controversy over the election of John Leslie to the chair of mathematics in Edinburgh which caused much excitement in the General Assembly. Theology and politics played a greater part than mathematics. Leslie was a contributor to *E.R.* He and Stewart and others were freely accused of heresy. Cf. Cockburn's *Memorials*, pp. 186–95, and Horner's article in *E.R.* xiii, Art. VII.

32. *Rum and Black Virgins:* probably alluding to the clergyman in question obtaining a chaplaincy connected with the West Indies.
   Henning: cf. Jeffrey's letter (*Life*, ii. 86) of Oct. 1803 to Horner: 'All we reviewers are getting our heads modelled by Henning, and propose to send him to London to complete the series, by the addition of your vast eyebrows.' John Henning (1771–1851): modeller and sculptor.

- Thomas Thomson (1768–1852) was one of the founders of the *E.R.* and occasionally acted as editor on Jeffrey's behalf. He only contributed three articles (in 1803–4), being a busy advocate (and intimate at the bar with Walter Scott) and becoming more and more devoted to antiquarian legal studies. His chief life-work was done as deputy clerk-register of Scotland, 1806–39. He succeeded Scott as President of the Bannatyne Club in 1832. S. called him 'Jus' to distinguish him from his medical friend John Thomson whom he called 'Pus'; he was also called 'Timotheus' by S. and Jeffrey, for no apparent reason, but presumably with some allusion to Dryden's *Alexander's Feast*.

It was through Bobus, the lifelong friend of Lord Holland from
Eton days, that S. was introduced to Holland House, where he
quickly captivated Lady Holland as at once an invaluable acquisition for her famous dinner-parties, a staunch Whig, and a
sincerely sympathetic friend. His letters throw so much light
upon the characters of both Lord and Lady Holland that I only
add a few brief notes here. Henry Richard Fox (1773–1840)
succeeded as 3rd Baron Holland when only just a year old, and
was brought up in intimacy with his uncle Charles James Fox,
whose liberal principles became the mainspring of his political
life. At the age of 21 he met Elizabeth Lady Webster (1770–
1845), daughter of Richard Vassall, a Jamaican planter, wife
since the age of 16 of an elderly Sussex baronet, whose dullness
she found intolerable. They became lovers and, after a divorce
granted by the House of Lords, were married in 1797. She was
beautiful, intelligent, vivacious, and domineering, often a trial to
her children, devoted to her husband as he to her. Lord Holland
was too much crippled by gout to undertake any of the more
active ministries of state, but was a member of the Cabinets of
Lord Grenville (1806–7) as Lord Privy Seal, of Lords Grey and
Melbourne (1830–40) as Chancellor of the Duchy of Lancaster,
and an assiduous and influential leader of the Whig Opposition
in the House of Lords during the long period of Tory government. His charm and his complete unselfishness won the friendship of men and women of every rank and party.

- The word looks like 'burners', but S. meant 'buriers' and spelt
it with two r's.

34. sc. daughter of Henry Mackenzie (1745–1831), author of *The
Man of Feeling* (1771), &c.

- The article in question must have been *E.R.* xiii, Art. V, reviewing *Hints towards forming the character of a Young Princess* (2
vols., 1805), but it does not seem to deserve the reprobation of
Elmsley and S.

- Anne Bannerman: Letter 100.

- Southey was in Edinburgh in Oct. 1805 and Jeffrey sent him the
review of his poem *Madoc* which he had written for the *E.R.*
Oct. no. xiii before meeting him for the first time. They met on
civil terms, but Southey's attitude was that which is usual in the
genus irritabile vatum towards their critics. 'We talked upon the
question of taste, on which we are at issue; he is a mere child
upon that subject.' Cf. Cockburn's *Life of Jeffrey*, i. 169.

35. Henry Reeve (1780–1814) studied medicine at Edinburgh, was a
member of the Speculative Society, the debating society, founded

in 1764, to which Jeffrey, Scott, Horner, Scarlett, and many other leading spirits belonged (see Cockburn's *Life of Jeffrey*, i. 53), and contributed two articles to *E.R.* iii, Arts. XV, XVI. After the foreign tour referred to in this letter he settled at Norwich as a successful physician, but died at the age of 34. His wife was a sister of Mrs. Sarah Austin, the editor of S.'s letters. His son was Henry Reeve (1813–95), who edited the *Greville Memoirs*, 1856, and was editor of *E.R.* for forty years (1855–95).

– Sir Thomas Bernard (1750–1818) was a notable philanthropist, a liberal benefactor of the Foundling Hospital, where, on his recommendation, S. was appointed alternate evening preacher in March 1805, and originator and Treasurer of the Royal Institution in Piccadilly, where, at his instigation, S. was invited to give his celebrated lectures on Moral Philosophy.

– S. wrote 'glutean' for the more usual 'gluteal'. The gluteal muscles are those of the buttock.

– P. corrects to '1807' and '1806'. S.'s double mistake is very odd.

– The allusion is to Napoleon's swift transference of the Grand Army from Boulogne to the Danube and the capitulation of Ulm on 17 Oct. Dr. Reeve was in Vienna from 30 Sept. till after the battle of Austerlitz (2 Dec.), and saw Napoleon at Schönbrunn. His *Journal of a Residence at Vienna and Berlin in the eventful Winter 1805–6* was published by his son in 1877.

37. No doubt the younger Archibald Alison: cf. p. 37.

– John Richardson (1780–1864), an intimate friend of Jeffrey, a solicitor who migrated from Edinburgh to London in Jan. 1806 and practised as a parliamentary solicitor for many years. He was of a retiring but most amiable character. His elder daughter married Henry Reeve in 1841, but died in 1842. Cf. Cockburn's *Life of Jeffrey*, index.

– Henry Hallam (1777–1859) became an intimate friend of the Hollands and of Lord Lansdowne. Of independent means, he devoted himself to history and gained a great and lasting reputation by his *Middle Ages* (1818), *Constitutional History* (1827), and *Literature of Europe* (1837–9). S. refers to an article by Hallam in *E.R.* xiv, Art. II, on Payne Knight's *An Analytical Inquiry into the Principles of Taste*, which went through two editions in 1805. S. evidently fears that Knight will have taken offence when they hoped that he would write for the *Review*. But the fear was not realized; Knight reviewed Falconer's edition of Strabo in *E.R.* xxviii (July 1809). Richard Payne Knight (1750–1824) was a wealthy, sceptical, learned connoisseur and collector, especially of bronze and coins of which he left a magnificent collection to the British Museum.

Gerrard Andrewes (1750–1825) was Rector of St. James's, Piccadilly, from 1802 and Dean of Canterbury from 1809 till his death. He declined the Bishopric of Chester in 1812. He seems to have been an amiable man and an effective preacher (*D.N.B.*). S.'s application was unsuccessful.

38. The *Peter Plymley Letters* were published from the summer of 1807 to the early part of 1808 in four successive pamphlets and ran at once into many editions. Though S. stated in the preface to his *Works* (2nd ed., 1840) that the Government took pains, without success, to discover the author, the authorship was an open secret from the first.

39. The review of Davy: *E.R.* xxii, Art. VIII. *The Bakerian Lecture on some Chemical Agencies of Electricity*, by Humphry Davy, Esq., Sec. R.S. The article was probably by John Playfair. Jeffrey wrote the review of *Letters from England* by Don Manuel Alvarez Espriella, *E.R.* xxii, Art. VII. (This book was really written by Southey.) Hoyle's *Exodus; an Epic poem in Thirteen Books*; reviewed by Thomas Campbell, *E.R.* xxii, Art. VI, an amusing article which makes legitimate fun of a dull imitation of Milton's manner. It is instructive to see the kind of 'levities' to which S. objected.

39. S.'s article on Methodism, *E.R.* xxii Art. V. Cf. Brougham's *Life and Times*, i. 262: 'The attacks on the Methodists by Sydney Smith gave great offence to a large and powerful body, the Evangelical party, especially in England. They complained, and most justly, that he had confounded the Calvinistic with the Arminian Methodists, charging the former with all the views of the latter, which such men as Wilberforce and Henry Thornton, Babbington, Stephen, and Macaulay were just as incapable of falling into as Sydney Smith himself The Review suffered not only from this great mistake, but from the tone of levity on sacred subjects almost unavoidably assumed by anyone arguing against great and manifest errors, sometimes of a ludicrous description. There were frequent complaints in Edinburgh, much strengthened by the known, and indeed absurd, opinions of William Drummond, who was a frequent contributor, though only upon classical questions.'

William Drummond (1770?–1828) was an eccentric amateur of letters and religious history and philosophy, as well as for a few years an M.P. (1795–1802) and diplomatist (1801–9).

40. Missions: S. wrote this article for the April no., *E.R.* xxiii, Art. IX.

– Mr. M. is Jeffrey's cousin, the Rev. Robert Morehead. He married a sister of Jeffrey's first wife. There are some letters both to

Mr. and to Mrs. Morehead in *Jeffrey's Life and Correspondence*. His *Discourses on the Principles of Religious Belief, as connected with Human Happiness and Improvement* were highly praised by Jeffrey in *E.R.* xxvii, Art VII.

41. Bishop's Lydiard was where S.'s father spent the last years of his life.

  – Amelia Alderson (1769–1853), daughter of a leading Norwich doctor, married in 1798 John Opie (1761–1807), the painter, whose memoir she wrote, 1809. She wrote some sentimental poems and novels which at the time touched the feelings of S. and other educated persons, and charmed innumerable friends of various social and religious circles, from Godwin and Mary Wollstonecroft to Elizabeth Fry, George Borrow, and Walter Scott. Now and then she sent her MSS. to S., who said, 'Tenderness is your forte, and sentiment your fault' (*Amelia*, by Menzies-Wilson and Lloyd, 1937). She was intermittently a Quaker.

  – *The Bishop:* sc. of Norwich, Henry Bathurst (1744–1837), who 'was distinguished throughout his life for the liberality of his principles, and for many years was considered to be "the only liberal bishop" in the House of Lords' (*D.N.B.*).

42. S.'s visit to Howick on this occasion was the beginning of his life-long intimate friendship with Lord and Lady Grey, with whom he had become acquainted in the Holland House circle as Lord and Lady Howick.

  – Sir James St. Clair Erskine (1762–1837) combined a military and political career, being M.P. from 1781 to 1805 when he succeeded, as 2nd Earl of Rosslyn, his uncle, Alexander Wedderburn, notorious among self-seeking politicians, who was created Baron Loughborough on becoming Lord Chief Justice in 1780, was Lord Chancellor 1793–1801, and created Earl of Rosslyn on his retirement. As a soldier Erskine served in various Mediterranean posts, being Commander-in-Chief Mediterranean in 1798. He became an intimate friend of Wellington and was Lord Privy Seal and Lord President of the Council in successive cabinets of Wellington.

  – Drum, the home of the Somervilles, near Edinburgh, was sold by Scott's friend the 15th Baron, in lots between 1800 and 1809. In 1808 the house belonged to Robert Cathcart, W.S., Lord Rosslyn being merely a tenant.

43. *little Vernon:* eldest son of Bobus (1800–73), afterwards a Minister under Melbourne and Palmerston, created Baron Lyveden, 1859. *Lady Affleck:* Lady Holland's mother. Her first husband died in 1795, and in 1796 she married Sir Gilbert Affleck, Bt., who died in 1808. She was beautiful and amiable, and 'she and Miss Fox,

between them, did all they could to make up for Lady Hollands' maternal short-comings' (*C. of H. H.*, p. 191). She died in 1835.

– *the Mufti:* James Whishaw (1764–1840), 'trusted counsellor of the Whig leaders in their long years of exclusion from office, and a familiar figure in their social life during the brightest days of Holland House and Lansdowne House' (W. P. Courtney, *The Pope of Holland House*, p. 19). He was described as 'a short, stout man with a cork leg, very lame, and with a rather surly manner', and both S. and Lady Holland comment on his 'caution' in expressing opinions; but he was justly esteemed for his integrity and generosity. He was affectionately called 'the Pope' and 'the Mufti'. The phrase 'in high leg' is quoted from this letter by *O.E.D.* as meaning 'in high spirits', but no other example is given.

44. Sc. *E.R.* xxv, Art. II, on the Curates Bill, Art. V on the Irish Popery Laws.

– *cheerful day:* Gray's *Elegy*.

– Thornton-le-Clay, the principal village in the parish of Foston, was just outside Foston Rectory.

– S. published 2 vols of *Sermons by the Rev. Sydney Smith, A.M., Late Fellow of New College, Oxford, Rector of Foston in Yorkshire, Preacher at the Foundling, and at Berkeley and Fitzroy Chapels, London.* Cadell and Davies, 1809. They were reviewed with bitter scorn in the *Quarterly Review.*

45. I do not know who the young gunpowder pupil was, but conjecture that his name was Fawkes.

46. Walter Scott was the prime mover of this 'confederacy', which was soon a London one, John Murray the publisher, William Gifford, George Ellis, Canning, &c. See the letter of Scott to Ellis, which gives the best account of the origin of the *Quarterly Review*, which first appeared in Feb. 1809: Lockhart, *Life of Scott*, ch. xviii. Cf. also Cockburn's *Life of Jeffrey*, i. 189 ff.

– 'This review' was presumably Art. IV of *E.R.* xxvi (Jan. 1809) on the Proceedings of the Society for the Suppression of Vice.

– *Bill: E.R.* xxv, Oct. 1808.

– *full:* Sc. his list of chaplains.

– Sheridan and Grey were mutually antipathetic; hence no doubt S.'s mode of speaking of one whom Grey had long known very well in politics and society.

– Barbarina Ogle (1768–1854), daughter of Admiral Sir Chaloner Ogle, married in 1789 Valentine Thomas Wilmot of Farnborough Place, a guardsman and, like herself, a lover of horses. They had nothing else in common except a daughter, afterwards Mrs. Sullivan. Mrs. Wilmot was greatly admired in Whig circles and artistic society, wrote four quasi-historical dramas, of which one was produced by Sheridan in 1815, translated poems of Petrarch, &c. Mr. Wilmot died in June 1819, and in Dec. his widow married Thomas Brand (1777–1851), a Whig M.P., 1806–19, who had become 20th Baron Dacre in Oct.

- Charles Richard Vaughan (1774–1849; knighted) 1833 was a younger brother of Henry Vaughan, better known as the court physician Sir Henry Halford. He had gone to Spain with Brougham's friend Sir Charles Stuart, the diplomatist, afterwards (1828) 1st Baron Stuart de Rothesay. In 1809 he published *A Narrative of the Siege of Saragossa*. He was an able and much-travelled diplomatist, especially as envoy to the U.S.A., 1825–35.

47. The letter is undated and unaddressed, but was written between Christmas 1808 and the New Year.

- *tusks:* P., which omits Brougham's name, prints 'trunks', apparently to improve S.'s picture. Below 'scoundrel' is replaced by 'Tory', to mitigate his ferocity.

- Don Juan: sc. John Allen.

48. Charles Brudenell Bruce (1773–1856), 3rd son of the 1st Earl of Ailesbury, whom he succeeded in 1814. He was M.P. for Marlborough, 1796–1814, created Marquess of Ailesbury at the Coronation of George IV, who had had his father and his uncle the Duke of Montagu as tutors.

- Henry Luttrell (*c.* 1765–1851), natural son of the 2nd Earl of Carhampton, was one of the most celebrated wits and diners-out of the day, one of the intimates of the Holland House circle, and a great friend of Rogers and Thomas Moore.

- Jane Maxwell (1749?–1812), wife of the 4th Duke of Gordon, was for years one of the leaders of society in Edinburgh and London, a confidante of Pitt, a great match-maker, the patroness of Burns. For many years she lived apart from her husband, who was a great landowner, but quite unfitted to be the husband of his brilliant, ambitious, and warm-hearted Duchess.

- Wordsworth: the allusion is to the concluding paragraph of Jeffrey's article on Burns, *E.R.* xxvi. Art I, in which he contrasts the simplicity of Burns with that of the 'new school of poetry' with their 'stuff about dancing daffodils', &c.

- *Brougham's attack:* Brougham's article, 'Don Pedro Cevallos on the French usurpation in Spain', *E.R.* xxv, Art. XIV.

- Alexander Baring (1774–1848), created Baron Ashburton 1835, negotiator of the Ashburton Boundary Treaty with the U.S.A. He published a pamphlet against the Orders in Council in 1808, reviewed, probably by Jeffrey in, *E.R.* xxiii, Art. XIII, and became head in 1810 of the great firm of Baring Brothers founded by his father, Sir Francis Baring.

Samuel Romilly (1757–1818) of Huguenot family, intimate friend of Dumont and through him of Bentham and Lord Lansdowne, devoted his powers chiefly to law-reform. He was Solicitor-General in the 'Ministry of All the Talents' in 1806. He supported Catholic Emancipation and abolition of the slave trade and, in general, all liberal and humanitarian causes. He was a cogent speaker in Parliament and in the law courts. He was greatly respected and loved by his friends, but had a tendency to melancholy, and on the death of his wife, to whom he was devoted, he cut his throat, 2 Nov. 1818.

49. *Mufti:* see above p. 43.

– John William Ward (1781–1833). son of the 3rd Viscount Dudley and Ward, whom he succeeded in 1823, was one of the young Englishmen who were sent to reside with Dugald Stewart and listen to his lectures on Moral Philosophy as a substitute for the Grand Tour during the Napoleonic Wars: Lords Lansdowne and Palmerston were others. This was how S. became acquainted with him. He was a good scholar and a man of parts, who more than once refused political office, but was made an earl and became Foreign Secretary in 1827 in Canning's Ministry. He became more and more eccentric and absent-minded and lost his reason a few months before his death. He was a great friend of the Sydney Smiths. Cf. M., p. 416.

50. This is the only allusion, as far as I know, to S.'s shyness on his first introduction to Holland House.

52. S. refers to the review of his sermons in the *Quarterly Review,* ii. Art. XII, a bitter and contemptuous attack, mainly on the ground of doctrinal insufficiency.

53. Sc. S.'s review of Parr's *Characters of the late Charles James Fox, by Philopatris Varvicensis,* 2 vols., 1809. This article was reprinted by S., *Works,* ii. 341.

– See p. 55.

54. *Suggestions on the Cortes,* a pamphlet printed in 1809, but never published.

– Corrected in P. to 'a Utopia'.

– *I beg . . . time:* Georgina Anne Fox (1809–19). She was Lady Holland's favourite child and was adored by Allen, who by his own desire was buried close to her and her father, 'the objects of his dearest affection' (*C. of H. H.* p. 310). S. was mistaken in the sex.

– *Lauderdale:* see p. 59: cf. Thomas Moore's squib:

> Bright Peer! to whom Nature and Berwickshire gave
> A humour endowed with effects so provoking

That whenever the House is unusually grave
You may always be sure that Lord Lauderdale's joking!

- *My own Pybus*: Sydney's brother-in-law, Charles Small Pybus (1766–1810), M.P. for Dover, a Lord of the Treasury in Pitt's administration, who published in 1800 a fulsome, polished, portentously prosaic and absurd epistle in heroic couplets, called *The Sovereign*, addressed to the Tsar Paul and dedicated to King George III. The notice of this book in the *Gentleman's Magazine*, vol. lxx, pt. ii, p. 854, is worth recalling: 'Mr. Urban's Reviewers are not a match for a Lord of the Treasury in putting together so small a number of lines, on fashionable paper, in fashionable type, with his *own portrait*, not that of his *hero* – for so *small* a price as ONE GUINEA, or, *with the portrait*, £1. 11. 6. Unfortunate experience has shewn that the subject of this poem was unhappily chosen.' Paul was assassinated in 1801.
- *you:* the pronoun is suppressed in P.
- Massena: one of Napoleon's ablest generals, at this time especially noted for his share in the battle of Wagram. Samuel Whitbread (1758–1815), son of the founder of the brewery, was a friend of Lord Grey at Eton, and married his sister in 1789. He became M.P. for Bedford in 1790 and was until his death one of the most eloquent of its members and most active, and often rash, in opposing every sort of abuse and oppression. He died by his own hand, 6 July 1815.
55. Henry Webster (1793–1847), 2nd son of Lady Holland by her first marriage, entered the Army in 1810, was wounded at Vittoria, and fought at Waterloo. He married Grace Boddington, daughter of a rich M.P., in 1824 and was knighted later. (*C. of H. H.*, p. 55).
- Charles Richard Fox (1796–1873), son of the Hollands before their marriage. He had recently been kicked by a horse when hunting at Ampthill. He joined the Navy in the summer, but changed to the Army in 1815. He was restless and often discontented, but had some of his father's charm and fun, and was befriended by the Duke of York and the Duke of Clarence whose 2nd daughter, by Mrs. Jordan, Lady Mary Fitzclarence, he married in 1824. When William IV came to the throne, he was made aide-de-camp to Queen Adelaide, and held posts in the Ordnance. His hobby was collecting, especially coins; his collection of 11,500 Greek coins was bought after his death by the Royal Museum of Berlin.
- Cf. Horace, *Odes*, II. i. 24, *atrocem animum Catonis*.
56. S. uses the French word because the French translation of Ben-

tham's *Principles of Morals and Legislation* was far more familiar than the original. Bentham and Dumont were both friends of the Hollands, but Dumont was more in evidence and was a member of the King of Clubs.

- S. alludes to Bentham's *Table of the Springs of Action*, in which fourteen species of pleasures and corresponding pains are catalogued.

- George Granville Leveson-Gower (1758–1833) became 2nd Marquess of Stafford 1803 and 1st Duke of Sutherland 1833. He married Elizabeth, Countess of Sutherland, 1785, adding most of that county to his already enormous estates, which he administered with great liberality. He was a great patron of art, and supported Catholic Emancipation and the Reform Bill.

- John Crewe (1742–1829), a Whig M.P., created a Baron 1806. His wife, Frances Greville, was famous for beauty, gambling, and intellectual charm, and a great friend of Fox.

57. Undated, but evidently part of the same episode as Letter 178. One regrets the absence of Lady Holland's intermediate one.

- This letter is so complete and faithful a family picture, that I have not been able to resist the temptation to insert it. The joyous and joy-giving father, the tender and devoted wife and mother, the happy children, sensible of their happiness, are all placed before us in these few words. [Note in P.]

58. *account*: in *The Annual Register* for 1806.
   This is inaccurately stated. Lord Grenville was an auditor of the Exchequer and on the motion of Fox (4 Feb. 1806) a Bill was passed allowing him to appoint a deputy in order that he might hold office as First Lord of the Treasury. Lord Ellenborough, Lord Chief Justice, was taken into the Cabinet.

59. James Maitland, 8th Earl of Lauderdale (1759–1839) born at Hatton House, Midlothian, and educated mainly in Scotland, entered Parliament as M.P. for Newport, Cornwall, in 1780, and was a supporter of Fox, and one of the strongest opponents of war with revolutionary France. He succeeded to the Earldom in 1789 and was a Scottish representative peer from 1790 till he became Lord Keeper of the Seal of Scotland in the Ministry of 1806 and was created a Baron of the United Kingdom. He led the Scottish Whigs till the trial of Queen Caroline, when he strongly supported the Government, and became a Tory, voting against the Reform Bill of 1831. In spite of his violent temper and eccentricity he was an intimate friend of the Hollands. He was 'the Noble Lord' of Burke's celebrated *Letter* (1796). He had four sons, none of whom married; his 3rd daughter was grandmother of A. J. Balfour.

60. In Mar. 1811 Lord Holland raised the question of government prosecution for libels in the House of Lords and Lord Folkestone in the Commons, but without success as far as voting went.

- Sir Nash Grose (1740–1814), Judge 1787–1813. Apparently S. alludes to his allocutions from the bench. His only extant 'lecture' is the *Charge to the Grand Jury of Herts*, 1796.

61. So the MS., as frequently.

Lord Sidmouth brought in a Bill for the licensing of Dissenting ministers on 9 May 1811. It was opposed by Lord Holland and others, and petitions against it came pouring in from Dissenting Congregations. Lord Liverpool and the Archbishop of Canterbury argued that the advantages of requiring Dissenting ministers to afford some proof of their qualifications would not outweigh the discontent aroused by the alleged attack upon the liberties of the Dissenters, and the Bill was negatived without a division on the second reading, 21 May.

- Henry Addington (1757–1844), friend from childhood of Pitt, entered Parliament 1783 and became Speaker 1789–1800. When Pitt resigned rather than give up Catholic Emancipation, Addington succeeded him with his support, 1801. He negotiated the Peace of Amiens, 1802, but when the war was resumed in 1803 his feeble administration led to Pitt's return to office. He was created Viscount Sidmouth 1805, was Home Secretary in Lord Liverpool's Ministry 1812–21, and adopted the severest methods of dealing with the economic and political discontent following the long war. His father had been Chatham's doctor and confidant; and he himself was nicknamed 'the Doctor', though bred for the law.

- So MS., and 'accomodation' and 'beleive' and 'Psalsms' below. S. alludes to his brother Robert's return from India, after about seven years as Advocate-General.

62. P. omits 'atheism'.

63. *Charles*: Cf. p. 55.

We are . . . etc.: the attempts of Joseph Lancaster (1778–1838), the Quaker schoolmaster, and of Samuel Whitbread, M.P., to establish elementary schools on the basis of undenominational Christian teaching stimulated the Church to a great effort to establish a national system of Church schools, The National Society was founded with this purpose in 1809, and the movement spread rapidly in the next few years. In 1811 Rev. Andrew Bell (1753–1832), ex-army chaplain and founder of pupil-teacher system in Madras, was appointed Superintendent of the Society. Bell and Lancaster became watchwords in educational controversy. For S.'s doubts of the Church expressed in a more judicial spirit cf. the contemporaneous letter of Horner to Malthus in the *Memoirs of Horner*, ii. 97.

– Son of the Archbishop of York, Archdeacon of the West Riding.

64. A large coach inn of which the sign was a bull standing beside a monstrous human mouth, but the name a corruption of Boulogne Mouth (Harbour), dating perhaps from Henry VIII's capture of Boulogne in 1544. *G.M.* 1818 (1), p. 310.

65. Brougham and the rest had failed at the General Election, but all except Curran obtained seats with little delay. John Philpot Curran (1750–1817), Irish patriot and friend of Grattan, one of the greatest orators of his day, and as famous in his day as S. for his wit. His last public act was to stand for Parliament for the borough of Newry in 1812 in the interest of Catholic Emancipation, but he retired before the end of the poll, 17 Oct.

66. James Abercromby (1776–1858), 3rd son of Gen. Sir Ralph Abercromby, was at this time a Commissioner in Bankruptcy and M.P. for Calne. He became Judge Advocate-General in 1827, Chief Baron of the Exchequer of Scotland in 1830, Speaker of the House of Commons 1835–9, when he was created Baron Dumfermline. He was a frequent diner at Holland House.

– *Excellence :* so the MS. P. corrects to 'Grace'.

67. At York, for the murder of Horsfall, an employer who had invoked the soldiery to shoot down Luddite rioters, who up till then had only wrecked machines.

– *Antonio ;* Lady Holland's page.

– Bobus had broken down in his maiden speech in the House of Commons.

68. S.'s sister (1774–1816), who after the death of her mother in 1802 devoted herself entirely to her father until her own death in 1816.

– *if you . . . lurch :* Bobus died within a fortnight of S.: see *M.*, p. 462.

– Grattan introduced the Roman Catholic Relief Bill to which S. here refers on 30 Apr. 1813 and it passed the second reading by 245 votes to 203. On 11 May Canning had given notice of three clauses which he proposed to move as additions to the Bill in Committee, and these passed the first reading on 19 May. But on 24 May in Committee, Abercromby in the chair, the Speaker, Abbot (afterwards Lord Colchester), moved an amendment excepting the right to sit and vote in either House of Parliament from those conferred on Roman Catholics by the Bill: and on this amendment being carried by 251 votes to 247 the Bill was dropped.

69. *We . . . north:* I cannot identify the persons in this paragraph.

great-minded leader: Jeffrey, whose first wife had died, to his lasting grief, in 1805, made the acquaintance in 1810 of Charlotte Wilkes, a great-neice of the notorious John Wilkes, whose parents lived in New York. On 29 Aug. 1813 he sailed for America, in spite of the war between England and America (1812–14), married Charlotte in October, and returned to England in Feb. 1814. During his absence Murray and Thomas Thomson managed the *E.R.*

70. *Jeffrey . . . them:* eight lines of the MS. are thoroughly obliterated no doubt to remove some 'jesting' of S. which was 'not convenient'.

- *Grafton:* he was actually baptized Windham, after William Windham: the statesman (1750–1810). Lady Holland was his godmother. After a year or two at Dr. Bond's private school at Hanwell he entered the Charterhouse on the nomination of the Archbishop of York in 1825 (not, as R., 1823), went as a pensioner to Trinity College, Cambridge, Oct, 1831, was sent down for insubordination, but allowed to migrate to Caius, July 1835, and took his B.A. 1836. He was for a time a clerk in the Audit Office at £90 per annum. His passion was for horses. He was called 'the Assassin' for killing a bull-dog in his rooms at college. He was a sore trial to his parents and was ultimately given an allowance by his father on condition of his keeping away from his mother's residence. He died 7 Dec. 1871. He is not mentioned in *M.* after his infancy. Cf. Letter 960.

71. *Patronage* which was published in 4 vols., London, 1814, and reviewed by Jeffrey in *E.R.* xliv, Art. X (Jan. 1814). Jeffrey, like Scott, had the highest opinion of Maria Edgeworth and had praised her *Tales of Fashionable Life* enthusiastically in 1809 and 1812.

- *Eunice* was the first of the *Tales of Fashionable Life*. S. does not elsewhere allude to Maria's 'odious father'; in reviewing his *Essays on Professional Education* in *E.R.* xxix (Oct. 1809) he had called him 'manly, independent, liberal'.

- So the MS., but 10 March was Thursday.

72. 'Dry' was a nickname of William Drummond: see p. 240.

73. Woolbeding House was the seat of Lord Robert Spencer, a mile from Midhurst. S. seems to allude to a story about the infancy of that Lord Robert Spencer (1640–1702) who became 2nd Earl of Sunderland on the death of his father at the battle of Newbury in 1643. He had a later adventure in 1688, when he fled to Holland disguised as a woman.

The 'Gilt Room' on the first floor of Holland House, fully described by the Princess Marie Liechtenstein in her *Holland House*, ii. 13 ff.

74. *E.R.* xlvii (Jan. 1815), which was evidently out early - a rare event. It contained Jeffrey's celebrated review of *The Excursion* (Art. I). and that of *Waverley* (Art. XI).

  – Art. II, *On the Light of the Cassegrainian Telescope, compared with that of the Gregorian.* By Capt. Henry Krater, 1813–14. Art. V, on *Scotch Husbandry*, was by James Cleghorn (1778–1838), farmer, actuary, and journalist.

  – *Carnotist:* the article (V) was by Brougham.

  – S. wrote 'Mr. Simon'. M. Simond was uncle to Jeffrey's second wife and is several times mentioned in Cockburn's *Jeffrey's Life and Correspondence*, but not in connexion with any book of travel of this date. Nor is there any article in *E.R.* for 1814 which accounts for S.'s remark. In the List of New Publications in *E.R.* xlvii, however, there is *Letters from Albion to a Friend on the Continent written in the Years 1810–13.* 2 vols., small 8vo.

75. Sc. a member of the family of the baronetcy, Scott of Ancrum, co. Roxburgh. Probably S. is merely indicating that he believes the author to be Walter Scott.

  – Craigcrook, about 3 miles NW. of Edinburgh. According to Cockburn's *Life* (i. 234) Jeffrey gave up his tenancy of Hatton, about 9 miles west of Edinburgh, 'in the autumn of 1814 and in the spring of 1815 transferred his rural duties to Craigcrook, where he passed all his future summers'.

  – *Lady Mary Bennet:* younger daughter of the 4th Earl of Tankerville. She married in 1831 Sir Charles Monck, Bt. (1779–1867), and died in 1861.

  – George Philips (1766–1847), son of a Manchester cotton merchant who bought the Sedgley House estate in 1785, was a friend of Mackintosh, with whom S. became intimate after his settling in Yorkshire, visiting him often at Sedgley and afterwards at Weston House, Shipston-on-Stour, which he built when Manchester became too smoky for him. Philips entered Parliament in 1812 and was an M.P. almost continuously till 1834. He was created a baronet in 1828. His three granddaughters, with whom S. used to romp, became respectively Countess of Camperdown, Lady Carew, and Countess of Caithness (R., pp. 237–8). On this visit with Douglas to Sedgley Park S. preached at Prestwick Church on 12 Jan. Miss Leycester of Toft was staying at the house and denied S.'s assertion that he would make her cry at church. Many years afterwards she told S.'s biographer that she 'could hardly look at the pulpit through her gathering tears' (R., p. 196).

76. *parish:* the allusion is to the attempt of Lord Holland to obtain for S. the living of St. Paul's, Covent Garden, in the gift of the Duke of Bedford.

– *suspension:* Sc. of the Habeas Corpus Act. This measure was passed in Mar. 1817 in consequence of the panic into which Parliament was thrown by 'bread and machinery' riots and the violent language of Cobbett and other Radicals, and, finally, the breaking of the Prince Regent's coach window on his return from opening Parliament. The 'doggrel rhymes' were those of William Hone (1780–1842), *John Wilkes's Catechism, The Sinecurist's Creed, The Political Litany*. Hone was prosecuted for blasphemous libel, but in spite of the efforts of the Lord Chief Justice, Ellenborough, he was acquitted. 'England about to be divided', &c., alludes to the reported intention of the Radicals to overthrow the constitution and to divide up landed estates into small holdings. The 'one armed apothecary' is Viscount Sidmouth, Home Secretary at the time, who had just issued instructions to the lords-lieutenant and magistrates throughout the country to arrest writers and publishers of seditious or blasphemous libels. Grenville and Fitzwilliam were leaders of the Old Whigs, who as landowners and quite the reverse of revolutionary supported the Ministry in their repressive measures at this time, though Fitzwilliam (p. 91) was removed from his lord-lieutenancy of the West Riding for his public censure of the 'Peterloo massacre' in 1819.

77. *to live:* P. alters to 'prolonged his life'; I cannot suggest a reason. Philip Nicholas Shuttleworth (1782–1842), at this time Fellow and Tutor of New College, Oxford, became Warden in 1822 and for the last year of his life Bishop of Chichester. His ex-pupil Henry Fox as an undergraduate at Christ Church kept up his intimacy with him and on his unanimous election as Warden wrote (*Journal*, p. 146): 'I am sure he will acquit himself most nobly. He is as high minded and liberal as possible, and there is nobody to whom I feel so indebted.' He is reputed to have invented the 'railway' for passing the wine across the fire-place at New College.

79. *here:* Sedgley Hall, Prestwick, the home of Mr. (afterwards Sir) George Philips (p. 75).

80. Mackintosh was appointed Professor of Law and General Politics at the East India College at Haileybury in Feb. 1818, a post he held till 1824. He only lectured on two days in the week, and continued to take a considerable part in the debates of the House

of Commons besides writing articles for *E.R.* and a good deal of desultory work. His health was always delicate and, as he says in the very interesting fragment of autobiography which his son incorporated in *Memoirs of Sir James Mackintosh*, he had a habit from childhood of day-dreaming which no doubt accounts for his failure to fulfil the promise of his gifts whether as orator, statesman, historian, or philosopher. There is no evidence as to the particular reason for S.'s expression of pity in the text, but it probably alluded to the disparity between Mackintosh's talents and the humble appointment which he had just accepted.

81. George Tierney (1761–1830) was one of the earliest intimates of Holland House and devoted to Lord and Lady Holland to the end of his days. Son of a wealthy merchant and educated at Eton and Peterhouse, Cambridge, he was called to the Bar, but bent on a political career. He entered the House of Commons in 1788, was ridiculed as 'the friend of humanity' in the *Anti-Jacobin*, fought a duel with Pitt in 1798, and gradually became the leader of the Whigs in the House of Commons, but had neither the family prestige nor party aptitude to force his way to high office and was never in the Cabinet till Canning's brief ministry of 1827. Lord Ilchester quotes Lady Caroline Lamb as writing 'he is the most agreeable man in England', and noting 'his beloved glassy eyes, bushy brows and satisfactory mouth' (*H. of H.*, p. 336).

82. Botherby is the name under which Byron in *Beppo*, stanza 72, ridicules the amiable versifier William Sotheby (1757–1833), great in the Dilettante Society and among the 'Blue-stockings'; often Walter Scott's host in London. *Beppo* was just out and Jeffrey had reviewed it in *E.R.* lviii. and had quoted the reference to Botherby: of the Turkish harem –

> But luckily these beauties are no 'blues',
> No bustling Botherbys have they to show 'em
> 'That charming passage in the last new poem'.

83. *Brougham's pamphlet: A Letter to Sir Samuel Romilly M.P. upon the abuse of Charities.* This went through many editions in 1818 and along with other contributions to the controversy was reviewed in *E.R.* lxii (Mar. 1819), Art. XII. The Bishop was George Henry Law (1761–1845), Bishop of Chester 1812–24, of Bath and Wells 1824–45. He and Lord Lonsdale were benefactors of St. Bees College; the college was treated more or less as Lord Lonsdale's property.

85. John Barrow (1764–1848), Second Secretary of the Admiralty for many years and founder of the Royal Geographical Society,

created a baronet 1835. He was private secretary to Lord Macartney in the first British embassy to China in 1792, and wrote several travel-books which were reviewed in *E.R.* The new NW. expedition was that under Capt. (afterwards Rear-Admiral Sir) William Edward Parry, who had commanded a brig in the expedition of 1818 under Capt. (afterwards Rear-Admiral Sir) John Ross. There is a long article on these expeditions (while the second was in process) in *E.R.* lxii (Mar. 1819), Art. V.

85. Thomas Erskine (1750–1823), Lord Chancellor in the 'Ministry of All the Talents', perhaps the most brilliant advocate ever for defence and one of the wittiest of talkers. Byron described him as 'the most brilliant person imaginable, quick, vivacious and sparkling, he spoke so well that I never felt tired of listening to him, even when he abandoned himself to the subject of which all his dear friends expressed themselves so much fatigued – self'. He was as vain as his eldest brother the 11th Earl of Buchan, the antiquarian friend of Scott, and lacked the sterling character of his other brother Henry, the friend of S. and Jeffrey, himself the most brilliant advocate at the Scottish bar. His vanity and lack of character spoilt his later years. His first wife died in 1805. On 12 Oct. 1818 he married Sarah Buck at Gretna Green, and vainly tried to divorce her in 1820 on the ground of insanity.

 – Henry Torrens (1779–1828) saw much military service abroad and became aide-de-camp to the Prince Regent in 1812, Major-General 1814, K.C.B. 1815.

87. *Hallam's . . . Europe in the Middle Ages* was first published in 1818, and reviewed in *E.R.* lix (Sept,). Art. V.

 – No doubt Rogers and Moore.

 – Probably Lady Georgiana Morpeth.

 – *The Bride of Lammermoor:* published with *The Legend of Montrose*, as the 3rd series of *Tales of my Landlord*, 4 vols. At the end of vol. 4 the author stated that he was 'retiring from the field'. At the same time the news was widespread of Scott's very serious illness: but in fact he had already begun to write *Ivanhoe*.

89. Thomas Moore had held the sinecure of Admiralty registrar at Bermuda since 1803. In 1819 he was rendered liable for £6,000 by the defalcations of his deputy there, and took refuge abroad till 1822, when the debt had been paid. Moore declined the help offered by Rogers, Jeffrey, and other friends.

 – This letter was reproduced in *Archibald Constable and His Literary Correspondents*, iii. 131, and quoted in part by R., pp. 214–15.

91. William Wentworth-Fitzwilliam, 2nd Earl (1748–1833), friend of Charles James Fox and Lord Carlisle, a Whig statesman of

very independent and impetuous character, of some Radical sympathies and unrestrained utterance. He was appointed Lord-Lieutenant of the West Riding, when the 11th Duke of Norfolk was dismissed for proposing the toast 'Our sovereign's health – the majesty of the people' at the celebrated political banquet at the Crown and Anchor Tavern in Jan. 1798. He was in turn dismissed in 1819 for holding in conjunction, with the 12th Duke of Norfolk and others, a meeting of some 20,000 persons at York which called for an inquiry into 'the Peterloo massacre'. He had been a very popular Lord-Lieutenant of Ireland 1794–5 and was Lord President of the Council in the Ministry of 1806–7.

92. *sad event:* the death of 'Gina'. Georgiana (more correctly Georgina, but known as Gina) was born in 1809 and died in 1819. She was Lady Holland's favourite child, and was adored by Allen, who by his own desire was buried close to her and her father, 'the objects of his dearest affection' (*C. of H. H.*, p. 310).

95. William Smith (1756–1835) was M.P. for most of the years 1784–1830, constantly advocating the claims of the Dissenters, parliamentary reform, the abolition of the slave trade. He was also patron of the painters Cotman and Opie.

97. Lady Charlotte Campbell (1774–1861) was youngest daughter of John 5th Duke of Argyll and of Elizabeth, one of the three famous Gunning sisters. She, too, was noted for her beauty. She married Col. John Campbell, on whose death in 1809 she was appointed one of Princess Caroline's ladies, and was one of the most effective witnesses for the defence of Caroline's character in the trial of 1820, In 1818 she married the Rev. E. J. Bury (1790–1832), and from 1822 to 1842 published anonymously a number of popular sentimental novels and some books of devotion. In 1838–9 a *Diary illustrative of the Times of George IV* was published anonymously (it was alleged without her knowledge) and sold like wildfire.

100. *poor—:* I can find no article in the *Q.R.* for 1820 to which S.'s remarks seem applicable. It is possible that the paragraph has been interpolated from another letter.

101. Alluding to the Chillingham cattle of Lady Mary's father, Lord Tankerville.

– *Southey: Life of Wesley* (1820).

102. *Kenilworth.*
Heneage Finch, 5th Earl of Aylesford (1786–1859), was Tory M.P. for Weobley, 1807–12, when he succeeded to the earldom. He married, 23 Apr. 1821, Augusta Sophia, daughter of George Greville, 2nd Earl of Warwick, a niece of Bobus's wife.

103. Elizabeth Grey married J. C. Bulteel in 1826; Georgiana did not marry.

– Sc. Lady Georgiana Morpeth. Her 3rd daughter, Harriet Elizabeth, married George Granville, 2nd Duke of Sutherland, in 1823, and was later Mistress of the Robes to Queen Victoria.

104. *E.R.* lxxi (Oct. 1821), Arts VI and VIII. Art. VI ends with a fervid eulogy of Scarlett.

– *E.R.* lxxi, Art. VII. No article on Suard appeared. It appears from this letter that the July no. lxx was not out by 7 Aug.

106. *Mary:* the Hollands' daughter, born 1806. She married in 1830 the 3rd Baron Lilford (1801–61).

107. Michael Angelo Taylor (1757–1834) was the son of the successful architect, Sir Robert Taylor (1714–88), who founded b y bequest the Taylor Institution for modern languages at Oxford. He was in Parliament with short intervals from 1784 till his death, an active committee-man, especially in regard to the paving and lighting of London. His wife was Frances Anne, daughter of the Rev. Sir Henry Vane, Bt.

– Allen's congratulations were on S. being given the living of Londesborough in the E. Riding of Yorkshire by the Duke of Devonshire for a term of years. See p. 109.

– Viz. Archdeacon Wrangham and Canon William Vernon, the only two of the clergy to support S. in a counter-petition to that of a crowded meeting of the clergy of Cleveland at Thirsk in Mar. 1825 against Catholic Emancipation (R., p. 243). Francis Wrangham (1769–1842), Archdeacon of Cleveland 1820–8, and of E. Riding 1828–41, was a wealthy clergyman, an early literary friend of Wordsworth, a classical scholar and prolific author of verses, especially translations, of sermons, and miscellaneous writings.

– William Venables Vernon (1789–1871) was fourth of the eleven sons of Archbishop Vernon (Harcourt 1831) and ultimately his heir. He entered the Navy in 1801, left it and went to Christ Church, Oxford, in 1807, took Orders in 1814, and with the living of Bishopsthorpe became his father's chaplain. In 1824 he was made a residentiary Canon of York. 'He was one of two clergymen who ventured to sign Sydney Smith's petition to Parliament in 1825 in favour of Catholic Emancipation' (R., p. 249). He is chiefly remembered as the founder and first general secretary of the British Association, which held its first meeting at York in Sept. 1831. He married 11 July 1824 Matilda Mary Gooch. In 1861 he succeeded his brother George to the Harcourt estates and removed to Nuneham. He was father of the statesman Sir William Harcourt (1827–1904).

108. Undated. Not earlier than 1824 as the paper bears a watermark of that year, nor after S. had set up a carriage in London, which he did as a Canon of St. Paul's. He often stayed with Bobus at 20, Savile Row. I am inclined to place the letter in the summer of 1825 when the Greys and S. were in London.

– *an happy match:* Lady Granville writes from Paris in Oct. (*Letters*, i. 360) an amusing account of Mary Fox's brilliant *début*: 'She *débuttéd* at a little soirée on Monday. Prince Frederick of Prussia did not admire, he immediately fell over head and ears in love. . . . In short, Mary is a sort of sky-rocket in Paris. I see her with my London eyes . . . a bright, good, amiable little thing – rather too precise, but a perfectly amiable little soul.' Lady Cowper alludes to the same incident in a letter of Oct. (*Lady Palmerston and her Times*, by Lady Airlie, i. 125).

– Possibly 'Locker': presumably the new Earl's major-domo. Henry Howard (1757–1842) of Corby Castle, Cumberland, a Roman Catholic Whig and antiquary. In this year he published *Remarks on the Erroneous Opinions Entertained respecting the Catholic Religion*.

– William Ord (1781–1855), M.P. for Morpeth 1802–30, for Newcastle 1835–52, a Whig and friend of the Greys and Hollands.

– *Lord Milton:* Charles William Wentworth-Fitzwilliam (1786–1857) eldest son of the 2nd Earl Fitzwilliam, was M.P. for Malton in 1806 and for Yorkshire 1807–30. He resembled his father in politics and temperament, and proved a difficult man to deal with both in the ministerial confusion on the death of Canning and in the crisis of Lord Grey's Reform Bill: cf. Lady Granville's *Letters* and Greville's *Memoirs*. Here, of course, S. is merely playing on his name and the poet's but Lady Holland would feel a certain aptness in the play.

– *Ryders:* John Stuart-Wortley (1801–55), eldest son of the 1st Baron Wharncliffe was Tory M.P. for Bossiney 1823–32, and for the West Riding 1841–5, when he succeeded his father. Like his father, he took a mediating line on the Reform Bill. He married, 12 Dec. 1825, Georgiana Ryder, daughter of the 1st Earl of Harrowby.

109. James Warren Doyle (1786–1834), Bishop of Kildare and Leighlin, the ablest and most eloquent champion of Catholic Emancipation of his day, and an exemplary diocesan. He published letters on the state of Ireland in 1824–5.

– *Memoirs of Captain Rock the celebrated Irish Chieftain . . . written by himself* was written by Moore. Published in April 1824, it had great success, as Moore's *Diary* testifies, especially among Whigs and Roman Catholics. S. reviewed it in *E.R.* lxxxi, Art. VII.

Admiral Sir Sidney Smith (1764–1840), celebrated for the defence of Acre in 1799. After retirement he lived mostly in Paris; in early life he was able to pass for a Frenchman.

– *This letter . . . it:* Cf. *M.*, p. 255: 'The only purchase he made for himself in Paris, though he brought us all a gift, was a huge seal, containing the arms of a peer of France which he met with in a broker's shop, and bought for four francs: this he declared should henceforth be the arms of his branch of the Smith family.'

110. The celebrated French actress, for 33 years the favourite of the Comedie Française and Parisian society from Napoleon onwards. Lady Granville often writes of her 'perfect' acting. Cf. Letter 472.

– John Crocker Bulteel, (d. 1843) of Flete House Devon, M.P. for South Devon 1833–4, High Sheriff 1841, married 13 May 1826, Elizabeth 2nd daughter of Lord and Lady Grey. Lady Granville writes on 22 Aug. 1830, 'the Bulteels, the happiest couple I ever saw, devoted to each other, fond of all the same things, their children and place, drawing like artists, singing like nightingales' (*Letters*, ii. 61).

– *Mr. Bea:* Perhaps 'Beaumont' or 'Beauclerk': the MS. is torn. Lord Dudley died unmarried.

111. *7 o'clock:* P. correctly supplies 'at the Ambassador's'.

It seems probable that S. makes a slip in writing Sir Charles for Sir Thomas Hardy, as the latter (1769–1839, Nelson's captain) and his wife were friends of the Granvilles and in Paris at this time. Lady Hardy was a daughter of Admiral Sir George Cranfield Berkeley (1753–1818), who in 1874 married Emily Charlotte Lennox, a sister of the Duke of Richmond. Her story, mainly from her diaries, is well told in *Nelson's Hardy and His Wife*, by John Gore (1935).

– I cannot identify Mr. and Mrs. Ellis: neither Agar Ellis nor Charles Ellis (afterwards Lord Seaford) had a wife at this date to be called Mrs. Ellis. Possibly S. meant Ellice. Edward Ellice (Letter 679) married a sister of Lord Grey.

– Lady Caroline Wortley, daughter of John Crichton, 1st Earl Erne, married James Archibald Stuart Wortley in 1799. Lady Granville writes of her, 5 Dec. 1824: 'Lady Caroline Wortley adores Paris and she is to me like a moonlight night after a hot day, refreshment and repose.' Her husband became 1st Baron Wharncliffe this year.

– Ralph Sneyd (1793–?) succeeded to the family estate of Keele

Hall, Staffs., in 1829 and was High Sheriff in 1844. He was a lively witty visitor and correspondent of Lady Granville (*Letters, passim*).

– Perhaps James Abercromby, the future Speaker, rather than his son Ralph who would be one of the 'two or three attachés'.
Edward Stanley of Cross Hall, Lancs., related to the Earl of Derby (1789–1870), married in 1819 Mary, daughter of the 8th Earl of Lauderdale: she died in 1877.

– John Hobart Cradock (1799–1873), a son of General Sir John Francis Cradock who was created Baron Howden 1819. John Cradock joined the Grenadier Guards soon after Waterloo and was aide-de-camp to Wellington in Paris; in 1824 he was an attaché at Berlin and from 1825 to 1826 to Lord Granville in Paris. He afterwards had a varied and adventurous career as a diplomat at Navarino, Antwerp, Spain, S. America. He married in 1830 Catherine, daughter of Count Skavonsky. He was extremely handsome and, as S.'s 'Crevecœur' implies, noted for his flirtations. Cf. Lady Granville's *Letters, passim*. He succeeded as 2nd Baron Howden in 1839, but had no children.

113. Dorothea Bland (1762–1816), known as Mrs. Jordan, the favourite actress of comedy of both the public and the critics. From 1790 to 1811 she was the mistress of the Duke of Clarence (William IV), to whom she bore ten children, one of whom, Mary, married Lord and Lady Holland's eldest son, Charles (Letter 175).

– Elizabeth Farren (1763–1829), married in 1797 the 12th Earl of Derby as his 2nd wife.

– F. H. Alexander Baron von Humboldt (1769–1859), the greatest traveller and all-round man of science of his age, courted by rulers and academies, principal founder of modern physical geography and meteorology, younger brother of the famous philologist Karl Wilhelm von Humboldt (1767–1835).

– Georges Baron de Cuvier (1769–1832), celebrated especially for his classification of the animal kingdom, held many high offices in the University of Paris and in the State, and was made a peer of France by Louis Philippe in 1831.

– *Prince Talleyrand*: this most supple and sagacious of statesmen was a friend of Lord Holland ever since, as an undergraduate, he visited Paris in 1791.

114. Mme de Bourke, the widow of Edmond Comte de Bourke (1761–1821) of Irish family settled in Denmark, Danish ambassador in London 1814–19, in Paris 1820–1. Mme de Bourke figures as a lively outspoken friend of Lady Granville in the latter's *Letters, passim*.

So the MS.; 'daughter-in-law' P. Actually 'step-daughter', her mother being Caroline, widow of Sir George Berriman Rumbold. This daughter Caroline married in 1828 Col. Adolphe de St. Clair of the Garde de Corps and died in 1847. Cf. Lady Granville's *Letters*, ii. 3.

– *Letter to the Electors upon the Catholic Question: Works*, iii. 315–53.

115. But not of the French names of the menu, which S. spells in his own phonetic manner. Macreau = Maquereau: Harricaux = Haricots.

116. I do not know which member of the Vane family this is; perhaps the Vane mentioned by Creevey (*Papers*, p. 438) as a satellite of Leach. Mrs. Taylor was daughter of the Rev. Sir Henry Vane, who was created a baronet in 1782.

– *Lingard*: Allen, in *E.R.* lxxxiii (Apr. 1825), Art. I and lxxxvii (June 1826), Art. IV, severely criticized Lingard's accounts of the Anglo-Saxon period and of the Massacre of St. Bartholomew in his *History of England*. John Lingard (1771–1851) was a temperate Roman Catholic of Gallican views, *persona grata* to Popes Pius VII and Leo XII, but not to the ultra-papalists. From 1811 till his death he lived in the village of Hornby, 9 miles from Lancaster, where he was much beloved, and was frequently visited by Brougham and others of the Northern Circuit. In 1839 the Hollands induced Lord Melbourne to grant him £300 from the privy purse of the Queen.

– *The lady*: Mary, daughter of William Rigby of Oldfield Hall, Cheshire.

– Mackintosh lived for some time at Lord Holland's seat at Ampthill Park on his retirement from his professorship at Haileybury in 1824.

117. The title is omitted in P. Published anonymously in 3 vols. by Hunt and Clarke, as a sequel to *Truth*, published the year before; both novels being written, according to the Preface, 'in defence of Deists, not of Deism; and surely the line may be drawn'. The book is so unreadable that it seems strange that the author, William Pitt Scargill (1787–1836), should have eked out a small income as a Unitarian Minister by such means. Some of his short essays contributed to periodicals and collected by his widow (1837) are (as the *D.N.B.* says) 'brisk and readable'. Apparently a slip for 'Three', the book being *Three Months in Ireland: by an English Protestant*.

118. So the MS. Frederick John Robinson (1782–1859), 2nd son of the 2nd Baron Grantham, was M.P. for Ripon 1807–27 and held many offices. He was Chancellor of the Exchequer 1823–7,

created Viscount Goderich and Secretary of State for War and the Colonies Apr. 1827, and succeeded Canning as Prime Minister in August. He resigned in Jan. 1828, held office again in Lord Grey's Government, and was created Marquess of Ripon in 1833.

– The Lord Chancellor, Lord Lyndhurst, who succeeded Lord Eldon in April, and did not in fact lose his office in the change of Ministry in Aug.

– It is impossible to be certain of the figure written: the '300' is followed by a very minute 'o' and then a wavy line, which probably stands for punctuation.

– *Cleopatra*: probably Lady Lyndhurst. Sarah Garay Brunsden (*c.* 1795–1834) was the beautiful and sparkling widow of Lt-Col.. Charles Thomas, who was killed at Waterloo. In Mar. 1819 she married John Singleton Copley (1772–1863), who was knighted the following June on becoming Solicitor-General, and created Baron Lyndhurst as Lord Chancellor a few weeks after this letter. She exercised great fascination among men of all ages; e.g. Henry Fox at 27 years (*Journal*, 355 foll.), Lord Grey at 63 (Greville, *Memoirs*, ii. 86). An alleged attempt at violent love-making by the Duke of Cumberland was a society scandal: but Lord Lyndhurst always refused to play the jealous husband, being himself somewhat of a charmer.

– William Wilberforce (1759–1833), the famous champion of the slaves, as charming as he was good, was M.P., mostly for Yorkshire, from 1780 to 1825, when he retired owing to failing health.

– A medicine for the bite of a mad dog, discovered by one William Hill of Ormskirk, which 'made Ormskirk famous' (*V.C.H. Lanc.* iii. 261).

119. George Hibbert (1757–1837) became a leading West India merchant, influential with Pitt and other statesmen. He was Whig M.P. for Seaford 1806–12, but after the Reform Act supported the Conservatives. He was one of the founders of the West India Docks; also of the London Institution, being F.R.S. (1811) and a great collector of books, prints, pictures, and rare plants. He was a member of the Roxburghe Club, and edited for the Club in 1819 Caxton's translation, *Six Bookes of Metamorphoses by Ovyde*. He married Elizabeth Fonnereau of Huguenot descent, sister of a wealthy and artistic solicitor Thomas George Fonnereau. She in 1829 inherited Munden in Herts. from her uncle Roger Parker; this afterwards became the home of S.'s daughter Emily, who married Nathaniel Hibbert on 1 Jan. 1828. Emily (1807–74) 'resembled S. in character more closely than any of his other children' (R., p. 263). The pair were remembered by Bar-

barina, wife of Lord Grey's 3rd son, Admiral Sir Francis Grey, and granddaughter of S.'s friend Lady Dacre, in *A Family Chronicle*, p. 191: 'She was very clever, extremely cultivated and well-read, and having passed her life with clever people at home and clever people in Society, was a delightful companion. ... Mr. Hibbert was, I think, the most agreeable man I ever met, full of cleverness and knowledge, very original in his views, and with that rare and valuable gift of making those he talked to feel as if they were clever too.' Their daughter, Elizabeth Margaret, married Henry Thurstan Holland (1825–1914), son and heir of Sir Henry Holland and stepson of Saba, created Viscount Knutsford in 1895; she died in 1855.

- Lord Lyndhurst, who became Chancellor in April of this year.
- Courtenay (1775–1843) was the youngest of the four brothers and went after S. to Winchester in 1783. He ran away twice, but survived his miseries to go up the school and win more than his share of prizes, till he left in 1792 to become a writer in the East India Company's offices at Calcutta. Here he became a leading Oriental scholar, and rose to be a Judge of the Supreme Court, and amassed a fortune. We know even less about his quarrel with the E.I.C. than about his brother's with Sir George Barlow in 1810, which S. evidently has in mind here. From a letter of Caroline Fox to her nephew Henry, of 11 Apr. 1828 (kindly supplied by Lord Ilchester), we learn that Courtenay was expected in that month, and that he had been reinstated in his judgeship, 'from which he had been very unjustly suspended', and was therefore only coming on leave of absence for three years. He died in 1843 (not 1839, as stated by R., p. 16).
- *1782:* So the MS. – unaccountably.
- *Captain Howard:* Frederick George (1805–34), 2nd son of the 6th Earl of Carlisle, 'accidentally killed. 18 Nov. 1834' (*Burke*).

120. John Russell, 6th Duke of Bedford (1766–1839), M.P. for Tavistock 1788–1802, succeeded to the dukedom in 1802 and was Lord-Lieutenant of Ireland in the 'Ministry of All the Talents'. He rebuilt Covent Garden Market 1830, was mainly interested in agriculture and botany, but also enriched Woburn Abbey with many works of art. He was father of Lord John Russell the statesman.

121. *Longleat:* The seat of the Marquess of Bath, near Warminster.
- The *Memoirs of the Duke of Rovigo* were published both in the original French and in translation in London 1828. Anne Jean Marie René Savary (1774–1833) was one of Napoleon's chief generals and diplomatists and stuck to him to the end, being on the *Bellerophon* which brought him to Plymouth after Waterloo. He was created Duke of Rovigo in 1807.

place: Oakley Park. Glos.

- Lady Hardy: Letter 470. This proved a false report, but Lord John, now a bachelor of 36, seems to have courted, with diffidence unlike his political character, both Emily, born in 1809, and Louisa, born in 1808, till he was firmly rejected by the latter in 1834. For the whole story see *Nelson's Hardy and His Wife,* by John Gore. Lord John married in 1835 Adelaide, sister of S.'s friend Lister, the young widow of the 2nd Lord Ribbesdale and mother of four children; she died in childbirth in 1838. See *C. of H. H.,* p. 202. He afterwards married, in 1841, Frances 2nd daughter of the 2nd Earl of Minto (1815–98).

- Edward Maltby (1770–1859), Bishop of Chichester 1831, of Durham 1836, a contemporary of S. at Winchester.

122. Edward John Littleton (1791–1863), created Baron Hatherton, 1835. At this time he was M.P. for Staffordshire. He was Chief Secretary in Ireland, 1833–4.

- Two of these were the 4th Duke of Newcastle, Henry Pelham Fiennes Pelham Clinton (1785–1851), the most bigoted Tory of his time, and George 2nd Baron Kenyon (1776–1855), to whom the Duke addressed an open letter: see *G.M.,* Sept. 1828. The third may have been Lord Winchelsea, or Lord Teynham, or Lord Bexley.

- A meeting was held at Penenden Heath in Kent on 24 Oct. to protest against the impending Catholic Emancipation. It was organized by the Kentish Club, one of the 'Brunswick' Clubs inaugurated at Dublin, and addressed by Lord Bexley (Nicholas Vansittart, 1766–1851. Chancellor of the Exchequer 1812–23), Lord Teynham, *et al.,* and in opposition by the R.C. Bishop of Kildare (p. 256), Cobbett, *et al.* The protest was carried with acclamation, but the anti-Catholic agitation had very little popularity.

- Henry William Paget (1768–1854), the distinguished soldier who, as Lord Uxbridge, lost a leg at Waterloo and was immediately created Marquess of Anglesey. He was Lord-Lieutenant of Ireland in 1828, but would not suppress the agitation for Catholic Emancipation as the King and the Duke of Wellington's Ministry required, and was recalled early in 1829.

- Jeremy Taylor's celebrated tract on *Liberty of Prophesying* ends with this story, which he believed to be of Jewish origin, but which was in fact Persian: see Heber's *Life of J. T.* prefixed to his *Works,* published in this year 1828. Owing to carelessness the story became incorporated in Benjamin Franklin's writings: *M.,* p. 270.

- *Horton:* see p. 155.

123. Nevertheless Lady Mary (1807–84) did marry, 30 July 1829, Charles Wood (1800–85), Whig M.P. for Great Grimsby. He was in the House of Commons 1826–66, member for Halifax 1832–65; hence his title on being created a Viscount in 1866. He held various offices and was a sound and industrious administrator, especially as Secretary of State for India, 1859–66.

  – Edward Grey (1782–1837) was Lord Grey's youngest brother. He succeeded Bishop Blomfield in 1828 as rector of St. Botolph, Bishopsgate, became Dean of Hereford in 1830 and Bishop of that diocese in 1832. He married 3 times and had 17 children, of whom 13 survived him; he was therefore an appropriate object of his brother's notorious nepotism. Cf. *G.M.* for Sept. 1837.

  – Letter 521.

124. Letter 522.

125. *Love:* P. has 'Easter-dues' – probably substituted from some other letter or from some remembered sally. In a letter of 5 Dec. to Lord Holland, Caroline Fox writes: 'Sydney's waterdrinking system certainly does not diminish his animal spirits. He dined at home again yesterday, and was full of irresistible fun and nonsense, that disarms criticism and makes Bobus laugh till he cries.' (I owe this quotation to Lord Ilchester.)

  – *George:* Lord Morpeth.

127. Henry George Grey (1802–94), eldest son of the 2nd Earl, Viscount Howick from 1807–45, when he succeeded as 3rd Earl. He entered Parliament in 1826 and was all his life an active Whig of advanced and independent views. He was Secretary for War 1835–9, for Colonies 1846–52.

128. Lord Grey presided at the first annual meeting of 'the London University' recently established as a non-sectarian institution. *A.R. 1829 Chron.*, p. 119.

  – *about her:* William Cavendish (1808–91) was a cousin of the 6th Duke of Devonshire whom he succeeded as 7th Duke in 1858, having succeeded his own grandfather as 2nd Earl of Burlington in 1834. He was 2nd wrangler and 8th classic at Cambridge, and a Liberal M.P. from 1829 to 1834. He married Blanche Georgiana (1812–40), 4th daughter of the 6th Earl of Carlisle on 6 Aug. 1829. He, like others of his family, was notably taciturn, but affectionate and honourable, and, though, taking little part in politics, filled many public positions, Chairman of the Railway Commission 1865, Chancellor of London, Cambridge, and Manchester (Victoria) Universities, &c.

129. The scrawl is no doubt meant for 'detained', though it might as easily be taken for 'deterred' or 'debarred'. The word *accident* is underlined – an unusual thing with S. and probably implying

irony here. The Duke of Wellington resided much at Walmer Castle after he succeeded Lord Liverpool as Warden of the Cinque Ports in Jan. 1829.

- *two Sons:* Charles 'was given command of a regiment stationed at Halifax, Nova Scotia in July 1829'. He sailed in Sept., but returned a year later on being appointed an equerry to Queen Adelaide (*C. of H. H.*). Henry paid one of his reluctant visits to England, July to Dec.

- I do not know to what scandal S. is referring. The notes of exclamation suggest that the 'great friend of yours' is ironical.

130. *Apostates:* alluding to the vote on Catholic Emancipation.

- *abuse:* The Crown took proceedings against the scurrilous *Morning Journal* for libelling the King, Parliament, the Prime Minister, and the Lord Chancellor, with reference to Catholic Emancipation, and the journal was suppressed; Robert Alexander, the editor, being sentenced to one year's imprisonment and a fine of £300 (Greville, i. 346). Robert Bell (1800–67), editor of *The Atlas*, was also indited for libelling Lord Lyndhurst to the effect that he or his wife had trafficked in the Chancellor's ecclesiastical patronage. The jury found him guilty of the fact, but not of malice, and recommended him to the mercy of the court. Accordingly he was not brought up for judgement. Bell wrote and edited many popular books, especially *The English Poets*, 24 vols., 1854–7. He was a friend of Thackeray.

- S.'s nephew Robert Vernon Smith (later Lord Lyveden). He had already 3 sons and later had another. The only daughter was Evelyn Elizabeth (1829–73).

131. Augustus Wall Callcott (1770–1844), the painter, R.A. 1810 knighted 1837. He married Maria Graham (*née* Dundas), widow (1785–1842), in 1827. She wrote, among other books, *Little Arthur's History of England* (1835). She was a close friend of Caroline Fox (*C. of H. H.*, p. 108.)

- Louisa Petty-Fitzmaurice, only daughter of the 3rd Marquess of Lansdowne, married in 1845 James Kenneth Howard (1814–82) and died in 1906.

- Lord Lansdowne's eldest son, born 1811, died, long before his father, in 1836. Macaulay, staying at Bowood a few months after S., wrote to his father: 'Lord Kerry is quite a favourite of mine, – kind, lively, intelligent, modest, with the gentle manners which indicate a long intimacy with the best society, and yet without the least affectation' (*Life*, ch. 3).

- Jeffrey became Dean of the Faculty of Advocates in 1829, Lord Advocate 1830, Judge of the Court of Session 1834.

- Louisa Georgiana, the elder daughter of Lord and Lady Bathurst.

Zoë Talon (1784–1850), daughter of an intriguer of the Revolution and Empire who had died in exile, married the Comte du Cayla but was living apart from him in the family of the Prince de Condé. She was introduced to Louis XVIII by the ultra-royalists in order to supplant his favourite Décazes, whose royalism was too tolerant for them. Louis lavished favours upon her, including the château of St. Ouen, near Paris, and she was his go-between with his brother and heir Charles Comte d'Artois and the politicians and ecclesiastics around them. On Louis's death she was pensioned and wrote her memoirs in retirement.

132. Controversy on Bentham and Utilitarianism and James Mill's *Essay on Government* was carried on between the *E.R.* and the *Westminster Review*, through four numbers of either, Macaulay being the chief assailant. The *W.R.* had started in 1824, as a Radical as well as Utilitarian organ, with a denunciation of the moderate Whig policy of *E.R.* Macaulay's attack on Mill was much too scornful, but Mill, who held an influential post in the India House, supported the appointment of Macaulay to the Indian Council in 1833.

133. George Nugent-Grenville, Baron Nugent in the Irish peerage (1789–1850), was grandson of George Grenville the Prime Minister of 1763–5, and 2nd son of the Whig leader who became Marquess of Buckingham in 1784. His mother was daughter of the 1st Lord Nugent of Carlanstown in the Irish peerage; the barony was granted to her in 1800, with special remainder to this 2nd son George (the elder son Richard being heir to the marquisate). George succeeded to the barony in 1812. He was a strong Whig, a Lord of the Treasury in Grey's Ministry 1830–2, High Commissioner to the Ionian Islands 1832–5. He published *Memorials of John Hampden*, 1832, and other books. He was, as S.'s reference here implies, a big fat man.

– Sydney Owenson (1783?–1859), daughter of the actor-manager Robert Owenson (1744–1812). She had a considerable vogue as novelist of Irish life and writer of travel books, both before and after her marriage (1812) with Sir Thomas Charles Morgan, M.D. (1783–1843), himself a writer on moral philosophy.

134. Lafayette, who had played a conspicuous part in the Revolution of 1789, commanded the National Guard in that of 1830, and suggested the revival of the Republic. The American Minister was William C. Rivers.

– 'The new Beer Bill' was introduced as part of the budget in March 1830, and the whole of the Beer Tax was repealed as from 10 Oct. There was considerable opposition on the part of brewers and publicans and in Parliament, and much prognostication of increased drunkenness, but the case for repeal, clearly put by the Chancellor of the Exchequer, Henry Goulburn, and wittily enforced by Brougham, was too strong to be resisted.

135. *Grey's appointment:* as Prime Minister. In the debate on the Address on 2 Nov. the Duke of Wellington met Lord Grey's demand for Reform with an uncompromising refusal. On 7 Nov. Sir Robert Peel, Home Secretary, cancelled the acceptance by the new King and his Ministers to the Lord Mayor's banquet on the 9th on the ground of danger from disturbance of the peace; and the Duke put Apsley House in a state of defence. The caution of the Government was greatly ridiculed and resented as King William was very popular. The Government was defeated on 16 Nov., on a motion about the Civil List, and promptly resigned. Lord Grey's Ministry was formed by 19 Nov.

– The word 'poor' is omitted in P. The spelling of the names Goderich, Melbourne, Russell, Macaulay is characteristic.

– Charles Gordon-Lennox, 5th Duke of Richmond (1791–1860), served in the Army under Wellington, was M.P. for Chichester 1812–19, succeeded to the dukedom 1819, and was Postmaster-General 1830–4. He only accepted this post, with a seat in the Cabinet, after refusing that of Master of the Horse. Lord Grey intended to make him Master-General of the Ordnance, but according to Greville (ii. 65) this appointment of a 'half-pay lt-col.' was too 'unpalatable to the Army'. The Duke though a lively and popular man and a lavishly hospitable magnate, was not a statesman.

– Greville (ii. 65) called the appointment 'bad' because Graham was 'inconsiderable', but he proved a very good administrator at the Admiralty 1830–4 and 1852–5. James Robert George Graham (1792–1861) was a model landlord at Netherby in Eskdale, a student of politics and economics, a highly polished but too elaborate orator, and, except among his tenants, too 'aristocratic' in manner to be popular.

– He was actually the 2nd Lord Minto's younger brother. George Elliot (1784–1863) served in the Navy under Nelson, was Secretary to the Admiralty 1830–4, and a Sea Lord 1834–7. He subsequently held several naval commands and was made a K.C.B. in 1862. S. was probably thinking of his cousin Charles Gilbert (1801–75), who after active service in the Navy 1815–28, held various posts under the Foreign and Colonial Offices and was made a K.C.B. in 1856.

– *John Russell:* he was made Paymaster-General at once, and a member of the Cabinet in June 1831, introducing the Reform Bill three times before it was passed in June 1832.

Macaulay was made a Commissioner of the Board of Control 1832. Thomas Babington Macaulay (1800–59), historian, essayist, orator, author of *Lays of Ancient Rome,* and chief architect of the criminal and educational codes of British India, was the son of Zachary Macaulay (1768–1838), one of the chief-slave aboli-tionists. He became a Fellow of Trinity, Cambridge, 1824, a mainstay of *E.R.* from 1825, was M.P., on and off, 1830–56. He was member of the Supreme Council of India 1834–8, Secretary of War, 1839–41, carried the Copyright Act of 1842, was Pay-master of the Forces 1846–7, created Baron Macaulay 1857.

– This note, undated and unstamped, was evidently enclosed in some other letter. The date 'August. 1830' is pencilled on it, but the only 'Letter to Mr. Swing' which is extant (*M.*, p. 237, 1st ed.; p. 287, 3rd ed.) appeared in the *Taunton Courier* of Wed., 8 Dec. The 'Letters' were reprinted as handbills, of which the one reprinted in the *Memoir* is still extant in K.

136. Henry Hunt was a Wiltshire farmer who became a Radical agi-tator, was often imprisoned, presided at the 'Peterloo' meeting of August 1819, contested several seats for Parliament and finally was M.P. for Preston Dec. 1830–3, being a thorn in the side of the moderate Reformers, and 'alienated even from his former friend Cobbett' (*D.N.B.*). William Cobbett (1762–1835) was self-educated, but became a first-rate journalist and essayist, and the most powerful agitator for Reform. He became M.P. for Oldham in 1832. His best-known works were *Cobbett's Weekly Political Register*, 1802–35, his *English Grammar,* 1818, and *Rural Rides,* 1830.

– Jeffrey was appointed Lord Advocate at the end of Nov. or be-ginning of Dec. 1830, and in consequence stood for Parliament 'within a few weeks' (Cockburn, *Life of Jeffrey*, i. 312). He was returned for the Forfarshire Burghs, on which occasion he was pelted by some of the supporters of his opponent. He was un-seated in March on a legal point, but elected for Lord Fitz-william's borough of Malton on 6 April, but Parliament was dis-solved on 23 April. He was returned once more for the Forfar-shire Burghs in June, and resigned in May 1834 on being made a Scottish Judge.

137. *Ely:* Bowyer Edward Sparke (1760–1836) was Dean of Bristol 1803–9, Bishop of Chester 1809–12, Bishop of Ely 1812–36.

– *Lichfield:* John Chappel Woodhouse (1748–1833) was Dean 1807–33.

– William Conygnham Plunket, 1st Baron Plunket (1764–1854), a brilliant advocate and orator, created a baron on becoming Chief Justice of the Common Pleas in Ireland 1827. He supported

Catholic Emancipation and was Lord Chancellor in Ireland, with one break of 5 months, from 1830 to 1841. There is a judicious account of him in *D.N.B.*

- *this measure:* The Reform Bill passed its second reading in the House of Commons by one vote, but was thrown out in Committee. The King reluctantly took Grey's advice and dissolved Parliament.

138. *Mr. Dyson:* This is Sydney's fun. The speech was one of his own.

- Charles James Blomfield (1786–1857) had lately been elected a Fellow of Trinity and afterwards became Bishop successively of Chester (1824) and London (1828). He is said to have written articles on classical subjects for the *Quarterly* as well as the *E.R.*, and in 1813 he and Prof. Monk (afterwards Bishop of Gloucester) established the *Museum Criticum*.

    S. was given a prebend at St. Paul's by Lord Grey Sept. 1831. His letter to S. is given by R. p. 293, as follows:

    'Downing St. Sept. 10th 1831

    'My dear Sydney, – You are much obliged to Dr. Bell for not dying, as he had promised. By the promotion of the Bishop of Chichester to the See of Worcester, a Canon Residentiary of St. Paul's becomes vacant. A snug thing, let me tell you, being worth full £2000 a year. To this the King, upon my recommendation, has signified his pleasure that you should be appointed, and I do not think it likely that you can be *dis*-appointed a second time by the old bishop coming to life again, like Dr. Bell. Mr. Harvey, tutor to Prince George of Cambridge, will have your stall at Bristol.

    I am, my dear Sydney,
    Yours very sincerely,
    GREY.'

- S. 'read himself in at St. Paul's on Oct. 2' (R.), and this letter was written before the Lords threw out the Reform Bill on 8 Oct. S. was back at Combe Florey on 6 Oct.: so if this letter was written from Bristol, it must have been on S.'s journey home between 2 and 6 Oct.

140. Henry Edward John Howard (1795–1868), at this time prebendary and succentor of York Cathedral, was made Dean of Lichfield in 1833, and held several lucrative livings. He translated Claudian and edited the LXX version of the Pentateuch, wrote Scripture history, and contributed largely to the restoration of Lichfield Cathedral.

Rev. George Caldwell (1779–1848) was for many years a Fellow and Tutor of Jesus College, Cambridge. He took orders in 1817, but never held a cure.

- Wrangham: p. 107. Wood: Grey's son-in-law.
- A minor incident in the Reform agitation, which reached a new peak in the Bristol riot. On 31 Oct. Sir F. Burdett presided over a large meeting in Lincoln's Inn Fields at which it was resolved to found a 'National Political Union'. The extremer elements demanded manhood suffrage and the ballot, and a meeting was announced for 7 Nov. at White Conduit Fields (so named in *The Times*, evidently the same as Lamb's Conduit Fields of S.: the names survives in Lamb's Conduit St., W.C.1). The Government thereupon warned the neighbouring parishes to enrol special constables and had troops ready to intervene in case of disorder. The meeting was then called off and only an inconsiderable crowd gathered at the rendezvous and required no serious compulsion to disperse.
- Robert Ferguson (1776–1840) of Raith House, on a hill overlooking the Forth, was son of William Berry (uncle of the Misses Berry), who took the name Ferguson on inheriting Raith from his uncle, and was noted for his improvements on the estate and his hospitality. Robert carried on the tradition and, being a man of wide culture and Lord-Lieutenant of Fife, his house was called by Wilkie, the artist, 'the Holland House of Scotland'. He was a Whig M.P. He was succeeded, for a few months, by his brother Sir Ronald Ferguson, also a Whig M.P. and a distinguished soldier.
- The word can hardly be anything but 'Circuit'. I cannot explain the sentence, though it obviously alludes to the recent Bristol riots. There were of course trials of rioters at Bristol and other scenes of riot, and some of the rioters were hanged. But it looks as if S. were suggesting the d'sfranchisement of Bristol as a warning.

141. Littleton should be Lyttelton. This 'earnest speech' (*D.N.B.*) was characterized by Greville (ii. 226) as 'very foolish'. William Henry, 3rd Baron Lyttelton (of the 2nd creation) (1782–1837), succeeded his half-brother in 1828. He was a Student of Christ Church 1798–1812, Whig M.P. 1806–20. His widow, daughter of the 2nd Earl Spencer, was for some years governess to Queen Victoria's children.

- Sc. Camperdown. Robert Dundas Duncan (1788–1857) succeeded his father as Viscount Duncan 1804, and was created Earl of Camperdown 1831. He moved the address in the Lords 6 Dec.

Dudley Ryder (1762–1837) was M.P. for Tiverton 1784–1803, when he succeeded as 2nd Baron Harrowby. He was a very well-informed and active parliamentarian and held office in many ministries, refusing the Premiership on Goderich's resignation in 1827. He was created Earl of Harrowby in 1829. He was liberal-minded, disinterested, conciliatory. His greatest achievement was in persuading 'wavering' peers to secure the passage of the Reform Bill. He married in 1795 Susan Leveson-Gower (1772–1838), daughter of the 1st Marquess of Stafford.

- George Hamilton-Gordon, 4th Earl of Aberdeen (1784–1860), best known as Prime Minister during the Crimean War, began life as an ardent Phil-Hellene, founding the Athenian Society in 1803 and reviewing Gell's *Topography of Troy* in *E.R.* xii (July 1805), Art. I. He figures in Byron's *English Bards* . . .

> First in the oat-fed phalanx shall be seen
> The travell'd Thane, Athenian Aberdeen.

S. elsewhere refers to him as 'the Exquisite'. He was a man of the highest character and refinement, but, as S. indicates and in Greville's words (vi. 400), 'a very bad speaker'.

- The new Reform Bill came before the Lords on 26 March. The question of creating peers to secure its passage had been discussed in the Cabinet and in private for months. It came to a head on 7 May, when on the king refusing Grey's request, the Ministry resigned. The Duke of Wellington failing to form a Ministry, and the country seething with excitement, the king recalled Grey on 12 May, yielded on 18 May, and the Bill was carried finally without the creation of peers on 4 June.

142. *you or I:* A curious confusion of thought. S. must mean that Lord Grey must say to his colleagues that they must decide between good, viz. forcing the Bill through by the creation of peers, or evil, viz. resigning and losing the Bill. S 's carelessness is also shown by the fact that he first closed his quotation at 'falls', then deleted the quotes, but inserted them before the next sentence, which in fact continues Grey's imagined speech.

- William Ord: cf. Letter 454.

143. Charles Robert Cockerell (1788–1863), son of the architect Samuel Pepys Cockerell (1754–1827), was perhaps the finest architect of his day for originality, learning, and taste. He laid the foundations of his art by 7 years of travel and exploration in Greece and Italy. He designed the Taylorian at Oxford (1842), completed the Fitzwilliam at Cambridge (1845), and St George's Hall, Liverpool (1847). He became Surveyor of St. Paul's Cathedral in 1819, architect to the Bank of England in 1833,

R.A. 1836. For his relations with S. see p. 174.

144. Many 'Political Unions' were formed in 1830–2 in imitation of that formed by Thomas Attwood at Birmingham in Jan. 1830 'to obtain by every just and legal means such a reform in the Commons' House of Parliament as may ensure a real and effectual representation of the lower and middle classes of the people in that House'. These unions were viewed with great alarm by many and Grey and Melbourne were constantly urged to prosecute them and the trade unions.

  – Great friends of Henry Fox abroad, 1822, and often dined at Holland House. J. N. Fazackerly (1787–1852), M.P. 1812–37. 'A sensible man and a moderate Whig' (Greville).

  – Sir Thomas Lethbridge, Bt. (1778–1849), M.P. for Somerset 1806–12 and 1820–30, had vehemently opposed Catholic Emancipation at a meeting in Devonshire in 1829, but was one of the many M.P.s who supported the Duke of Wellington's Government in their volte-face in March. The writer of *A.R.* 1829, violently anti-Catholic, singles him out for scathing comment (p. 25). His youngest son, Thomas Prowse, succeeded S. as rector of Combe Florey.

145. Louis Constant (b. 1778) was *valet de chambre* to Napoleon from 1800 till April 1814, when owing to a misunderstanding he did not accompany Napoleon to Elba. S.'s reading was probably in the 'Life of Napoleon by de Bourrienne with notes from (among others) the Memoirs of Constant', in the *National Library*, a compilation conducted by Rev. G. R. Gleig, that indefatigable biographer.

  – This was a novel *The Refugee in America,* published by Frances Trollope (*née* Milton) (1780–1863) later in the same year, 1832, as her first book *Domestic Manners of the Americans.* She took to writing to meet the financial disasters of her husband. The *Domestic Manners* had great success undiminished by American resentment at its too prevalant tone of ridicule. Mrs. Trollope subsequently wrote nearly as many and, at the time, as popular novels as her famous son.

  – It is possible that this was the father (a silk merchant of London) of William Henry Guillemard (1815–87), a schoolmaster and Hebrew scholar who as vicar of St. Mary-the-less (1869–87) 'introduced the Oxford movement to Cambridge' (*D.N.B.*).

146. *The Bishop of London:* Charles James Blomfield (1786–1857) was a conscientious bishop who tried to avert strife between the extreme High Church and Low Church parties, and took a leading part in practical ecclesiastical measures such as building new churches, dividing livings to diminish the scandal of pluralities,

&c. Peel, the Prime Minister, was sincerely anxious that the
Church should set its house in order in its own interests; and at
this time events were leading up to the Ecclesiastical Commission
of 1835 and the Church Acts of the next two years. The Bishop
had approached the Dean and Chapter of St. Pauls' with reference
to London livings.

– Dawson Warren (1771–1838) of Trinity College, Oxford, was
Vicar of Edmonton 1795–1838.

– The curate was the vicar's son, Rev. E. Blackburn Warren, who
succeeded him in the living.

147. *Combeflorey, Taunton:* On 16 May Brougham introduced two
Bills in the House of Lords, one dealing with Pluralities, the
other with Non-Residence. The latter 'provided that all rectors,
curates and other inferior dignitaries should reside upon their
livings, except for two months in the year, under pain of for-
feiture of treble the amount of the value of the living for the time
they were absent from it' (Brougham ap. *Hansard*). No Acts on
these and other proposals were passed till after the Commission
of 1835; and the three months' leave of absence was left untouched.

148. Anne Louisa, daughter of Senator William Bingham of U.S.A.,
married in 1798 to Alexander Baring, who was created Baron
Ashburton in 1835. Both this Mrs. Baring and her daughter-in-
law Lady Harriett were noted as hostesses of the cultivated *élite*
at their town and country houses.

– *Chancellor of the Exchequer:* John Charles Spencer (1782–1845),
Viscount Althorp till he succeeded as 3rd Earl Spencer, was the
most popular, respected, and reluctant politician of his day.
Hunting, racing, prize-fights, horse- and hound-breeding, and
farming were his chosen pursuits. Nothing but his sense of duty
induced him to enter and stay in Parliament. He was a very lame
speaker; but as a plain country gentleman of evident sincerity,
unselfish goodwill, and practical sense 'he exercised', as Greville
(v. 231) says, 'in the House of Commons an influence and even a
dominion greater than any Leader either after or before him'.
He was quite indispensable to Lord Grey's Ministry, and when
he resigned the Chancellorship of the Exchequer on 7 July 1834,
in the stormy debate on the Irish Coercion Bill, Grey resigned
too. When Lord Melbourne succeeded as Prime Minister, Althorp on his entreaty and that of Grey and of 206 M.P.s withdrew his resignation; but on his succeeding to the peerage on 10
Nov. the King dismissed the Ministry. S. is writing immediately
after Althorp's resignation and before he knew of Lord Grey's –
which he much regretted: see Letter 664.

149. *George:* Lord Durham. His impatience for more radical reforms was often embarrassing to his father-in-law.

– *intended:* Wyndham remained a thorn in his father's side to the end. In the following July he was under sentence of expulsion from Trinity, Cambridge, but for his father's sake allowed to transfer to Caius. S.'s impassioned appeals to Christopher Words-worth, the Master of Trinity, may be read in Vol. 2 of *Letters*, pp. 616–20.

– The new Poor Law of 1834 substituting the workhouse, with its separation of married folk, for the system of outdoor relief, was extremely, and rightly, unpopular, though it was enacted with the consent of both parties as necessary to avert national bank-ruptcy. It was based on Bentham and its most powerful advocates were Brougham and Althorp.

– Frederick Gerald Byng (1784–1871), 5th son of the 5th Viscount Torrington, was a clerk in the Foreign Office 1804–39, and gentleman-usher of the Privy Chamber 1831–71. but principally a popular man about town and diner-out. His nickname was in general use.

150. Perhaps the Hon. E. R. Petre (1795–1848). Sheriff of Yorkshire, 1830–1.

– Lady Sarah Sophia Fane (1785–1867), eldest daughter of the 10th Earl of Westmorland and of Sarah, daughter and heiress of Robert Child the banker, married George Villiers, 5th Earl of Jersey, at Gretna Green in 1805. She was one of the leaders of fashion and most incessant talkers of her day, who figures fre-quently in Greville's *Memoirs* and Lady Granville's *Letters* and elsewhere, and was the model for Lady St. Julians in Disraeli's *Coningsby.*

151. Henry John Ridley: prebendary of Bristol (1816–32), of Nor-wich (1832–4) He was given the living of Kirkby Underwood in 1827 by his relative Lord Eldon,, *G.M.* (Jan. 1835, p. 104), so far from mentioning suicide, speaks of 'the short period of time allotted to him by his Maker.'

– Samuel Butler (1774–1839) was a successful headmaster of Shrewsbury from 1798 to 1836, when he was made Bishop of Lichfield and Coventry.

153. The words (or word) before 'see' are illegible: the text is the best conjecture I can make, following the *ductus litterarum*, but it is far from satisfactory.

– *Bankrupt:* S. means Bishop Phillpots, and the allusion is ap-parently to the negotiations of the Bishop first with the Tory Government and then with the Whigs by which he tried to keep the rich living of Stanhope when he became Bishop of Exeter:

see *D.N.B.* and Greville (ii. 95) 'Dishonest bankrupt' is absurd, even in a private letter of Sydney Smith.

– *greatest fool:* Probably Bishop Carr, who was translated from Chichester to Worcester in 1831, 'in fulfilment, as it was understood at the time, of a promise made by the late king' (*D.N.B.*) whom he attended during his last illness. He took little part in politics, but voted against Catholic Emancipation. There seems to be no evidence for S.'s phrase.

– *honest man:* The Hollands' friend Bishop Maltby, who succeeded Carr as Bishop of Chichester. According to *D.N.B.* 'his liberality of action was sometimes misconstrued'. According to S. (p. 177) 'an excellent man and a great fool'.

– *insignificant man:* Joseph Allen (1770–1845) was made Bishop of Bristol in Oct. 1834. He had been tutor to Lord Althorp at Trinity College, Cambridge. He was a Canon of Westminster 1806–34, Bishop of Bristol 1834–6, of Ely 1836–45.

154. Sir Benjamin Brodie (1783–1862) attended George IV and was sergeant-surgeon to William IV and Victoria; made a baronet 1834. He was eminent in various fields of surgery and medicine.
On the fall of the Whig Ministry Brougham had asked his successor Lyndhurst for the reversion of his post as Chief Baron, without salary, but retaining his pension as Chancellor. The request was of course refused. Brougham was not reinstated as Chancellor when Melbourne returned to power in May.

– Sir Stephen Hammick (1777–1867), surgeon-general extraordinary to George IV and William IV, made a baronet 1834.

155. Robert John Wilmot (1784–1841) was son of Sir Robert Wilmot, Bt., and first cousin, through his mother, of Lord Byron, whose *Memoirs* he took part in destroying in the interest of Augusta Leigh. He was M.P. for Newcastle-under-Lyme 1818–30, Under-Secretary for War and Colonies 1821–7, Governor of Ceylon 1831–7. He married in 1806 Anne Beatrix Horton (the subject of Byron's 'She walks in beauty . . .'), and in 1823 added Horton to his name; succeeded to the baronetcy 1834. He wrote pamphlets and lectured on social and political subjects.

– This Lady Williams might be Diana Anne, widow of Sir James Hamlyn-Williams, 2nd Bt., of Clovelly Court, Their son, the 3rd Bt. (1791–1861), married in 1823 Lady Mary, daughter of the 1st Earl Fortescue of Castlehill. I cannot identify T——. Malthus died 23 Dec. 1834.

156. John Fitzgibbon, 2nd Earl of Clare (1792–1851), school-friend of Byron, was Governor of Bombay 1830–4.

– *Lord* ——: I have found no allusion elsewhere leading to the identification of this person. It is quite possibly a jest of S.

Actually Lord Heytesbury (1779–1860) was nominated Governor General by Peel, but the Ministry fell before he could take office, and Melbourne appointed Lord Auckland in his stead.

156. This reads oddly of one of the doughtiest champions of reform and liberty in parliamentary history. But rumour had long been busy with Lord John's matrimonial aspirations (p. 121), and he was to marry Lady Ribbesdale in April.

– This is quite at variance with Lord Duncannon's established reputation: cf. especially Greville's remarkable eulogy (*Memoirs*, v. 445–8). John William Ponsonby (1781–1847), eldest son of the Earl of Bessborough in the Irish peerage, was Viscount Duncannon by courtesy till July 1834, when he was created Baron Duncannon. He was an influential Whip to the Whigs in opposition, one of the framers of the Reform Bill, an excellent Commissioner of Woods and Forests, and a highly esteemed Lord-Lieutenant of Ireland in the last two years of his life.

– Constantine Henry Phipps, 1st Marquess of Normanby (1797–1863); bore the courtesy title of Viscount Normanby (1812–31) as son of the 1st Earl of Mulgrave, whom he succeeded in 1831. He was a Whig M.P. who supported Canning in 1826–7. He was Lord Privy Seal in Melbourne's Ministry 1834, Lord-Lieutenant of Ireland 1835–9 where his liberal policy towards the Catholics met with bitter opposition both there and in England. He was created Marquess of Normanby in 1838, and was Secretary for War and the Colonies for a few months in 1839, Home Secretary 1839–41, Ambassador at Paris 1846–52, Minister at Florence 1854–8. In early life he wrote 'a number of romantic tales, novels and sketches avowedly founded on fact' (*D.N.B.*). His addiction to the theatre comes out in Lady Granville's *Letters*. S.'s remark was occasioned by Lord Normanby's marriage on 12 Aug. to Maria Liddell, daughter of the 1st Baron Ravensworth. Edward Ellice (1781–1863) was commonly called 'the Bear' or 'Bear Ellice' – a nickname said to be given him by Brougham (who himself was sometimes called 'the Brush'; cf. Lady Granville's *Letters*, ii. 284) alluding to his connexion with the fur trade of North America. He was son of a Montreal merchant and himself a first-rate man of business with great commercial and landed interests in Canada and New York State. He was a Whig of independent and sagacious views, succeeded Duncannon as Whip in Grey's Government, and greatly helped to pass the Reform Bill by raising funds for electioneering; took office reluctantly and refused a peerage, but was confidential adviser to several cabinets and intimate with leading French statesmen; the first chairman of the Reform Club, 1836. He married in 1809

Hannah Althaea, youngest sister of Lord Grey, who died in 1832. In 1843 he married the widow of Lord Leicester (Coke of Norfolk); she died in 1844. He was very popular and entertained lavishly at Glenquioch, Inverness.

157. This is what S. wrote with his usual indifference to niceties. Anglo-Massilian would have been pedantic, except to a scholar. Carlyle uses Marseillese.

   – Daniel Whittle Harvey (1786–1863) was an eloquent Radical M.P. of dubious honesty. A well-to-do attorney with a rich wife, he made several unsuccessful attempts to join the bar, but was rejected on grounds of fraud, even after a Committee of the House of Commons exonerated him in 1834. He was effective as the first Commissioner of the Metropolitan Police 1840–63: he also founded the *Sunday Times* and other newspapers. Like S. here, Greville in July 1834 (iii. 50) links him with Brougham, whose 'political character', he says, 'is about on a par with Whittle Harvey's moral character'.

   – A Church Commission was appointed on 4 Feb. 1835; its first report was presented on 17 March.

158. *her infidelities . . .;* Elizabeth Leveson-Gower (1765–1839), succeeded her father the 18th Earl of Sutherland as countess in her own right in 1766. In 1785 she married George Granville Leveson Gower (1758–1833), who became 2nd Marquess of Stafford in 1803 and in the last year of his life was created Duke of Sutherland. By inheritance and marriage he owned enormous estates and devoted himself to their improvement and that of his tenants, though his methods were the subject of great controversy. He supported Catholic Emancipation and the Reform Bill, and was a great patron of art. I have found no other reference to the 'infidelities' of the Duchess.

159. *Boroughs:* on 5 June Lord John Russell introduced a Bill for the reform of municipal government necessitated by the Reform Act of 1832. After much discussion in both Houses it was finally passed on 7 Sept.

   – Sir Henry Halford (1768–1844), physician to George IV, William IV, and Victoria, created a baronet in 1809.

   – *things:* The M.S. has been torn in breaking the seal.

   – *prelate:* P. has 'peer'. The name Copplestone (S.'s spelling of Copleston) is omitted in P. Copleston was Bishop of Llandaff as well as Dean of St. Paul's.

160. This and the next letter were written to Mrs. Austin, the future editor of S.'s *Letters*, in editing which she suppressed her name, owing no doubt to editorial modesty.

Sarah Taylor (1793–1867), the youngest child, 2nd daughter, of the remarkable Norwich family of the yarn-maker and hymn-writer John Taylor and his beautiful and accomplished wife Susanna Cook, was herself a woman of great charm and character, and with her husband John Austin (1790–1859), whom she married in 1820, familiar with many of the legal, political, and literary *élite*. John Austin was regarded by his friends as the ablest of them all and, according to Brougham, would have out-distanced himself and Lord Lyndhurst in legal honours but for his excessive care for perfection: and his brother Charles (1799–1874), who made a large fortune at the parliamentary bar, said: 'John is much cleverer than I, but he is always knocking his head against principles.' He failed to attract as an equity draughts-man and as the first Professor of Jurisprudence at London Uni-versity, and it was owing to his wife's able exertions in editing his writings after his death that he became famous as a theoretic lawyer. She had from the first compensated for her husband's lack of success by a stream of excellent translations, chiefly from the German, and by articles in *E.R.* and other magazines. His health was not good, and they lived abroad for many years in Germany and France, but she, at least, spent some time in most years in England where she had many friends. The Revolution of 1848 drove them from Paris, to settle at Weybridge, where besides editing her husband's unfinished legal studies she wrote many articles, &c., and kept up a copious correspondence, especially with Guizot and other foreign friends. Her only child Lucie (1821–69) married, 16 May 1840, Sir Alexander Cornewall Duff-Gordon, 3rd Bt. (1811–72), assistant gentleman usher to Queen Victoria and a commissioner of inland revenue. Like her mother she was beautiful and intellectual, and with her husband did a good deal of translation; but from her 30th year was so affected by bronchitis that she had to go first to the Cape and then to Egypt, where she spent the last six years of her life and was almost worshipped by the Arabs for her affectionate ben-eficence. Her family letters from the Cape and Egypt were pub-lished and deservedly appreciated. In 1893 her daughter Janet Ross, well known for her Italian studies, published *Three Generations of English Women*, memoirs and correspondence of her mother, grandmother, and great-grandmother, from which most of the above account is taken.

161. *not yet over:* S. refers to the amendments of the Lords to the municipal government reform Bill accepted by the Government. Cf. p. 111.

162. *Derby:* so the MS.
163. *and blood:* see p. 33.
    This is very frank. There is no doubt that Howick had shown an impatient temper in politics after the passing of the Reform Act, and Greville writes on 27 June that Lord Grey, who was no longer in the Government, and Howick, who was Secretary for War, 'disagree on many points. Howick tells him nothing, and consequently he knows nothing. and this provokes him'. Howick always took an independent line in politics; but the Greys were a very happy family.
164. Carlin (1713–83), whose real name was Charles Bertinazzi, born at Turin, was for nearly half a century, the favourite comic actor, and especially impromptu harlequin, of Paris. I have not found the source of S.'s allusion; the story of the 'melancholy clown' is often told of Grimaldi.
  – p. 28.
  – Undated, but '1836' pencilled by an early hand. S. took the lease of 33 Charles St. at the end of 1835 and moved in in Feb. 1836.
  – The famous diplomatist, nicknamed the Great Elchi (Ambassador) from his extraordinary influence at Constantinople, Stratford Canning (1786–1880) was at this time M.P. for King's Lynn (1835–42). He had been made G.C.B. 1839, and was created Viscount Stratford de Redcliffe 1851.
165. *Mrs. Brown:* Lady Holland's maid and afterwards housekeeper, who 'died in her service and left her all her savings' (*C. of H. H.,* p 353).
  – Wyndham was between 22 and 23; born 16 Sept. 1813. In reply to this letter Melbourne gave him a clerkship in the Audit Office.
    Renn Dickson Hampden (1793–1868), elected a Fellow of Oriel in the period of Arnold, Newman, &c., a learned philosopher and theologian, and one of the most amiable and self-effacing of men, was outrageously persecuted by the Tories and the Tractarians for advocating the admission of Dissenters to the University. They used every effort to annul his appointment by Lord Melbourne to the Regius Professorship of Divinity, but without success. S. here refers to his inaugural lecture given on 17 March, which was reviewed with warm praise by Arnold in *E.R.* for April. Similar virulence was aroused when Hampden was made Bishop of Hereford in 1847; but he administered his see with exemplary devotion and charity.
166. Barbara Isabella, daughter of General William Kirkpatrick, the lively and devoted wife of Charles Buller, M.P. for West Looe, 1826 to 1830, when he resigned that pocket-borough to his son,

the better-known and brilliant politician, pupil and friend of Carlyle, and friend of Mill, Grote, &c., secretary to Lord Durham in Canada 1838, M.P. for Liskeard 1832 till his early death in 1848.

- *Lady Dacre:* From *A Family Chronicle*, p. 144. Cf. 68. The book was *Translations from Petrarch* which had come out in Nov. 1836.

167. William Lort Mansel (1753–1820), famous for his epigrams and mimicry, was tutor to Spencer Perceval at Trinity, Cambridge, and owed his appointments to the Mastership of Trinity, 1798, and the Bishopric of Bristol, 1808, to Perceval's recommendations to Pitt and to the Duke of Portland's Cabinet respectively. Perceval was Chancellor of the Exchequer from March 1807 till his murder on 11 May 1812, and Prime Minister from Dec. 1809.

168. Edward Stanley (1779–1840), brother of the 1st Lord Stanley of Alderley, was the devoted and enlightened incumbent at Alderley from 1805 to 1837 and a model Bishop of Norwich from 1837 till his death. He was the father of Dean Stanley. Caldwell: see p. 140.

- A neighbour of S. at Ashfield, Taunton. He and his brother Robert (1765–1842), a doctor and an ardent supporter of the Reform Bill, both lived near Taunton, and were no doubt nearly related to Alexander William Kinglake, the historian of the Crimean War, whose father was a banker at Taunton.

- Probably *A Dissertation on Gout* (1804), one of Robert Kinglake's medical writings.

169. Mrs. Pennington: an old friend of Jeffrey, four intimate letters to whom are in Cockburn's *Life of Jeffrey*. Her maiden name was Jane Grant, of Rothiemurchus. Jeffrey writes to her in 1828 at Malshanger, Hants. She married (1) in 1825 Col. Jervase Pennington, a retired Indian Army officer, and later (2) James Gibson Craig (1799–1886), Writer to the Signet and antiquary. Her girlhood is portrayed in her sister's *Memoirs of a Highland Lady* (ed. Lady Strachey).

- Richard Monckton Milnes (1809–85), son of a Yorkshire landowner of considerable political and social gifts who, refused office in 1809 and a peerage in 1856, was a Fellow Commoner at Trinity, an 'Apostle' with Tennyson, &c., and a prominent speaker at the Union. His vivacity, amiability, interest in politics, society, and good causes made him one of the most conspicuous men of his time, but he was too impressionable and many-sided to achieve high office in politics. He was equally at home with Rogers and Carlyle. He was the only suitor whom Florence Nightingale was tempted to accept. He married in 1851 Annabel, daughter of the 2nd Baron Crewe, and was created Baron

Houghton in 1863. He wrote political pamphlets and minor poetry, and first made Keats known to the general public by his *Life and Letters of John Keats* (1848) and his edition of the poems (1854). The *Life, Letters and Friendships of Richard Monckton Milnes first Lord Houghton*, by T. Wemyss Reid (1890) contains a large number of S.'s *mots* recorded by R. M. M. A biography with much new and interesting detail in two volumes by James Pope Hennessy came out in 1949–51.

170. No doubt Georgiana's brother Egerton. Probably S. wrote E. H. for short. There could be no reason for concealing the name in P.; and, if there had been, no initials would have been given. Egerton Venables Vernon Harcourt (1803–83) was a barrister and registrar of York diocese.

172. The 'mistake' was the proclamation issued by Lord Durham from Quebec on 9 Oct., the eve of his return to England, in which he censured with resentment Lord Melbourne's Ministry for abandoning him to his critics in Parliament over his conduct of affairs in Canada, especially his exiling some of the French Canadian rebels to Bermuda. Greville (iv. 96) wrote on 8 Nov.: 'For once the whole Press has joined in a full chorus of disapprobation'. Nevertheless on his landing at Plymouth, Lord Durham had a triumphant reception by the populace.

173. *Atheist*: sc. John Allen.
    In its early days *The Spectator* (founded 1828) had occasional illustrations. John Arthur Roebuck (1801–79), Q.C., M.P. for Bath most of 1832–47, for Sheffield 1849–68, 1874–9: a vehement independent, mostly radical, but a supporter of Palmerston's foreign policy, and ultimately a Tory P.C. He moved for the Committee on the Crimean campaign in 1855, and supported the South against the North in the American Civil War.

  – Charles Grant (1778–1866). eldest son of the leading evangelical and Indian statesman Charles Grant (1746–1823), a fine speaker in the House of Commons 1811–35, created Baron Glenelg 1835. He was Chief Secretary for Ireland 1819–23. He was one of Canning's last Ministry who joined Lord Grey in 1830 and as President of the Board of Control 1830–4 carried a reform of the East India Company's charter. He was Secretary for the Colonies 1835–9.

  – Gilbert Elliot (1782–1859), 2nd Earl Minto 1814; First Lord of the Admiralty 1835–41.

  – Quite illegible, if one were not certain who is meant. John Cam Hobhouse (1786–1869), friend of Byron and inventor of the phrase 'His Majesty's Opposition', was created Baron Broughton in 1851.

The word following 'Fergusons' is quite illegible, but is perhaps meant for 'situation' – rather an odd word for office. Robert Cutlar Fergusson (1768–1838) after a chequered career as advocate and Whig was Judge-Advocate-General in Melbourne's Ministry till he died the day after this letter was written. Macaulay did not succeed him, but soon afterwards became Secretary for War.

– S. fulfilled this threat in the *Third Letter to Archdeacon Singleton* with some of the sharpest of his ridicule (*Works*, iii. 252–5). Here S. has in mind two apostrophes of Jesus to Simon Peter: 'Simon, I have somewhat to say unto thee' (Luke vii. 40) and 'Simon, Simon, behold Satan desired to have you' (Luke xxii. 31). It is rather startling to find S. using words attributed to Christ in this manner; he probably did it inadvertently.

174. This and the following letter are copied from originals kindly lent by Mrs. Henry Noel. Cf. pp. 210–11. S.'s characteristic outspokenness was followed by harmony, to which full testimony is borne in a letter of Cockerell to Lady Bell, written in 1851, expressing the highest appreciation of S.'s character and services to the cathedral. (*M*.3, pp. 297–301.)

175. C. Hodgson was Receiver (i.e. bursar or treasurer) to the Chapter.

– From *Nelson's Hardy and his Wife* by John Gore (Murray 1935), by kind permission of the author, who adds (p. 199): 'with this testimonial to the character of Sir Thomas and to the charm and wit of Lady Hardy, he enclosed a gift more welcome even than sermons – a rhymed recipe for a salad'. Cf. p. 75.

176. This is the 'very *excellent* receipt for a salad' which Lady Holland, writing to Henry on 3 March 1840, says S. 'has put into verse' (*Eliz. Holland and her Son*, p. 183). The verses S. sent to Lady Hardy with the next preceding letter. It is natural to suppose that the rhymed version had not been long in circulation, though as early as 1823 S. had boasted to Lady Holland of his skill in dressing salads: p. 107. This scrap of paper is undated, but addressed to 33 South Street, the house which Lady Holland inherited from her mother in 1835 and in which she mostly lived from then till her death: *C. of H. H.* p., 191.

As this celebrated *Recipe for a Salad* has been generally printed with a bad mistake, 'brown' for 'crown' in l. 11, I take this opportunity of reprinting it with the correction from an early MS. copy made for S.'s friend Dr. Chambers, kindly lent me by his descendant, Miss Irene Chambers. William Frederick Chambers (1786–1855), physician to St. George's Hospital 1816–39, an eminent and candid doctor, who attended Lady Holland on her deathbed, Nov. 17, 1845.

Recipe for a Salad

To make this condiment your poet begs
The pounded yellow of two hard-boil'd eggs;
Two boiled potatoes, passed through kitchen seive,
Smoothness and softness to the salad give.
Let onion atoms lurk within the bowl,
And, half-suspected, animate the whole.
Of mordant mustard add a single spoon,
Distrust the condiment that bites so soon;
But deem it not, thou man of herbs, a fault
To add a double quantity of salt;
Four times the spoon with oil of Lucca crown,
And twice with vinegar procur'd from town;
And lastly o'er the flavour'd compound toss
A magic soupçon of anchovy sauce.
Oh, green and glorious! Oh, herbaceous treat!
Twould tempt the dying anchorite to eat;
Back to the world he'd turn his fleeting soul,
And plunge his fingers in the salad-bowl!
Serenely full, the epicure would say,
'Fate cannot harm me, I have dined today.'

Against the Ballot; included in S.'s *Works*, vol. iii. This pamphlet, published early in 1839, went through many editions and had its share in postponing the Ballot Act till 1868.

177. *Noggs:* the devoted champion of Nicholas Nickleby.

– Harriet Lewin (1792–1878) was the daughter of a retired Madras Civil Servant; in 1820 she married George Grote (1794–1871), the historian of Greece, leader of the 'philosophical Radicals', one of the founders and chief pillars of University College and London University. He was also a leading banker and economist, M.P. for the City 1832–41, and the most persistent advocate of the Ballot. Mrs. Grote was a woman of great charm, energy, and intellectual interests, and with her husband a close link between English and French Liberals.

– S. means Daniel Webster (1782–1852), the famous American lawyer-statesman-orator, who was on a visit to London at this time. He breakfasted with Monckton Milnes on 18 June, Carlyle being of the party (D. A. Wilson's *Carlyle*, iii. 72). S. no doubt met him on such an occasion. The name the 'Great Western' was suggested by Brunel's famous steamship built in 1838.

– Perhaps Mrs. Austin, to whom the compliment would be appropriate. I have no suggestions to replace the other blanks.

178. William Turnbull (1729–96) wrote a number of medical treatises and contributed to the *Dictionary of Arts and Sciences* (ed. 1778).

S. may refer to some treatise of his, but it is more likely that he refers to the son, William, who published a memoir of his father in 1805, and was probably a doctor in London at this time.

- Charles Edward Poulett Thomson (1790–1841), bred to commerce, entered Parliament in 1826 and soon established himself as a financial expert and free-trader. He was Vice-President of the Board of Trade in Lord Grey's Ministry of 1830, President 1834. He succeeded Lord Durham as Governor-General of Canada in 1839 with notable success, but died there in Sept. 1841 in consequence of a fall from his horse. He was created Baron Sydenham in 1840.

- *Mantalini*: evidently Lord Normanby, who had been Lord-Lieutenant of Ireland 1835–9, Secretary for War and the Colonies Feb.–Aug. 1839, and then exchanged the Colonial Office with Lord John Russell for the Home Office, till the fall of the Government in 1841. He was a clever, amiable, and liberal-minded man, frequently criticized for too great leniency towards malcontents, and for a 'frivolous theatrical manner', but popular and valued (*D.N.B.*). Curiously enough, Lord Redesdale (*Memories,* i. 136) writes of his 'Turveydrop-like pomposity'.

- George William Frederick Villiers (1800–70) succeeded his uncle as 4th Earl of Clarendon Dec. 1838. He had been Ambassador at Madrid 1833–9; at this time was Lord Privy Seal, 1839–41, afterwards Lord-Lieutenant of Ireland, 1847–52, and Foreign Secretary 1853–8, 1865–6, 1868–70. In every office he encountered the greatest difficulties and incurred much opposition, but his abilities, culture, amiability, and integrity made him most sought after as a colleague in government. His mother Theresa Parker was sister-in-law of S.'s friend Lady Morley.

- Lord and Lady Holland were staying at Lilford Hall in Northants, the home of their daughter Mary, at the end of Sept. when a fire broke out in the drawing-room at 7 a.m. She wrote: 'Everybody behaved well: even *I* did with composure and self-possession. Upon it bursting into my room, I went immediately to Papa, conveyed him in his rolling chair to a distant and safe room, roused Allen from a sound sleep, and remained quiet' (*C. of H. H.,* p. 258).

179. There was a rumour in the London papers on 22 Oct. that Brougham had been killed in a carriage accident near his home in Cumberland. It was started by a letter to a Mr. Montgomery purporting to come from B. Duncombe Shafto, who with his wife and Brougham's niece Miss Eden were in the carriage, but unhurt. *The Times* did not report the accident, but on 23 Oct. referred to the falsity of it and on 24 Oct. prefaced a long friendly

article on Brougham's personal gifts with a strong comment on the 'impudence and inhumanity' of the fabrication. On the 28th appeared a letter from Shafto denying that he had written to Montgomery or anyone else on the subject; but the notion persisted that Brougham himself was at the bottom of it. He was actually hurt in the accident, but not seriously.

– Sir James Clark (1788–1870) after being a naval surgeon practised in Rome 1819–26, visiting German spas, and becoming physician to Prince Leopold, afterwards King of the Belgians, through whom he became physician to Queen Victoria and a baronet 1837. He was much esteemed at court, but was hostilely attacked by the Marquess of Hastings (1808–44) for not having promptly scotched the scandal about his sister Lady Flora Elizabeth (1806–39), Lady-in-Waiting to the Duchess of Kent, who was falsely suspected of pregnancy by some of the court ladies, medically examined and exonerated in Feb., and died of a disease of the liver in July. Clark published a statement in self-defence in Oct., which is printed in *A.R.* 466 ff.

– Anne Maria (1783–1857), daughter of the 3rd Earl of Harrington, married in 1808 Francis Russell, Marquess of Tavistock (1788–1861), who succeeded to the Dukedom of Bedford in this month. She was a Lady of the Bedchamber 1837–41. Greville agrees with S. in thinking that Lord Melbourne might have 'put an extinguisher on' the scandal.

– Edward George Earle Lytton Bulwer (1803–73), created Baron Lytton 1866, remembered now as a prolific, ambitious, and popular novelist, ridiculed by Thackeray and other critics for his pretentious style. But he wrote much else, articles, plays, satire, &c., and was M.P. 1831–41, 1852–66, Secretary for the Colonies 1858, 1859. After a very successful Whig pamphlet in 1834 he was offered a lordship of the Admiralty by Lord Melbourne, but declined to abandon so much of his indefatigable literary labours.

– *against*——: it is tempting to suppose that the two unnamed parties to this imaginary dialogue were Bishop Phillpotts and Lord Lansdowne, and the reference to Lord Lansdowne in Letter 800 (not here included), together with S.'s acknowledged regard for him, lends colour to the supposition. But I have no evidence, and the dates are not easy to reconcile.

180. Catherine Stevens (*c.* 1800–76) married Col. Crowe in 1822, and lived mostly in Edinburgh. She wrote much between 1838 and 1859, two tragedies, a number of novels and short stories, and a treatise on *Spiritualism* in 1859. Her most successful books were *Susan Hopley or the adventures of a maidservant* (1841), which

S. praises in Letter 827, and *The Night Side of Nature* (1848), a collection of stories of the supernatural.

181. Lord Stowell began the practice of having the reports of cases in the Admiralty Court printed; and many of his judgments became famous and formed the foundation of much maritime law. The long war with France afforded immense material.

William Scott, Lord Eldon's elder brother, was Judge of the High Court of Admiralty 1798–1828, and M.P. for Oxford 1801–21; created Baron Stowell 1821. He was a Tory in grain and had the reputation of being both parsimonious and a great eater and drinker. He became acquainted with S. when S. took a cottage at Sonning in 1807, where he wrote the *Plymley Letters*. According to *M*., p. 151. he 'not unfrequently said "Ah, Mr. Smith, you would have been in a different situation, and a far richer man, if you had belonged to us." '

– Undated, but the date is fixed by the references to the deaths of Lord Durham, 28 July 1840, and or the Hollands' old friend Canon Marsh, 30 July.

– Francis Richard Grey (1813–90), 6th son of Lord Grey, married Elizabeth Dorothy, 5th daughter of Lord Carlisle. He was Rector of Morpeth 1842–90, Hon. Canon of Durham 1863–82, of Newcastle 1882–90.

– Rector of Winterslow, an old friend of the Carlisles and Hollands and tutor of Henry Fox in 1818.

182. S. means that he is rallying the cathedral clergy. He was no doubt composing the next letter at this time.

183. Sir Matthew Wood, Bt. (1768–1843), of humble origin, a very active municipal and political reformer. Lord Mayor of London 1815–17, champion of Queen Caroline. His baronetcy in 1837 was the first honour bestowed by Queen Victoria.

188. *give* ——: The Bishop of London.

189. Probably Mrs. Austin: see p. 159.
As far as I know this collocation of cabbages and kings is spontaneous. If so, it was probably the source (possibly unremembered) of Lewis Carroll's phrase in *Alice Through the Looking-Glass* which has become proverbial.

190. S.'s letters to Hale are all addressed to 'The Very Revd Archdeacon Hale'. William Hale Hale (1795–1870) was curate to Blomfield at St. Botolph's, Gracechurch St., 1821, and domestic chaplain to Blomfield as Bishop of Chester 1824–8, and of London 1828. He was Preacher at the Charterhouse from 1823 till 1842, when he became Master. He became a Prebendary of St. Paul's in 1829, Archdeacon of St. Albans in 1839, of Middlesex and a Residentiary Canon in 1840, Archdeacon of London in

1842. He became Almoner on the death of Hawes in 1846. He held 'the rich living of St. Giles, Cripplegate, 1847–57' (*D.N.B.*). He edited various ecclesiastical documents and published articles and sermons. Though a Tory and, like S., opposed to the policy of the Ecclesiastical Commission, he took up S.'s work in reforming St. Paul's, often, in S.'s opinion, with more zeal than discretion.

- *Bishop:* sc. the Dean, who was also Bishop of Llandaff (Copleston, p. 159).
- William Hawes (1785–1846). As Almoner he had charge of the choir-boys. He was a Chorister at the Chapel Royal 1793–1801, a Gentleman of the same 1805, Master 1817. He was a Vicar Choral, Almoner, and Master of the children at St. Paul's from 1813 till his death. But he was best known as an editor and publisher of songs and producer of concerts and operas. (*D.N.B.*)
- Sc. the Bill to be moved in Parliament as the result of the Ecclesiastical Commission.
- Sc. the 'fines' payable on renewal of the leases, from which the emoluments of the Prebendaries were derived.
- Sc. the fees collected from visitors to the Dome and the Whispering Gallery, &c. This money went partly to pay the Minor Canons.

192. *long:* S. is criticizing *Susan Hopley*, the most successful novel of Mrs. Crowe (p. 180), which was dramatized in 1884 by George Didbin Pitt, a forgotten dramatizer of popular tales.

195. I include this letter as a specimen, alas too rare! of the relations between these two brothers (cf. Letter 233); but also for the clear view of the normal English attitude towards politics – a view common enough, but never better expressed.

196. A large quantity of forged Exchequer bills were put into circulation by a man named Rapallo who had advanced money to Louis Napoleon for his abortive attempt to revive the Empire at Boulogne in Aug. 1840.

- *Lord Monteagle:* Thomas Spring-Rice (1790–1866), an Irishman, Whig M.P. 1820–39, Secretary to the Treasury 1830–4, Chancellor of the Exchequer 1835–9. He was twice thought of as candidate for the Speakership, but on both occasions rejected in favour of more advanced Liberals (Abercromby and Shaw Lefevre). He resigned in 1839, received the office of Controller of the Treasury (almost a sinecure), and was created Earl of Monteagle. He was industrious, voluble, warm-hearted, without the force of character for success in high office.
- William Empson (1791–1852), Professor of Law at the East India College, 1824–52, married Jeffrey's daughter Charlotte in 1838.

He was a school-friend and later a supporter of the views of Thomas Arnold, the famous headmaster of Rugby. For many years a contributor to *E.R.*, he succeeded Macvey Napier as editor in 1847.

197. *No. 862:* from the original in the possession (1930) of C. F. Bell, Esq., a cousin of the recipient to whom I owe the following information.

Louisa Bithia Courtenay (1812–1904) was the only daughter and eldest of four children of Philip Courtenay (1785–1841), himself the natural son by a French mother of Rev. John Warner (1736–1800; *D.N.B.*). Her mother was Louisa. daughter of Hugh Bell, an Irish merchant in London. Courtenay became a Q.C., a bencher of Lincoln's Inn, and M.P. for Bridgwater (1837–41), but was chiefly known as a devotee of finance and gastronomy. He figures in both aspects of Crabb Robinson's diaries; e.g. as Wordsworth's 'factotum' for investments and as a *convive* of Samuel Rogers, at whose table S. met him. In 1839–40 he lost heavily in the banking crisis; in Mar. 1841 his 2nd son William Hayley went down in the S.S. *President*; in June he lost his seat in Parliament. So, when he died on 10 Dec. 1841 from an overdose of morphia, Crabb Robinson was convinced, in spite of the verdict at the inquest, that he had committed suicide. His 3rd son Francis was private secretary to Lord Dalhousie in India (1847), a notable amateur tenor and a friend of Rossini.

Louisa Courtenay 'became a typical great lady of the old school, with widespread acquaintance amongst the famous people of her day'. She was a friend of Peacock; probably the model for his 'Miss Ilex' in *Gryll Grange* (1860) and certainly for his son-in-law Meredith's 'Aunt Bel' in *Evan Harrington* (1860).

Accouchment: Albert Edward, son and heir, was born on 9 Nov.

198. Macaulay's essay on Warren Hastings appeared in *E.R.* Oct. 1841. He was Secretary at War from Sept. 1839 till Peel's Ministry came in (Sept. 1841).

— *niece:* Catherine Stephens (1794–1882) was a famous concert and opera singer, who retired in 1835. In April 1838 she married the Earl of Essex, who died the following April aged 81. She had 'a character for virtue, kindness and generosity such as few actresses have enjoyed' (*D.N.B.*). On her death her niece Esther Matilda Johnstone inherited her property of over £71,000 (*Complete Peerage*).

— *Tower:* Greville concurs and says that the destruction of quantities of old arms, 'useless and unsaleable', was rather welcome. But the Crown Jewels, &c., were only rescued with great exertion, and some of the buildings were burnt out. There is a detailed account of the fire, which was judged to be accidental, in *A.R.*

— From *Rogers and his Contemporaries* by P. W. Clayden (1889), ii. 215.

— *volumes:* the 2nd edition of his *Works* (1840).

200. Queen Victoria paid her first visit to Scotland 1–15 Sept. 1842, visiting the Duke of Buccleuch at Dalkeith, Lord Mansfield at Scone, Lord Breadalbane at Taymouth, and Lord Willoughby at Drummond Castle. She travelled by sea. Peel's Government had been nervous owing to Chartist disturbances in N. England, but the visit was an unqualified success.

— Jeffrey who was never robust, had been very ill in the previous winter and had leave of absence from the Scottish bench from November. He was in England – London, Torquay, Haileybury (with his daughter and son-in-law) – till May 1842.

201. This title does not appear in the catalogue of the British Museum or the Bodleian.

— The names of Rogers, Macaulay, and Hallam are omitted by P., but can be restored with certainty. S. more than once refers to Macaulay's notorious 'waterspouts of talk'. The irritability of Rogers was also notorious. Sir Henry Holland. S.'s son-in-law, writes of him (*Recollections*, p. 209): 'He could be, and ever was, generous to poverty and real distress; but intolerant to all that presented itself in social rivalry to himself. The usurpation by others of talk at a dinner table, or the interruption to one of his own anecdotes, was sure to provide some access of bitterness bitterly expressed.' Of Hallam, his intimate friend of forty years, Holland writes (ibid., p. 227): 'His latter years were clouded by a paralytic seizure, which I mention only from the effect on him, rarely found in such cases, of diffusing a placid gentleness over the sterner qualities of his mind. He still indeed clung to society; but submitted patiently to the altered condition of his appearing in it. A physician can best estimate the moral rectitude expressed in this gentle acquiscence, supervening on a mind disputative and dogmatic in its natural bent.'

202. *Mrs. ——:* perhaps Mrs. Meynell; but the description better suits Mrs. Grote, who may well have been in Rome again as she was in the previous autumn.

203. *Mrs. Austin:* P. omits the name. Cf. Letter 693.

— *Semiramis:* the opera of Rossini, first published at Venice in 1823.

204. *Bacchanals:* the incident here mentioned is described in *The Illustrated London News*, vol. 1, no. 26. Five women of the streets were arrested by the police while molesting Rogers in Waterloo

Place and soliciting alms. In the police-court two of them alleged intimacy with Rogers, one of them the receipt of 10/- a week, the others of frequent gifts of money. All were sent to the House of Correction for a month with the threat of three months hard labour if brought up again. – I owe this reference to Mr. R. H. W. Case of 17 Airlie Gardens, W. 8.

– So the MS., for 'not the only'.

– John Ponsonby (*c.* 1770–1855) was Lady Grey's eldest brother. He succeeded as 2nd Baron Ponsonby in 1806, and was created a Viscount in 1839. He was Ambassador at Constantinople 1832–7, at Vienna 1846–50. He married in 1803 Lady Frances Villiers, daughter of the 4th Earl of Jersey, whom Lady Granville describes in 1812 as 'beautiful beyond all description'.

– Lady Morley was Frances, only daughter of Thomas Talbot of Gonville, Norfolk. In 1809 she became the 2nd wife of John Parker, 2nd Baron Bovingdon of Bovingdon, Devon, who was created Earl of Morley in 1815. He was a supporter of Pitt and Caning, and afterwards of Lord Grey's Reform Bill. Lady Morley was noted for her 'waggery' (Creevey) and high spirits. Lady Granville (Oct. 1825): 'She falls upon the flatness and ennui of London Society like rain upon a parched field.' Some of S.'s most amusing letters are written to her; Henry Fox calls her husband 'dull and pompous' (*Journal*, p. 91); he was an old Oxford friend of Lord Holland.

– *Lays of Ancient Rome*, first published in 1842, at once attained great and deserved popularity.

– The earliest reference in *O.E.D.* to the Dodo as extinct is dated 1874, and alludes, curiously enough, to 'the Dodo race of real unmitigated . . . Toryism'.

205. *Dogmersfield Park:* the seat of Sir Henry St. John-Mildmay, 4th Bt. (1787–1848), at Winchfield, Hants. His younger brother Humphrey married Lady Ashburton's daughter Anne Eugenia, who died on 8 March 1839 at Nice, as the result of her clothes catching fire.

206. Harriet Martineau (1802–76), the prolific popularizer of social, economic, and political information, mainly through short stories, by means of which, in spite of deafness and ill health, she rose from utter poverty to modest affluence. She was greatly valued in political, literary, and philosophical circles, including Comte whose Positivism she successfully introduced to the British public in 1853. Her *Autobiography* (written in 1855 but not published till 1877) is full of sound sense and just judgements. Like S. she strongly disapproved of the publication of private letters, and

she expressly forbade the publication of hers by her will.

- The Archbishop invited Gil Blas's criticism of his preaching, but resented it when given.
- William Vesey-Fitzgerald (1783–1843), 2nd Baron (I.) 1832, created Baron (U.K.) 1835. As a Tory M.P. he held various ministerial posts.

207. *My . . . this month:* cf. pp. 174–5. There is a painfully indignant (undated and unpublished) letter from Mrs. Sydney to Saba about the 'testamentary papers' left by Courtenay, in which apparently many legacies were mentioned, but Sydney's name did not appear. Whether Bobus was also omitted we do not know. S. evidently took a calmer view of the matter, and may even have thought that the two papers were not intended to be Courtenay's complete will.

- *Bulteel:* Lady Grey's son-in-law: cf. p. 110. This was evidently one of the Bishop of Exeter's numerous clashes with patrons and clergy of his diocese: but even with the kind aid of Mr. O. M. Mozer, Hon. Archivist of Exeter Cathedral, I have been unable to find any trace of the affair.
- Sc. Doctors Commons, or the College of Advocates, the corporation of ecclesiastical lawyers located in St. Paul's Churchyard. The Queens' (or King's) Advocate was the principal law officer of the Crown in the College. William Adams, LL.D., was one of the counsel for the prosecution in Queen Caroline's case, and the father of the first editor of *The Complete Peerage,* George Edward Cokayne (1825–1911), who took his mother's name on her death in 1873.

208. *Address delivered at the anniversary meeting of the Geological Society of London on Feb. 17, 1843:* one of the great number of Murchison's published addresses.

- Belvoir Castle in Leicestershire, the home of the Duke of Rutland, which had been entirely rebuilt after a fire in 1816. The Belvoir hunt is one of the celebrated 'Shires'.
- *Pamela . . . rewarded:* the point is that Lady Cowper had been so intimate with Lord Palmerston for many years before their marriage (in fact they had been intimate from childhood) that the scandalmongers assumed adultery: thus Greville (ii. 324) in 1832 calls her Palmerston's 'mistress' *sans phrase*. But Lady Cowper's reputation was never seriously challenged. She was a model wife and mother. After her husband's death in 1837, Palmerston earnestly wooed her and, though she naturally hesitated to marry again at her age, there is no doubt that the marriage was a love-match and completely happy to the day of his death. At the same time Brougham's jest probably implied the suspicion

that Palmerston would have seduced her if she had not been impregnable. *Pamela or Virtue Rewarded* is the title of Richardson's first famous novel (1740).

Emily Mary Lamb (1787–1869) was the younger and devoted sister of William, afterwards the Prime Minister Lord Melbourne, and of Frederick, afterwards Lord Beauvale and Ambassador at Vienna. She married in 1805 Peter, 5th Earl Cowper (1778–1837), the handsome, worthy, unambitious owner of Panshanger, near her own home of Brocket. She had great charm all her life, and was an ardent Whig and after her marriage with Palmerston the chief hostess of political society.

– Trentham Hall in Staffordshire, a seat of the Leveson-Gowers, at this date of George Granville, 2nd Duke of Sutherland, whose wife was Harriet Elizabeth Georgiana, 3rd daughter of the 6th Earl of Carlisle, who became First Lady to Queen Victoria in 1837.

209. Cf. note p. 26.

– William Whewell (1794–1866), one of the greatest Masters of Trinity (1841–66), was at this time also Vice-Chancellor of Cambridge University. He had won his way from humble origin by force of intellect and character, was 2nd Wrangler 1816, Fellow of Trinity 1817, Prof. of Mineralogy 1828–32, of Moral Philosophy 1838–55. He published many works on mathematics, science, and philosophy, was a somewhat violent but never malicious controversialist, was twice happily married and had many friends, including S.'s friend Mrs. Austin (cf. *Three Generations*, &c.).

210. I know of no treatise of Seneca with this title, though he often expresses the Stoic estimate of riches. S. probably alludes to some book of moral extracts, such as Sir Roger L'Estrange's *Seneca's Morals*, of which many editions came out between 1690 and 1850.

– Charles Anderson Worsley Anderson-Pelham (1809–62) was son and heir of the 1st Earl of Yarborough, and like his father a supporter of Melbourne. He succeeded to the earldom in 1846, but was an invalid for some years before his death.

211. *maximus minimus:* Jeffrey.

– *Bishop of Durham:* Maltby. S. alludes to the split in the Scottish Church which came after years of controversy over patronage, when on 18 May 1843 470 ministers resigned their livings and joined the Free Church.

– Helen Sheridan (1807–67), the eldest of the three beautiful and gifted grand-daughters of the dramatist, married in 1825 to the 4th Baron Dufferin (1794–1841); their only son was the states-

man, the 1st Marquess, Viceroy of India, &c. She married again
in Oct. 1862 'on his deathbed, at his earnest request' (*D.N.B.*)
George, Lord Gifford (1822–62), eldest son of the 8th Marquess
of Tweeddale (1787–1876), who died in Dec. of the same year.
She wrote anonymously both in prose and verse, especially songs
of great charm, which were published in 1894 by her son, Her
next sister, 'the Norton' of this letter, was the celebrated Caroline
(1808–77), whose poems, mainly inspired by the style of Byron,
had a great vogue, and whose unhappy marriage in 1827 to the
Hon. George Norton (1800–75), brother of the 3rd Baron Grant-
ley, became notorious through his unjustified action for crim.
con. against Lord Melbourne (1836) and suggested the subject
of George Meredith's *Diana of the Crossways* (1885).

— *to see* ——: probably Thomas Moore who paid a visit to Combe
Florey in the first week of August.

— *to* ——: it is possible that S. wrote 'Norton'.

212. *Milnes:* see note p. 169.

215. James Alexander Stewart-Mackenzie (1784–1843), son of Admiral Keith Stewart and grandson of the 6th Earl of Galloway,
added the name Mackenzie on marrying in 1817 Maria, daughter
and co-heiress of Lord Seaforth, Baron Mackenzie, widow of
Vice-Admiral Sir Samuel Hood (1762–1814), and a friend of Sir
Walter Scott. He was Governor of Ceylon 1837–40, High Commissioner of the Ionian Islands 1840–3.

— George Bell (1770–1843) an eminent lawyer and professor at
Edinburgh, and, like his brother, Sir Charles (1774–1842), the
distinguished neurologist, an intimate friend of Jeffrey.

— James Tate (1771–1843) was appointed Master of Richmond
School (Yorks.) 1796. I have not found the date of his ordination,
but he was appointed rector of Marske in 1808 and held that
living, while still residing at Richmond, till he was appointed by
the Crown a Canon Residentiary of St. Paul's in 1833 – promotion not unconnected with his support of Catholic Emancipation to which S. alludes. He was then appointed to the living
of All Saints Edmonton in 1839 on the death of the vicar, Dawson Warren. He had two sons, James and Thomas, both of whom
became Scholars of Trinity College, Cambridge. Thomas (1802–
63) succeeded his father as vicar of Edmonton 1 Dec. 1843 and
held the living till his death. He had been curate to his father.
Meantime Thomas Warren, son of the previous vicar Dawson
Warren (who died 17 Dec. 1838), had been curate to his father
and presented by him to the recently established St. Paul's
Church, Winchmore Hill, the first of the many district churches
erected in the ancient parish of Edmonton. But, as we learn from

Letter 966, Thomas Tate on becoming vicar ejected Thomas
Warren and took charge of St. Paul's into his own hands.

216. I cannot identify this 'measure'. Parliament was in recess from
the end of Aug. till 1 Feb. From the following sentence it would
seem that S. was invited to take part in some proceedings which
would involve his personal attendance, and from the next sentence I am inclined to guess that a meeting about the American
debts was in prospect. But there is nothing in either Wemyss
Reid's or Pope-Hennessy's biography of Milnes to throw light
on the subject. Milnes had his finger in many pies, mostly of a
benevolent intention.

  – In 1842–3, in consequence of land speculation, &c. (pilloried by
  Dickens in *Martin Chuzzlewit* which came out in numbers from
  Jan. 1843 to July 1844), many American States defaulted to their
  bondholders, and some, including Pennsylvania the richest,
  actually repudiated their debts. A storm arose, and S., now too
  well-off to be seriously inconvenienced by the loss of a few bonds,
  plunged into the fray in the spirit of his *Peter Plymley* and other
  campaigns for just dealing. He sent a petition to Congress dated
  7 March 1843, which he later published in the *Morning Chronicle*
  and followed with two letters on 3 and 22 Nov.: the whole being
  then published in a pamphlet which had a rapid sale. (I know of
  only two copies of this pamphlet, both of the 2nd ed. 1844, in
  the British Museum and the Bodleian). He was met with a storm
  of abuse in America, but also with the support of Webster,
  Everett (the minister in London), Ticknor, and other leading
  Americans. Letters poured in on him by every post for some
  weeks, and parcels of apples, cheese, &c. All of the States except
  Michigan and Mississippi discharged their debts before the end
  of 1845. This episode in S.'s life is described in *M.*, pp. 349–58.

  – A light pencil-mark is written across 'eyes' and the words 'pain
  is' are written above, doubtless by Lady Grey.

217. *on me :* so the MS.

218. *4th coming :* so the MS. This abbreviation is eccentric, even for S.
  Nassau William Senior (1790–1864), grandson of Aaron Señor,
a Spaniard naturalized in England, was one of the most influential political and economic authorities of the time, and intimate with S. and many of his friends. He refused various offices
and honours, but served on many commissions, and was mainly
responsible for the Poor Law of 1834. S. called his house in
Kensington Gore the chapel-of-ease to Lansdowne House
(*D.N.B.*).

219. *Cecil:* perhaps one of the Holland or Hibbert children?
  Harriet Martineau was very ill both in 1829 and again from 1839

to 1844 when 'she tried mesmerism and recovered' (*D.N.B.*);
she resumed her literary labours and lived till 1876. In Oct. 1843
a number of her friends and admirers subscribed £1,400 as a
Testimonial, as described in her *Autobiography* (ii. 180–1): and
S. 'said that everybody who sent me game, fruit and flowers was
sure of Heaven, provided always that they punctually paid the
dues of the Church of England' (ibid. 179).

- Adelaide Kemble (1814?–79), daughter of Charles Kemble the
actor, was one of the greatest English singers both in opera and
song. She married Edward John Sartoris in 1843 and thereafter
sang only in society, and published some tales and sketches.

220. *My son:* Wyndham: p. 70.
George Augustus Selwyn (1719–91), the celebrated wit and
darling of Society, friend of Horace Walpole, the 1st Lord
Holland, the 5th Earl of Carlisle, &c. The first two volumes of
George Selwyn and his Contemporaries, by J. H. Jesse, consisting
mainly of letters to Selwyn, came out in 1843, the last two in 1844.

221. Samuel Jones Loyd (1796–1883), one of the richest and most influential bankers, virtually author of the Bank Act of 1844, created Baron Overstone in 1860.

- Thomas Tate: p. 292.

222. So the MS This is an unusually long passage of its kind for S.,
who was evidently nettled by Melbourne's well-known manner.

- *Life in the Sick Room: Essays by an Invalid* was published anonymously, but the authorship was instantly recognized. The essays
were written in a burst of self-expression towards the end of five
years of apparently incurable illness, from which in fact Miss
Martineau rapidly recovered in 1844 by means of mesmerism.
The book sold well at first, but was soon forgotten. There is a
copy in the British Museum. In her *Autobiography* Miss Martineau frankly criticized not the statements of fact, but the crude
and morbid state of mind betrayed. But during these years of illness she had written some of her most popular and lasting books
such as *Deerbrook, Feats on the Fjord, The Crofton Boys.* For S.'s
criticism of the book see p. 225.

223. Edward Everett (1794–1865) was American Minister in London
from Nov. 1841 to Aug. 1845, and as a brilliant orator, strikingly
handsome and agreeable, was very well received in society. He
was an intimate friend of S.'s son-in-law, Dr. Holland.

- In the debate of nine nights (13–23 Feb.) on the Opposition
motion of Lord John Russell for a Committee of the House to
inquire into the state of Ireland, which was rejected by a majority
of 99. Greville (v. 162) reports that 'Howick spoke out and de-

clared at once he would make the Catholic the established religion of Ireland'.

224. S. refers to the *Correspondence of Burke* with Rockingham and others, edited by the 5th Earl Fitzwilliam and Sir Richard Bourke (a relative of Burke, Governor of New South Wales 1831–7); 4 vols., 1844.

   – *Shelburne:* Emily (1819–95), eldest daughter of the Comte de Flahault and the Baroness Keith, married Henry (1816–66), 2nd son and the 3rd Marquess of Lansdowne, as his second wife, 1 Nov. 1843. Lord Shelburne succeeded his father as 4th Marquess in 1863.

   – *Kerry:* Augusta Lavinia Priscilla Ponsonby (1814–1904), 2nd daughter of the 4th Earl of Bessborough, married in 1834 the Earl of Kerry (p. 131).

   – Lord Abinger (p. 236) had been a widower since 1829 when in Sept, 1843 he married Elizabeth (*née* Steere) (1803–86) widow of Rev. H. J. Ridley, rector of Abinger. It is remarkable that this second marriage is not even mentioned in the *Memoir* of his father published by his son Peter Campbell Scarlett in 1877. He died in April 1844, being seized with paralysis in the evening of a day when he had sat as Judge of Assize at Bury St. Edmunds.

225. Anthony Ashley Cooper (1801–85) was an active M.P. as Lord Ashley from 1828 to 1851, when he succeeded his father as 7th Earl of Shaftesbury. His political interests were wholly philanthropic. He had been trying to have a Bill passed to limit the hours in factories to ten since 1833, and had at last carried an amendment in Committee to a Government Bill to this effect by 9 votes. But on the third reading the amendment was lost by 138 votes. There is an amusing account of Ashley convincing his step-father-in-law Palmerston of the real suffering of the factory workers in *Lady Palmerston and her Times*, ii. 74–5.

227. Joseph Phillimore (1775–1855), an eminent ecclesiastical and civil jurist, was Regius Professor of Civil Law at Oxford from 1809 till his death. He was commissary of the deanery of St. Paul's from 1834. He succeeded his and S.'s friend Horner as M.P. for St. Mawes 1817–26, and was M.P. for Yarmouth, Isle of Wight, 1826–30.

   – Eugène Robin (1812–48) was a French-Belgian poet and publicist who had asked Van de Weyer to obtain some particulars of S.'s life for an article which he was writing for the *Revue des Deux Mondes*.

228. Jane, daughter of Richard Huck-Saunders, M.D. (1720–85) married in 1800, as his 2nd wife, John Fane, 10th Earl of Westmor-

land (1759–1841). Three amusing references to her loquacity occur in Lady Granville's *Letters*.

229. *Caroline:* 3rd daughter of the Greys and widow of Hon. George Barrington, R.N. (1794–1835).

   – *Twiss:* John Scott (1751–1838) was a highly successful barrister and politician, and an obstinate enemy of reforms. He became Lord Chief Justice and Baron Eldon in 1799, Lord Chancellor 1801–6 and 1807–27, Earl of Eldon 1821.

230. Apparently a local doctor who attended Lord Grey at Howick, and neither of the two distinguished Wilsons of the medical profession, J. A. (1795–1882) and W. J. E. (1809–84).

INDEX